Welcor

BECKY WINTER

Welcome to *Quiet Spaces*. We hope you will find much of interest in the pages that follow. 'The journey' is a very rich theme for Christian spirituality and has been explored in a wide variety of different ways by our contributors. What does the journey mean to you? Why not write in and tell us? (See page 63 for details.)

It has been lovely to hear from readers and to include some of your letters. Visit our website at www.quietspaces.org.uk for more information about *Quiet Spaces* and to offer your thoughts and comments.

We hope that this edition of *Quiet Spaces* will provide food for the journey and good company along the way.

Becky Winter

PS: Have you thought of placing a subscription so that we can make sure you receive your *Quiet Spaces* regularly? Do you know anyone who might appreciate *Quiet Spaces*? You might like to think about buying a gift subscription for them. See page 64 for further details.

Be thou a bright
flame before me,
Be thou a guiding
star above me,
Be thou a smooth
path beneath me,
Be thou a kindly
shepherd behind me,
Today and for
evermore.

ST COLUMBA OF IONA

1

Published by
The Bible Reading Fellowship, First Floor, Elsfield Hall, 15–17 Elsfield Way, Oxford OX2 8FG
Websites: www.brf.org.uk and www.quietspaces.org.uk
ISBN 1 84101 448 6

Acknowledgments
Scripture quotations taken from the Contemporary English Version of the Bible published by
HarperCollins Publishers, copyright © 1991, 1992, 1995 American Bible Society, are used by
permission.

Scripture quotations taken from The New Revised Standard Version of the Bible, Anglicized
Edition, copyright © 1989, 1995 by the Division of Christian Education of the National
Council of the Churches of Christ in the USA, are used by permission. All rights reserved.

Scripture quotations taken from the Holy Bible, New International Version, copyright © 1973,
1978, 1984 by International Bible Society, are used by permission of Hodder & Stoughton
Limited. All rights reserved. 'NIV' is a registered trademark of International Bible Society. UK
trademark number 1448790.

Scriptures quoted from the Good News Bible published by The Bible Societies/HarperCollins
Publishers Ltd, UK © American Bible Society 1966, 1971, 1976, 1992, used with permission.

Extracts from the Authorized Version of the Bible (The King James Bible), the rights in which
are vested in the Crown, are reproduced by permission of the Crown's patentee, Cambridge
University Press.

'Arrival' by R.S. Thomas, from *Collected Poems*, published by J.M. Dent, a division of The Orion
Publishing Group. Reprinted by permission of the publisher.

Printed by Gutenberg Press, Tarxien, Malta

Quiet Spaces

CONTENTS

PLUS
Reflections, poems and quotes

Why 'The Journey'?

Becky Winter sets the scene.

One of the most powerful images of the Christian life is that of a journey. Indeed, the New Testament records that the early Christians initially referred to themselves as followers of 'the way'... Just as God led the people of Israel out of captivity in Egypt into the promised land, so the Christian life is seen as a slow process of deliverance from bondage to sin before being led triumphantly into the heavenly city.

ALISTAIR MCGRATH, *CHRISTIAN SPIRITUALITY*

This journey from captivity to the land of promise is the story of the journey of faith.

In his book *Hope in the Wilderness* (BRF, 2004), David Winter says:

When Jesus was about to leave his disciples he used the language of leaving and travelling to describe what was going to happen to him, and subsequently to them too. 'I am going,' he said, and 'where I am going you cannot follow me now, but you will follow afterward' (John 13:36). His journey to the Father, however, had a particular purpose: 'I go to prepare a place for you... so that where I am you may be also' (John 14:2–3). He was the one who went ahead to prepare the way, to ensure that when they came to the Father there would be a 'place'—a dwelling, a place to stay— especially for each of them.'

By these words Jesus sets the life of faith in the language of journey.

But the journey of life and faith is unlikely to be plain sailing all the way. Often the road seems hard and uphill, and we easily lose our way; the spiritual desert is a very real part of this journey. How do we survive the wilderness? What can we learn from fellow travellers? How do we see the 'pillar of cloud' by day and the 'pillar of fire' by night?

This pilgrimage—our travelling to and with God—is at the heart of the Christian story. ■

Beginning with journey's end

Somebody has said that to travel hopefully is better than to arrive, but so far as I'm concerned (and I think many people stand with me on this) the best part of travelling is getting there. When we talk of the joys of travel, most of us, I imagine, really mean the joys of seeing and experiencing new and different things, of being released from the familiar into new and exciting realms of experience. I suppose those who share that view make poor ramblers, because in truth the rambler goes nowhere. The main object of the exercise is the exercise itself.

It seems to me that there is sometimes a danger of pilgrimage becoming a kind of godly ramble. The medieval pilgrim may well have enjoyed the journey—certainly Chaucer's merry 'Canterbury Pilgrims' did—but the clear object of it all was to get to the place of blessing. So it is for today's pilgrim. We travel hopefully because we expect to arrive eventually at our destination. The walk is important, obviously, but the destination is supreme. If the Christian pilgrimage leads nowhere in the end—if it, too, is merely a kind of spiritual ramble—then the journey itself ceases to have meaning. We travel, in the words of the Church of England's new baptism service, 'within the company of Christ's pilgrim people', being 'renewed

Canon David Winter is a writer, speaker and broadcaster. He is a General Editor for BRF's 'People's Bible Commentary' series and has written many popular books. His most recent book for BRF is 'Old Words, New Life'.

Behind us lie the years of our earthly pilgrimage

They could only get to where they wanted to be by leaving where they were

The reward is just before our eyes

daily by his anointing Spirit' until in the end we 'come to the inheritance of the saints in heaven'.

This is truly to travel 'hopefully'—sustained by the unique and distinctive hope of our faith. But it is also to travel with a goal in mind and a destination ahead, and that goal is God himself, in his heavenly kingdom.

It's that destination, and the final leg of the pilgrim journey, that I should like to focus on, partly because this part of the Christian pilgrimage tends to be overshadowed by the actual business of the daily journey. The wilderness journey of the Israelites from slavery in Egypt to freedom in the promised land has always been seen as a model of all our journeys of faith. It was slow and arduous, with many setbacks and failures on the way, but eventually the people and their new young leader, Joshua, came to the river Jordan. Across its waters, swollen with the early autumn rains, stood the land God had promised them, 'flowing with milk and honey'. They could only get to where they wanted to be by leaving where they were, and inevitably that would involve crossing the river—all of them, men, women, children, the aged and infirm and babies in arms, not to speak of cattle and provisions.

Joshua, prompted by the Lord, addressed the people. 'When you see the ark of the covenant of the Lord your God being carried by the levitical priests, then you shall set out from your place. Follow it, so that you may know the way you should go, for you have not passed this way before' (Joshua 3:3–4). The priests in fact led the people to the Jordan, and as their feet touched the waters so the stream dried up and the ark was carried into the middle of the riverbed. Then all the people walked across, on either side of the ark (though at a respectful distance), until the entire nation had finished crossing over Jordan and stood at last on the soil of the promised land. This was the end of their pilgrimage, the completion of the long and arduous journey on which the Israelites had embarked 40 years earlier.

All our earthly pilgrimages end at Jordan. Behind us lie the years of our earthly pilgrimage. Like that of the Israelites, it has probably been marked by many moments of failure and sin, of doubt and even despair. It has doubtless also included days of rich blessing, when we felt very close to God and very sure of our journey. Now, ahead of us lies the promised land, the kingdom of heaven to which our Father has called us; but to get there we must cross the final hurdle, take the last steps of the long journey of faith. Like the Israelites of old, we need to follow closely the 'ark of the covenant of the Lord our God', because—also like them—'we have not walked this way before'. The last part of the pilgrimage may well seem, in prospect, the most daunting, but the reward is just before our eyes.

For the Israelites on the verge of Jordan, the ark represented the presence of God in the midst of his people. As the priests stood there on the riverbed, holding it high, the weary pilgrims had the assurance that 'the ark of the covenant of the Lord of all the earth' was with them on this strange adventure. For us, the words of the psalmist offer a similar assurance: 'though I walk through the valley of the shadow of death... you are with me'. At the final moment of our pilgrimage, we are not alone: 'your rod and your staff—they comfort me' (Psalm 23:4). We also have the words of Jesus, 'Where I am, there you may be also' (John 14:3).

All those who set out on the journey of faith, the Christian pilgrimage, must know in their heart of hearts that this is where it finally leads—to 'Jordan', to the dark river that must be crossed in order to enter the bright promise of what lies beyond. This was where Bunyan's 'Christian' arrived at the end of *Pilgrim's Progress*, and he found the river deep and wide; but sustained by the presence of 'the Lord of all the earth' and encouraged by the faith of those who had gone before him, he crossed it, as we shall. And 'all the trumpets sounded for him on the other side'. ■

We travel hopefully because we expect to arrive eventually at our destination. The walk is important, obviously, but the destination is supreme.

The spirituality
of walking pilgrimages

Canon John Crowe, before his recent retirement, was Team Rector of Dorchester Abbey near Oxford, a place of pilgrimage to the shrine of St Birinus. With some of his family a few years ago, he walked part of the pilgrim route to Santiago de Compostela and has led days on the theme of pilgrimages and shrines for the Oxford Diocese. In 1997 he was a route leader on the ecumenical pilgrimage through the British Isles to mark the 1400th anniversary of the arrival of St Augustine to Canterbury and the death of St Columba.

...one is often walking on one's own, giving opportunity for **personal reflection**

From prehistoric times it has been natural for people to walk to holy places. Walking gives the chance for reflection; it gives a sense of purpose, direction and goal. Most of the world's major religions share in this experience of significant journeying. It has always been part of the Jewish/Christian tradition—seen as a foretaste of the journey every individual makes from birth to death, from earth to heaven.

A recent study day in the Oxford diocese on 'Pilgrimage' drew a variety of responses on the spirituality of walking pilgrimages. They included 'Sense of goal/orientation', 'connection between past, present and future', 'sense of journeying, meeting, sharing and giving', 'holy places', 'sense of timelessness', 'searching for meaning', 'counter-culture', 'reflection on life experience' and 'effort, cost and commitment'.

Vivid memories of walking part of the camino to Santiago de Compostela with some of my family ten years ago echo those responses. There is a great difference between fast pilgrimages by plane and by coach and slow walking pilgrimages.

Despite the increased numbers of walking pilgrims to Santiago, one is often walking on one's own, giving opportunity for personal reflection. You then meet up with others or rejoin your own companions, and there's a natural sharing of experience along the way. Hunger, thirst, heat and rain, physical tiredness, exhilaration at the beauty of different places and days, all can lead to a reflection not possible in the rush of everyday life or in the busy schedule of the 10-day pilgrimage by coach.

You learn to travel light, to rejoice in the simple things of life: a bottle of cold, clear water is more satisfying than a bottle of wine or beer. Having a shower at the end of a hard day's walk is a luxury! Sleep comes easily despite a hard bed (or floor) and the snoring inevitable in the pilgrim hostels.

Testing and blessing on the way

The people of Israel, descendants of Abraham, knew themselves called to be God's pilgrim people. Their journey under the leadership of Moses from Egypt to the promised land developed this sense of calling. The 40 years in the wilderness was hard and testing for them. At times they wished they were back in Egypt: they often murmured against Moses. But they were also blessed by God and nourished in unexpected ways on their journey.

You learn to travel light, to rejoice in the simple things of life

Later, under King David's leadership, Jerusalem became established as their capital city. They found a focus for their religion in the temple, built by David's son, King Solomon. There was always a creative tension between the way they continued to see themselves as God's pilgrim people and yet saw

Walls confine; openness and freedom of spirit have to be fostered

the temple in Jerusalem as their national shrine, the centre of their worship and political life.

Prophets like Jeremiah warned them against making the temple a shrine independent of ethical behaviour. The temple shrine, which commemorated all that God had done for them in bringing them out of Egypt into the promised land, was not to be seen as a magical protection against the advances of neighbouring nations. Trusting in God, and obeying the commandments: these were of more importance than cities or temples.

In the New Testament we find Jesus, in his childhood and as an adult, making pilgrimages to Jerusalem, but as in the Gospel story we come towards his entry into Jerusalem, we find that Jesus had ambivalent feelings towards the temple. The religion there had lost its heart. He spoke out against it; he cleansed the temple and spoke of his body being God's temple.

Jesus taught in the synagogues but also to crowds and to the twelve disciples in the open air, often as they walked. There is a sense of freedom in the open air. Walls confine; openness and freedom of spirit have to be fostered.

Early Christianity was a religion with no temple, no shrines or sanctuaries. In New Testament times the return of Jesus and the end of the world were expected. There was no point in building churches or shrines. But as time went on, it was natural that devotion to the memory of Jesus led to Christians seeking out the places invested with memories of his earthly life, death and resurrection.

It was natural, too, for those early Christians to identify places associated with the witness unto death of apostles like Peter and Paul. Belief in the resurrection meant that these were not sad places, but holy places where the veil between heaven and earth had grown thin—holy places where God was especially present.

Developments after Constantine

The conversion of the Emperor Constantine to Christianity, in the early fourth century, led to much interest in the Holy Land. His mother, St Helena, over 70 years old by then, had been in the habit of going to the shrines of the martyred saints in Rome, and she travelled to Jerusalem and other holy places associated with Jesus.

The early years of Christianity in the British Isles are shrouded in mystery. Individuals like Alban were converted and were ready to witness unto death long before the conversion of Constantine. The Celtic saints went on long journeys, evangelizing in distant places, following the example of Abraham who had set out not knowing where he was going.

By the early seventh century, the period when missionaries like Augustine, Cuthbert, Boniface and Birinus were spreading the gospel throughout northern Europe, it was normal practice to mark the progress of the gospel and the achievements of these pioneer evangelists—whether martyred or not—by having shrines built over their tombs. By then, the shrine of St Alban, martyred in 209, had already been in existence for over 400 years.

Pilgrims started to make long journeys to the Holy Land, Rome and Santiago de Compostela. More were able to make shorter pilgrimages to local shrines commemorating those who had brought the gospel to Britain. What was their motivation?

A number of reasons can be given. They had to be ready to be away from their normal settled situation, leaving what was familiar to take up the role of an exile/stranger/outsider like Abraham and Jacob. They went to shrines to give thanks, to be sorry for sins they had committed and to pray for others and for themselves to be healed.

Pilgrimages could be open to abuse. Pilgrims were sometimes accused of forsaking responsibility to their families. Boniface warned nuns not to go on pilgrimages to the Holy Land because they would be corrupted on the way and fall into prostitution!

> ## The desert taught us about our **limitations**

What of today?

There are an increasing number of 'activity holidays' which have elements of a pilgrimage about them. Young people go round the world with their rucksacks to 'find themselves'. Bishop Richard Chartres, in an article in *The Guardian* in 1996, described a walk across the Sinai desert with a group of young people from the East

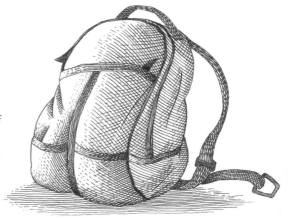

Lead, kindly light

Lead, kindly light,
amid the encircling gloom,
*   Lead thou me on;*
The night is dark,
and I am far from home;
*   Lead thou me on.*
Keep thou my feet;
I do not ask to see
The distant scene:
*   one step enough for me.*

JOHN HENRY NEWMAN
(1801–90)

End of London—Muslims, Christians and agnostics (the majority). It involved ten days' trekking, guided by local Bedouin, and sleeping under the stars.

As we quietened down and took our place in the landscape so we were able to open up to one another. It was possible to communicate at a deeper level and to hear things which would have been missed at home. The basis for dialogue is humility and mutual respect. The desert taught us about our limitations. It is a great leveller. The result was real dialogue between people who in other circumstances would have been wary of each other. Dialogue, rightly understood, is itself an experience of the way in which God communicates.

It is certainly true that away from the settled routine of life—often based on hierarchy in secular and religious environments—there is a sense of community and equality which is most refreshing. True pilgrims are more open to one another and to God.

Today, opportunities for pilgrimage are on the increase, many of them ecumenical: local day walking pilgrimages, a week or two following a particular pilgrim route, sleeping on the floors of church halls in this country, and of course longer pilgrim journeys overseas.

Walking pilgrimages are all-age, and open to all sorts of people—believers, those searching for meaning, those wishing to have 'time out' to make sense of a change of occupation, retirement or bereavement, as well as those who find going on pilgrimage regularly a good way of charging up their spiritual batteries. ■

For help with walking pilgrimages to Santiago de Compostela—maps, routes, hostels, excellent regular bulletins and other publications—contact the Confraternity of St James, 27 Blackfriars Road, London SE1 8NY. Email: office@csj.org.uk. Website: www.csj.org.uk

Signposts

This meditation is taken from 'Lighted Windows' by Margaret Silf (BRF, 2002).

This is the testimony given by John when the Jews sent priests and Levites from Jerusalem to ask him, 'Who are you?' He confessed and did not deny it, but confessed, 'I am not the Messiah.' And they asked him, 'What then? Are you Elijah?' He said, 'I am not.' 'Are you the prophet?' He answered, 'No.' Then they said to him, 'Who are you? Let us have an answer for those who sent us. What do you say about yourself?' He said, 'I am the voice of one crying out in the wilderness, "Make straight the way of the Lord,"' as the prophet Isaiah said…

'I baptize with water. Among you stands one whom you do not know, the one who is coming after me; I am not worthy to untie the thong of his sandal.' …

The next day he saw Jesus coming toward him and declared, 'Here is the Lamb of God who takes away the sin of the world! This is he of whom I said, "After me comes a man who ranks ahead of me because he was before me." I myself did not know him; but I came baptizing with water for this reason, that he might be revealed to Israel.' …

The next day John again was standing with two of his disciples, and as he watched Jesus walk by, he exclaimed, 'Look, here is the Lamb of God!' The two disciples heard him say this, and they followed Jesus.

JOHN 1:19–37 (ABRIDGED)

God guides us. But we who are guided by him are also called, as John was called, to 'prepare the way of the Lord'.

Imagine yourself walking along your local high street on a sunny morning. People all around you are going about their business—perhaps setting up their market stalls for the day, taking the children to school, opening up the shops. But in the middle of it all, one person is standing in the middle of the pavement, gazing up to the sky.

Give the scene another five minutes, and no prizes for guessing how the high street looks now! Some people are still getting on with the morning chores, but meanwhile a large crowd has gathered around the stranger on the pavement who is gazing at the sky. Nothing has been spoken. But they all want to know what it is that is so powerfully engaging the attention of this person.

I find God's guidance in those who point beyond themselves

It wouldn't matter now if the person who started it all were simply to walk away. The crowd is no longer interested in that person as such, but in whatever it was that was attracting that person's gaze.

Of course, it would be possible to instigate a scene like this just for the fun of it, staring at nothing at all, then walking away, leaving a fascinated crowd behind you, likewise staring at they-know-not-what. But John the Baptist isn't having a joke. His focus is firmly on the One who is going to have a profound effect on the world and its story from this moment on.

Yet what he actually does, at this moment at least, is not a million miles from the action of our person in the high street. He simply directs the attention of the crowds to something—Someone—beyond themselves. This gives me a very big clue about where I might discover God's guidance: *I find God's guidance in those who point beyond themselves.*

When I look back over the years, I can name several people who have been 'John the Baptist' for me. Without exception they have been people whose faces have been turned to God, and whose hearts have been focused on God, to such an extent that others were bound to notice and be attracted in the same direction. Usually, I suspect, they never realized the power of their witness. They have been people who were so free of any need for personal status and recognition that they could walk away when their task was done, entrusting the rest to God. And they haven't always been in the places where you might expect such people to be.

By contrast, I have also encountered people, and institutions, who appeared to be doing the opposite—pointing always to themselves rather than to the One who is beyond them. John shows us very graphically how to deal with this tendency towards a 'messiah complex' in ourselves and in others. His answer is a simple, honest, straightforward 'No'. 'No, *I'm* not the One you are looking for. I am only pointing in his direction. *I'm* not your destination. I'm just one of the sign-posts along your way.' There is a danger in listening to those who claim to have 'the answers' in their own right. There is an even greater danger in becoming such a person ourselves.

And when the awaited one actually appears, John readily lets his own disciples move on. He even encourages them to do so. 'Look, *that's* the man you are looking for. Follow *him*.' The Lord is bigger than all our lesser allegiances—even our allegiance to a particular faith tradition.

We are challenged always to point beyond ourselves

'Look, here is the lamb of God'

God guides us. But we who are guided by him are also called, as John was called, to 'prepare the way of the Lord'—to journey on in such a way that we (perhaps unconsciously) provide pointers to those who follow after. We are challenged to live constantly with our inner eyes fixed on God. We are challenged always to point beyond ourselves.

Where have you discovered pointers to God in your personal story? Which way is the finger of your own life pointing? ∎

The Journey

These prayers are written by Jenny Biggar, who is a BRF trustee. She works as a secretary and is a trained counsellor. Music making, cooking and writing are among her main enjoyments.

There are many different ways in which you can use these pages. The prayers are designed so that they can be used in addition to an existing pattern, as a way of weaving this issue's theme into all of the other things we offer to God. You may decide to use these prayers for one week, or you may like to repeat them week after week, adapting them to your own concerns and circumstances.

Monday

Heavenly Father, when you sent your Son to be one of us in order to bring us into your family and back to you, he too was born a baby.

I am sorry for the times I have ignored your complete humanity. Please forgive me.

Thank you for always being here with me, no matter what. Please help me to be more aware of you close to me, and vulnerable for my sake.

Heavenly Father, I pray for those starting out on a journey, whether as a newborn baby or as someone embarking on a new venture. Please provide them with companions who care and who will continue to stand by them through the bad times as well as the good.

Heavenly Father, may I be more prepared to be approachable, open and vulnerable this day and every day. Amen.

Tuesday

Heavenly Father, when he was still a tiny baby, your Son had to leave his home and become a refugee. He too knew what it meant to be an alien in a strange land.

I am sorry for the times I have turned away from your loving care and spurned your kingdom. Please forgive me.

Thank you for always being here with me, no matter what. Please help me to be more aware of your love that is always with me, regardless of how far I wander from you.

Heavenly Father, I pray for those forced to leave their homes. May they find safe refuge and a real welcome, and be enabled to build new homes.

Heavenly Father, may I realize more and more that your kingdom is my true home, and walk towards it this day and every day. Amen.

Thank you for always being here with me, no matter what

Wednesday

Heavenly Father, when your Son grew up he worked as a carpenter, and must have built, created and repaired all manner of things.

I am sorry for the times when I have missed opportunities to work for you, to build your kingdom and to repair relationships. Please forgive me.

Thank you for always being here with me, no matter what. Please help me to recognize the work you give me to do and undertake it joyfully.

Heavenly Father, I pray for those who cannot find work and who feel despised as a consequence. Show them what it is that you want them to do and open the way for them to achieve it.

Heavenly Father, may I find ways of working for your kingdom in everything I do this day and every day. Amen.

❖

Thursday

Heavenly Father, men in authority schemed to incriminate your Son and plotted to have him executed. His only weapons were truth and love.

I am sorry for the times when I have retaliated in anger at perceived wrongs or spoken against someone without establishing the truth. Please forgive me.

Thank you for always being here with me, no matter what. Please help me to be more and more committed to you and to openly declare this commitment, despite others' indifference, ridicule or opposition.

Heavenly Father, I pray for those who have been unfairly tried and imprisoned unjustly. Be especially apparent to them as they face prejudice and brutality.

Heavenly Father, may I understand your purposes in the hard times as well as the good, this day and every day. Amen.

❖

Friday

Heavenly Father, at the end of his life's journey your Son abandoned himself to you.

I am sorry for the times when I have been so frightened of losing control that I have relied solely on my own resources, instead of letting go in order to hold and be held by you. Please forgive me.

Thank you for always being here with me, no matter what. Please help me to trust you completely at every stage of my journey.

Heavenly Father, I pray for those who are dying. May they have the company of those who care and the time to say, 'Au revoir'.

Heavenly Father, may I let go and run towards you this day and every day. Amen.

Heavenly Father
may I understand your purposes
in the **hard times** as well as the good…

I learn to trust you in the stillness this day and every day

Saturday

Heavenly Father, after his cruel death your Son's body was buried and journey's end appeared to have been reached.

I am sorry for the times I have believed you absent, when I have not stayed still and listened for your voice. Please forgive me.

Thank you for always being here with me, no matter what. Please help me to be more aware of you always with me, and to find the inner stillness in which to hear you clearly.

Heavenly Father, I pray for those bewildered by absence and abandonment, who feel deserted on their journey. May they know the reality of you with them and be very aware of your presence directing them.

Heavenly Father, may I learn to trust you in the stillness this day and every day. Amen.

Sunday

Heavenly Father, you raised your Son from death and opened the gateway to life for us, life in all its fullness.

I am sorry for the times I have not lived your kingdom life to the full. Please forgive me.

Thank you for always being here with me, no matter what. Please help me to be more aware of journeying both with you and towards you, and to enjoy every moment.

Heavenly Father, I pray for those who have reached their journey's end. May they find that it is just the start of the real journey with you.

Heavenly Father, may I walk joyfully in your company this day and every day. Amen.

'Stand fast':

Iona and Saint Columba

This is an extract from *Pilgrims in the Kingdom* (BRF, 2004) by Deborah and David Douglas. Deborah, a trained spiritual director who has led retreats in the USA and Britain, writes here of a windswept visit to the island of Iona.

As I scramble up the lee side of the hill through heather and grazing sheep, I am breathless and exhilarated, a little scared, and wet to the skin—although whether from rain or sea spray it is impossible to tell. I have never been out in a gale before, and a gale here on this tiny Hebridean island off the west coast of Scotland means more than a 60-miles-per-hour wind: it blows right off the north Atlantic, elemental and wild, from just beyond the middle of nowhere.

This wind has already changed my life: I had planned to leave Iona this morning, but the storms have wrought havoc with the ferry schedules, and the locals only shrug when I ask when I will be able to return to the mainland. This is October; this is a remote and tiny island. I will leave when the weather permits and the Lord wills... For hours I have been swept before the wind, blown about like a leaf, from the abbey down to Columba's Bay and across the grassy, sandy reaches of the *machair* to the brow of this small hill.

The view from here is breathtaking in its timeless simplicity—rocks, heather, a wild chaos of surf at the far edge of the island, and then nothing but sea until it merges into sky.

I stand on Dun I (pronounced 'Doon Ee'), the highest point on the island. When I reach the summit, the force of the wind... actually knocks me

STONE CROSS, IONA ABBEY (JOAN MYERS) ▶

down. When I regain my feet, I experiment with my balance and discover that I can literally lean on the wind, invisible but tangible as earth or stone. I rock forward on the balls of my feet and bank into the wind, arms out, head high, poised for a moment on the muscled air like a carved figurehead on a sailing ship, surrendered to the sky, plunging ahead into the storm.

> ## There has been a recent explosion of interest in people's happiness and well-being

I have a powerful sense of being where edges meet and disappear: horizon and shore are no tidy boundaries here but points of passionate encounter. The air is full of the salt and wet of the sea; the sea is whipped by the wild air; the earth is buffeted by sea and sky alike. The very sky seems lowering to touch the ground. Nothing is static; everything is in motion. I almost feel as though I am present at creation before God separated the waters from the dry land. I definitely feel I am standing—precariously—on the very rim of the world.

I wonder if St Columba felt the same way. More than 14 centuries have passed since that intrepid middle-aged Irish monk arrived on the island with his little band of followers, but he is the reason that I, like thousands of pilgrims before me, have come to Iona.

One of the great figures of the early history of Christianity in Britain and Ireland, Columba, of noble birth and monastic training, established a monastery on Iona about AD563... to bring the light of Christ to the Western Isles. From this minute rocky stronghold, that light would spread throughout modern Scotland and down into much of north and central England, years before Pope Gregory I sent Augustine, the Archbishop of Canterbury, from Rome to convert the Anglo-Saxons in 597.

It is not clear why Columba left his beloved Ireland to start a new life in this wild place. Ancient records suggest political intrigue, possible exile, but whatever the particular reasons, such a journey would be consistent with the early Celtic tradition of setting out as wandering pilgrims to find the place of one's own resurrection. Like the desert fathers and mothers of Egypt, who strongly influenced early Irish monasticism, Celtic Christians often sought out isolated, barren places on the edge of the world to offer themselves to God so deeply as to receive as gift from the risen Christ their own spiritual death and rebirth.

However... the ancient notion of pilgrimage was not one primarily of flight to the edge but of return to the centre: the earliest Christian pilgimages were transforming journeys to Jerusalem... the very centre of the world...

Scholarly opinion divides on whether Columba and those early monks saw themselves as hermits or as missionaries: perhaps they lived as both. What can seem from the outside to be paradox is often experienced as balance, and the mystics report that the stillness at the heart of God is both our destination and the grace by which we seek it. Living at the edge may also be all about living from the centre. As T.S. Eliot reminds us, 'At the still point of the turning world' there is 'neither from nor towards... neither arrest nor movement'—only the light, 'a white light still and moving'.

It is that radiant, dynamic stillness that we seek whenever we step away from where we are: it may look like the very edge of the world, but it is also home. Perhaps Columba knew himself to be truly standing at the brink of everything and, simultaneously, rooted at the heart of it.

✝

Almost as abandoned to the whim of the wind as if I were attempting to navigate a coracle through the sea, I allow myself to be blown back down the lee side of Dun I and across the island again, south to Columba's Bay. One of the remarkable things about Iona is apparent here—a geological footnote that adds to the aura of the island's ancient mystery—the age of the rock from which it is made. Apparently the stone of Iona is among the oldest on the surface of the planet, thrust up eons ago from the very depths of the primordial sea. No fossil record exists here: this rock predates all life. Once there was a small marble quarry here, long since abandoned. The pebbled beach is strewn with fragments of white marble, polished into roundness by centuries of wind and sea. These mingle with tumbled bits of quartz, feldspar, hornblende, slate and epidote. The ones I like best are silvery green streaked with white, locally known as 'Columba's tears'. But the sea today is an awesome thing. The spray hurls itself a hundred feet in the air and stings like a whip. This is no day

I have a powerful sense of being where edges meet and disappear

to linger by the shore. Quickly I choose a pebble from the beach and thrust it into my pocket...

I battle my way, metre by stormy metre, past the grazing pasture called Eithne's Fold, where the monks kept their sheep. I press on past the remains of the ancient Augustinian nunnery, built in the early 13th century... Nearly tempted to drop to the ground and crawl by now, I stagger past Oran's Chapel and across the *Reilig Oran*, ancient burial ground of 60 kings—Scottish, Irish and Norwegian... These are some of the most famous, most atmospheric places on Iona, but I am seeking refuge from atmosphere at the moment, and I struggle with the church's heavy doors until at last I stand in the comparative quiet of the nave.

Inside the abbey, a group of tourists moves toward the altar at the east end of the church, so I, seeking shelter but not company, duck into a low doorway and up a dark and winding stone staircase to the tower. The narrow lancet windows are unglazed, and the ubiquitous wind roars into the space and whirls downward in a mighty draught. As I grasp at a stone window ledge for balance, I wonder what recklessness or sheer contrariness keeps me, in a gale on a flat island, obstinately seeking the highest points around rather than prudently lying low until the storm is over. Once again I wonder if this isn't part of the spell of Iona, this longing for higher ground, something Columba himself might have felt...

Even in the relative shelter of the tower, the wind whips my hair about my face and flaps the sleeves of my nylon rain jacket as though they were sails. As I stand braced against the sill of the narrow window, I notice what is carved into the stone lintel above it: 'Stand fast.'

As I make my way back down the corkscrew stairs, riding the current of captured wind like a cork in a whirlpool, I salute the memory of all the monks across the windswept centuries who have, in this remote and barren place of austere blessing, indeed stood fast—lived hidden lives of faith, rooted in God and abandoned to the wind of the Spirit.

Pilgrimage

The ancient notion of pilgrimage was not one primarily of flight to the edge but of return to the centre

✢

Long intrigued by the flowing lines and mysterious symbols of Celtic design, I have pored over ancient illuminated manuscripts and fragments of carved stone in museums in Ireland and Scotland. But those glimpses had not prepared me for the experience of actually standing in front of one of the

Pilgrims
in the Kingdom

0   50   100   150 kilometers

0   50   100 miles

ATLANTIC OCEAN

NORTH SEA

IRISH SEA

SCOTLAND

ENGLAND

WALES

THAMES

IONA
(St. Columba)

ST. ANDREWS

EDINBURGH
(St. Margaret)

LINDISFARNE
(HOLY ISLAND)
(St. Aidan & St. Cuthbert)

WHITHORN
(St. Ninian)

PENDLE HILL
(George Fox)

YORK
(Mary Ward &
Margaret Clitherow)

NORWICH
(Julian of Norwich)

ST. BEUNO'S
(Gerard Manley Hopkins)

LITTLE GIDDING
(Nicholas Ferrar
& T.S. Eliot)

COVENTRY CATHEDRAL

OLNEY
(John Newton)

PLESHEY
(Evelyn Underhill)

OXFORD
(C.S. Lewis)

LONDON
ALDERSGATE ST.
(John Wesley)

BEMERTON
(George Herbert)

CANTERBURY
CATHEDRAL

N
W   E
S

October storm, I am tempted literally to cling to the cross, and in that longing I receive, for a moment, another insight into the paradox of living on the edge and moving from the centre—a glimpse into what it might mean to 'stand fast'.

A radiant conviction of the 'real presence' of Christ and all the angels and saints is one of the most striking aspects of Celtic Christian spirituality: the cross stands firmly at the heart of that tradition, as deeply rooted and as steadfast in endurance as the stone cross standing before me. The Christian Celtic tradition is also characterized by the paradox I have felt so keenly on Iona—the stillness at the heart of the journey into God, the trust and peacefulness in the midst of the tumult...

Perhaps the key to the riddle lies, more than I had supposed, in the great stone crosses that stand like sentinels in the wind-scoured land. Perhaps it is only

huge carved freestanding crosses on the grounds of the abbey. One of these, St Martin's Cross, dates from the early eighth century and offers a marvellous example of its kind—massive Irish granite, three to four metres tall, beautifully carved with intricate designs, a circle joining the intersecting arms of the cross. It stands where it has stood for a thousand years, resolute against gales, Vikings and Victorian vandals. In the brutal winds of this

> The stillness
> at the heart
> of God is
> both our
> destination
> and the
> grace by
> which we
> seek it

in clinging to the cross of Christ, in finding our only true shelter standing fast beneath its arms, that we can hope to live either on the edge or from the centre.

✢

It is night, but still the gale roars. The restored medieval abbey, where a handful of pilgrims has gathered for evening prayer, is lit only by candles inside wrought-iron sconces…

Only traces remain in the north transept of the earlier church built by Reginald on this site in 1203. There are no traces at all of the church Queen Margaret is thought to have built here in 1072, restoring the earlier monastic foundation after the savage destruction caused by repeated Viking attacks from 794 to 986. Of the daub-and-wattle buildings erected by Columba, not a straw remains.

Columba's legacy was a tenacious one, however; for centuries the monastic community he founded maintained its spiritual leadership in the Western Isles. It was not until 1638 that the last bishop of Iona was deposed… After that, the abbey gradually fell into decay. By the middle of the 19th century, sentimental Victorian sightseers, chipping off bits of the high altar as souvenirs, had completed the ruin of the great church, among whose broken walls the islanders' cattle grazed…

However, in 1938 the Iona Community, under the formidable leadership of George MacLeod, a visionary minister of the Church of Scotland, undertook the daunting project of restoring the abbey.

The intention of the Community was not only to repair the fabric of the ancient buildings as a symbol of the conjunction of the spiritual and the material in modern life but also to create on Iona a centre from which to take those principles into the world. Presently, the Iona Community has an interdenominational, international membership of thousands. Their goal is not to recreate monastic life but to commit themselves to one another in the context of their ordinary lives, bound by a common discipline of prayer and work...

Tonight the ancient and enduring faith of those sixth-century monks burns in this place like a flame, more steadfast than the quaking candles in the choir, more robust in its silent witness than our thin voices raised above the wind.

I kneel in the choir and pray, 'May the shelter I seek be the shadow of your cross.'

✢

Upon waking the next morning, the first thing I notice is the silence. The wind still breathes (I wonder if it ever stops here) but in the merest sighing whisper compared to the groaning, screaming clamour of the past two days. The storm is over...

I climb to the top of Dun I and find (almost to my disappointment) that I can stand upright on the summit, this time neither bowled over nor held aloft by the powerful air. I find in my jacket pocket the small, smooth stone I picked up on the beach the day before, and I finger it idly...

I am beginning to realize that living on the edge involves us in constantly moving on: the horizon disappears as we approach it, is revealed in fact to be an illusion. There is no edge. There is no end. The sphere is unbounded. There is only the still point of the turning world. Our only hope of wholeness lies in the dynamic integration offered us by the cross...

Near the summit of Dun I, not a yard from where I stand, a heap of stones rises taller than I am—a cairn, or memorial marker, spontaneously created at sacred places by those who make pilgrimage to them. I gaze at the cairn for a long time, wondering how many thousands of stones compose it,

> **Living on the edge involves us in constantly moving on: the horizon disappears as we approach it, is revealed in fact to be an illusion**

holding in prayer all the people who have travelled to this place and marked their presence in such a small, concrete and anonymous way. I realize this cairn represents a whole communion of saints, a community of people to which I belong, although I will never meet them or even know who they are.

Carefully I add my stone to the pile and head on down the slope again, strengthened by my time in this place, light of heart and hopeful of the grace to stand fast and move on, ever deeper into the God in whom we have already arrived. ■

An apprentice
journey

Margaret Silf is an ecumenical Christian, trained by the Jesuits in accompanying others in prayer. She is a well-known writer and speaker and a contributor to BRF's 'New Daylight' Bible reading notes.

It was the first day at Medical School. Our daughter joined 200 other aspiring doctors to be addressed by the Dean, by way of an official welcome to the five years that lay between them and their hoped-for graduation day.

'Don't imagine that this is going to be some kind of ivory tower academic journey,' he told them. 'You should see yourselves rather as *apprentices* than students. We will spend the first two years teaching you some anatomy and physiology before you can be let loose on real patients, but after that your learning will be very much "hands on". You will learn, like apprentices, day by day, from those who have already mastered their craft.'

When my daughter told me about this little pep talk, I couldn't help comparing it with the Christian journey. Perhaps God, too, is asking us to engage in an apprentice journey rather than merely subscribing to a particular belief system. It's relatively easy to get our heads round the 'anatomy and physiology' of faith, by reading and studying the scriptures and attending Sunday worship. While that is an important starting point, we are also asked to go further—to apply what we have learned, in the real world among God's lost and lonely people. That's when the hard part starts, the stage when we become 'on-the-job disciples', *living* what we learn from the gospel, allowing the Christ-life to become incarnate in our own circumstances and situations. It's daunting! But we have the ultimate master craftsman as guide and teacher.

In earlier generations, the apprentice journey was commonplace. A young person would be apprenticed to a master craftsman, who would teach the apprentice the basic skills of the chosen profession. When the initial teaching phase was completed, the apprentices would become 'journeymen', so called because they would work as day labourers (from the French *journée*), travelling through the world, working day by day in different situations, in order to widen and deepen their experience. The journeyman stage offers no long-term security. It provides work on a daily basis in exchange for a bed, a meal and expert instruction. The one who is learning (whom we could, appropriately, call the 'disciple') travels in trust, never knowing what each new situation will bring, yet ready not only

to learn but to apply that learning in practice.

Perhaps it's no coincidence that Jesus was apprentice-trained himself, learning the craft of carpentry from his earthly father. Again and again in the Gospel narratives we find him teaching his disciples as a master craftsman might: first showing them, by his own example, his stories and his actions,

Jesus was apprentice-trained himself

what it means to be a fully human being, truly and constantly aligned to the heart of God; and then gently leading them into situations where they are asked to put into practice all they are learning, as they journey alongside him through the Galilean countryside and the hostile city streets of Jerusalem. What he is asking of them, and of us, however, is not so much that we learn to do exactly what he does, but that we seek to become more and more like who he is. He asks us to embody his values and attitudes more and more completely into our own life's decisions, reactions and relationships.

How do we do this in practice? Perhaps the finest 'tools' we have, and the only tools we really need, are the Gospel narrative and the gift of prayer. We can learn to 'inhabit' the Gospels, entering into every incident in a spirit

we never finish learning

of prayerful meditation, always asking ourselves the questions, 'How does this incident connect to my own life's circumstances? What is it teaching me about any specific situation in my life or in the world? How can I apply Jesus' values and attitudes in this situation?' And when the connections

> ... we might seal our prayer by asking for the gift of the Holy Spirit

become clear, we might seal our prayer by asking for the gift of the Holy Spirit who alone can empower us to make the love and wisdom of the Lord a reality in these actual situations.

The apprentice journey is quite unpredictable. Every new day will bring its own surprises and challenges, and will coax us beyond our comfort zone, but every new day is a new opportunity to learn from the Master and to grow more like him in the way

we do things, the way we relate to each other and the world, and the way we *are*. We won't stop learning and growing until the day we die, but the journey will reveal itself to be the only way we really choose to live.

Five years on, and the medical students were once more gathered, this time for graduation. The Dean addressed them once again. He told a story about two graduates he had met earlier in the week. He had asked both of them the same question as they stood in front of him on the raised dais in the university hall: 'What are you going to do next?' One grinned broadly and replied, 'I'm going to be a top surgeon!' The second replied, 'I'm going to turn left and walk very carefully down these three steps.' Both answers, it seems to me, ring true in our journey with God. It's right to have the big vision: we are called to be people who transform the world. And it's right to be acutely aware of our need of God in the simple next step that lies right in front of us.

On the apprentice journey with God, there is, of course, no graduation, because we never finish learning. Nevertheless we, who remain for ever disciples, are also sent out as apostles, to put God's teaching into constant practice. In one hand we hold the vision that turns earth into heaven, and in the other the simple question, 'What is the more Christ-like, the more loving thing to do next?' ■

Spiritual lessons:

The hidden life of the limpet

Julie Watson is a minister in secular employment, working full-time as a Principal Lecturer at the University of Teesside and serving as Assistant Curate in Redcar.

The limpet is one of the most well-known sights on the rocky coastline. Also called pointed hat shells, they are accepted as being one of the best types of shell for decorating sandcastles. In reality, the strong conical shell is an effective shape to resist the strength of pounding waves, as well as making life difficult (but not impossible) for predators who want the limpet for dinner.

To most people, limpets are simply stuck on the rock and appear to be rather boring: we only see them when they are out of water, and they don't do very much while they are trying to survive being dried out. When submerged in salty water, however, the limpet can move at a rate of 1.5 cm (just over half an inch in old currency) per minute. That may not seem very fast, but it is carrying its home on its back! As it grazes the surface of the rock, it feeds on algae by scraping them from the surface using iron oxide-hardened 'teeth'. The algae provide the nutrients to allow the limpet to lay down more shell and

Much of what we do spiritually is also hidden from all except God

strange to think that we don't see any action from the limpet because it is hidden; but it reminds us that much of what we do spiritually is also hidden from all except God.

Our own thoughts, feelings and prayers for others and ourselves are hidden from other people, as well as the time that we spend wrestling with problems and trying to understand and help other people in their struggles. There is the time that we spend trying to understand God and his will for us as we live our lives as Christians. There are times of pondering and worshipping God, whether for the beauty of creation or the amazing things that people have been able to make and the skills that they have learned. These are some of our hidden times and they are important for our spiritual growth even though no one else knows about them.

How much hidden time you have will depend on what else you have to do in each day and whether you enjoy being with other people or on your own, but however much or little you have, make good use of that time! ■

grow larger. If conditions are good, limpets can live up to 15 years.

Once the tide begins to ebb, the limpet returns home, each one having a place on a rock where there is a scar into which its shell fits perfectly. As the rock and limpets become once again visible to beachcombers, it appears as if they have not moved at all. It is quite

Forgiveness journey

Sue Atkinson is an author and speaker who is well-known for her work in the area of depression and self-esteem. Her book 'Climbing out of Depression' has been widely acclaimed and has stayed in print for over a decade.

I began a while ago on a journey towards forgiveness, as a woman neighbour was pushing and shoving me, egged on by her husband, both of them yelling at me, telling me what a horrible person I was. When I asked the woman not to touch me in her first aggressive lashing out, she could see how frightened and shocked I was, but she kept advancing towards me, prodding, poking, slapping, yelling.

In the chaos of my mind ('I must get out of her way, I must untie my dog so they don't hurt her, I must get back to the house') there was a small part of me that was saying, 'Maybe they are just lashing out at me because of some unhappiness in their lives?' In the chaos my mind said, 'You will need to forgive these people', but although that journey towards forgiveness almost started during the attack, it was a very long time before I could honestly say to myself that I had begun to *feel* forgiving.

Instant forgiveness?

Whenever that 'F' word is used, my memories of guilt-laden sermons come into play. Did Paul really mean that we must let go of all anger by the time the sun goes down on the same day that we experience some

> **When we forgive we ride the crest of love's cosmic wave; we walk in stride with God.**
>
> LEWIS SMEDES

abuse or hurt? (Ephesians 4:26). This has always bothered me. It paints a picture of a Father God I do not know. If some absolutely terrible thing is done to my child at dusk and I feel rage, does God not forgive me if I cannot forgive by the time the sun has set? Some would say 'yes'. This is disconcerting.

'If you don't forgive, God will not forgive you. It says so in the Lord's Prayer.' Really?

> **I turned to writing and painting to find my way through...**

Forgive and forget?

Any working towards forgiveness had to come from my inner self

In my journey towards forgiving, I found the words of Lewis Smedes very helpful. He says that we are unlikely to forget great hurts done to us. Indeed, if we are to forgive with any meaning, we need to *remember* the hurts! The quick 'I'm sorry', and the immediate response, 'It doesn't matter', just aren't appropriate for some of the very significant wrongs that may be done to us.

If forgiving is to happen, it needs thought (I know I deserve justice but I may never get it); time (as the days went by I began to see that my suffocating guilt was misplaced); dialogue, if that is possible; and, ideally, at least some sense of contrition from the perpetrator. I knew that I could not talk to these neighbours: I was far too frightened of them, and the advice from the diocese was not to involve the police (I was living in a clergy house). So any working towards forgiveness had to come from my inner self.

How do we forgive?

After days of tears and trying to talk myself out of my rage about the attack, I turned to writing and painting to find my way through to some sense of peace and forgiveness. It was hard to find words other than those of outrage, and it was prayer painting that helped me to start to think that one day I might even *feel* forgiving.

As I painted with my favourite brush, I didn't want colour—just black. I began at the top of the page and with each brush stroke I could feel my inner rage more intensely. All worry that I was in some way sinful, still to be so angry, disappeared as I painted with a much-loved friend beside me. I was furiously angry. I was resentful. I played in my mind with revenge. It was better to admit these feelings than to try to cover them up. There was no point in feeling guilty about this amount of anger and vengeance. It was a fact; this was how I felt.

Painting rage

As I worked down the page, I was still just stabbing at the paper, muttering my rage, but gradually sinking into a 'conversation' with God. I found myself painting trees. I painted the joy that my garden brought me. I painted my sense of having my safe space invaded, my haven desecrated by these 'monsters'.

Forgiving is a process

What the prayer painting did for me was to give my rage to God. I began to see that it is God who does the forgiving anyway. I knew I had truly started on the pathway to forgiving with my hand in the hand of God, not knowing where he would lead me.

Forgiving, I found, is not some one-off event that takes place soon after some drastic event. It is a process. For me, the forgiving started with some sense of 'letting go'. I let go of the hurt, more for the sake of

As I painted with my favourite brush, I didn't want colour—**just black**

When I befriend my anger and use it creatively, it can save my life.

DENNIS LINN

my own mental health than for anything to do with those who had wronged me. I let go in order not to become bitter and twisted.

Knowing that I was intending to forgive did not stop the nightmares or the terrible fear I felt whenever I went into the garden. I had to let time, relaxation and prayer heal those things gradually over many weeks and months.

Justice?

Lewes Smedes points out that we deserve justice after some wrong is done to us. But it is forgoing this right to justice that can be at the heart of forgiving. I deserved justice: I was doing nothing wrong, quietly gardening in my own garden on a sunny afternoon. But it soon became clear to me that I would never get any justice. Once I had accepted that, the way forward was clear for me to 'let go' and to go on walking my journey towards inner peace and forgiveness.

Don't forgive too soon

I'm still on that journey. It is my intention to forgive that motivates me to pray for that couple in their sadness and pray for myself that I continue to 'let go'. I'm aware that some might say that I 'should' have totally forgiven them and have forgotten everything about the attack. But that does not seem quite real to my experience—or the experiences of others I know who have been seriously abused.

Pushing people into forgiving seems to me to be rather a damaging thing. We need time to heal. We need time to connect with our inner self, acknowledging the depth of the hurt so that we know that our forgiving is also deep. It is a process that we go through with the Spirit beside us as we paint, think and write. The painting was, for me, the turning point, when I knew that by the grace of a loving Father I was walking with him along the road to forgiveness.

It is a long road. ■

Further reading

- *Forgive and Forget*, Lewis Smedes

- *Don't Forgive Too Soon*, Dennis Linn, Sheila Linn, Matthew Linn

- *Psychology for Christian Ministry*, Fraser Watts, Rebecca Nye, Sarah Savage

★ **SEE ALSO**

Quiet Spaces: Creation and Creativity for an introduction to prayer painting.

The enshrouding blackness
engulfs my being.
Alone.
Afraid.
My mind a whirlpool
ever inwards
towards an eternity of intolerable
pain.

I used to reach out
a hand
into the black unknown
in hope.
But my soul was torn from me,
and I hoped no more.

It was like a pit.
Unfathomable depth.
Tortuous grovelling.
My tears the only sound
in the impenetrable darkness.

I remember that pit,
and the fear,
and the hopelessness
of an eternal agony of mind,
and the soulless wandering
in uncharted desert.

Now I find myself at this oasis,
this unlooked for harbour,
this refuge.
I did not deserve that gracious act
to pluck me from that all-
powerful deep.

I had no hope,
but turning back along the path
I came,
I see a gracious hand
and a loving smile.
I see a guiding light
and feel a protecting wing.

Nestling in your warmth,
my cold heat has thawed.
The blackness of my soul
has blossomed into a million
blooms.

My tears have turned to jewels,
and my bitterness to honey.

But I remember the pit.
Keep me, O Lord,
safe
in the refuge of your wings.

SUE ATKINSON

On the road

This edited extract comes from 'Mark', by Dick France,
in BRF's 'People's Bible Commentary' series.

They were on the road, going up to Jerusalem, and Jesus was walking ahead of them; they were amazed, and those who followed were afraid.

MARK 10:32 (NRSV)

This verse is one of the most vivid pieces of descriptive writing in Mark's Gospel, and seems to preserve the impression of someone who was there at the time, who was himself part of the tableau this verse represents. Peter seems the most obvious candidate.

The scene is 'on the road', a phrase which has become a familiar theme in this part of the Gospel with its restless onward movement (8:27; 9:33; 10:17, 52). The goal is Jerusalem, now directly named in verses 32 and 33 (it was there only by implication in 8:31 and 9:31)—and we already know from 3:22 and 7:1 what sort of reception Jesus can expect in Jerusalem. Yet for all that Mark allows us to see Jesus striding purposefully ahead on the road, leading the way impatiently towards what he knows is his own death.

But Jesus' eagerness is not shared by his disciples, who are perhaps slowly beginning to realize that he means what he has said about what lies ahead. They follow him 'amazed', while an apparently larger group of fellow travellers are quite simply 'afraid'. The contrast between the determined leader and the reluctant followers is striking, the more so when we remember that it is his death, not theirs, which is the immediate prospect. ■

Lord, sometimes to follow where you lead is a bewildering and frightening business. Even when we are afraid help us still to follow, as your disciples did on the road to Jerusalem. Amen.

PRAYER

The desert speaks

The desert was created simply to be itself, not to be transformed by people into something else. So too the mountain and the sea. The desert is therefore the logical dwelling place for one who seeks to be nothing but her/himself—that is to say a creature solitary and poor and dependent upon no one but God.

THOMAS MERTON, FROM *THOUGHTS IN SOLITUDE*, BURNS AND OATES, 1975

In March 2004, Julie Watson joined a trek through the Sinai desert...

Welcome, travellers, welcome. Welcome to my world, for I am the desert in which you walk, following in the footsteps of thousands—seekers, pilgrims, runaways. However you arrived here, welcome.

I am old and shaped by wind and water, silent, empty and barren. I am the place that few seek, yet many find; for those who are driven to journey here are unaware that in the silence their own souls will shout more loudly. I have watched many journey across rock and sand, and seen their joy and tears. None can be unaffected by their time here, whether alone or with friends; each is silenced by the awesome power of the emptiness or perhaps simply by the absence of their usual busy world. Let me share with you some of my memories as I have watched the passing of time.

Long, long ago, a whole people passed through this desert—the children of Israel, a whole mass of humanity wandering after their God. Eventually they left the desert and entered their own land. Many years later I overheard another group: travelling from the east, they watched the night skies, seeking a special star that signified the birth of a great king. Soon after these magi, a young couple and their tiny baby passed through to

39

hide in Egypt for a time, escaping a massacre, and when it was safe they returned home. Many have come over the years by choice or compulsion, journeying for a few days or weeks, months or even years, learning the wisdom of the desert.

Today another group has entered the land. They are eager and keen to explore, but how will they manage as the desert begins to explore each one of them? They begin at speed but soon slow down as solid rock turns to soft, flowing sand—two steps forward and one slide back. Faced by a huge sand dune, some are overwhelmed. Tantrum Hill, it has been named by those who wrestled with themselves to complete the challenge, for there is no way forward except to climb the dune; and even in a group, each person faces it alone. Some approach with quiet determination, others with tears and tantrums. They climb, finding that when they reach what appeared to be the top, another dune awaits. Time slows as they crawl ahead, then stand speechless at the top, for it is only there that the beauty of my presence is revealed and they clearly see the brown barren ground and the bright blue of the sky. For

Many have come over the years by choice or compulsion... learning the wisdom of the desert

here there is no vegetation to mask the underlying rock and so the desert brings each one to face themselves and who they really are. Only now can they begin to understand the struggle and purpose of this journey.

Watching them descend slowly once again from the high peaks to the dry valleys, I wonder whether they will settle tonight. The thoughts that they have had will roll around in their minds, and sleep will be hard to find. The ground is hard too: lumps of granite protrude through the thin mattresses that they are trying to sleep on. In their sleeplessness, perhaps they will look up to the heavens around them and see the wonders encapsulated in the desert skies. For in the deep darkness stars have appeared, as if a child has sprinkled silver glitter over a huge expanse of thick black velvet. So many can be seen tonight that they are amazed, yet those stars have been above them every night of their lives. Before, they were in places filled with light, with comfortable beds and pleasant dreams; but now, in the deepest desert, the night reveals the beauty of the starlit darkness. They will remember this night, and that hidden things are as real as those that can be seen and known.

Weary, they wake, wondering who chose for them to come this way, facing another day of walking—today down a wadi, a dry riverbed. After a time they will think that they have seen enough of sand and rock and that the desert is truly barren; then they

My Lord God, I have no idea where I am going. I do not see the road ahead of me. I cannot know for certain where it will end. Nor do I really know myself, and the fact that I think I am following your will does not mean that I am actually doing so. But I believe that the desire to please you does in fact please you. And I hope that I have that desire in all that I am doing. I hope that I will never do anything apart from that desire. And I know that if I do this you will lead me by the right road, though I may know nothing about it. Therefore I will trust you always, though I may seem to be lost and in the shadow of death. I will not fear, for you are ever with me, and you will never leave me to face my perils alone.

THOMAS MERTON, FROM *THOUGHTS IN SOLITUDE*, BURNS AND OATES, 1975

> Many pass through the
> desert without leaving
> footprints, for their
> journey is deep within
> themselves

will be surprised by flowers blossoming where they are least expected. Even in the deepest desert there is life, not as obvious as in their other world, for here water is scarce and hidden underground, a treasure of more value than gold. Plants and trees grow, their roots seeking a suggestion of water, growing towards the place that will give them life, deeper and deeper, building strong foundations for growth, reaching up to the sunshine and the highest heavens. Here the trees provide rest for weary travellers, a small pool of shade from the burning sun, an oasis of peace in the challenge of the journey.

Soon they will enter my gallery— sculptures made from sandstone, eroded by wind and water day by day cutting through sand that became stone, to return it to sand again and so complete the cycle. They have walked through the desert being surprised by awesome views, becoming aware of their weaknesses and the strength of their endurance; they have huddled into corners and tried to hide behind rocks; they have stood on the highest peaks and rejoiced in their own being. Soon they will leave the desert and be confronted once again by colour and noise and the busyness of the life they left behind, but they will never be the same again, for they have passed through the furnace of the desert and have been changed for ever.

Many pass through the desert without leaving footprints, for their journey is deep within themselves. Many fear finding the darkest night of the desert. But do not be afraid, my travellers, for I welcome you; and if you dare to embrace the desert, you will find riches beyond your wildest dreams.

The wilderness and the dry land shall be glad,
the desert shall rejoice and blossom;
like the crocus it shall
blossom abundantly,
and rejoice with joy and singing...

I will make a way in the wilderness
and rivers in the desert.
ISAIAH 35:1–2a; 43:19 (NRSV) ■

St John of the Cross

David Barton has worked as a headteacher and as an education advisor specializing in RE. He is an Anglican priest and Warden of the Sisters of the Love of God, an Anglican contemplative community.

John of the Cross is someone whose name is recognized, and who is often referred to, but about whom very little seems to be understood. Salvador Dali named a painting after him, a haunting view of the cross brooding over the world, with just a glimpse of shadowy figures walking the shores of a lake, and John's phrase 'the dark night of the soul' is often quoted. Beyond its title, I am never really sure that the painting has any link to John at all. Dali's cross seems disengaged, unearthed almost. For John, the cross was always earthed, bound up with human life. And while the idea of a dark night has given us a vivid phrase to describe some of our deepest feelings of loss, I wonder if those who use it ever really understand

He took the loneliness and deprivation as a gift of emptiness, divinely given

the sense of *blessing* that is bound up in John's writing about this experience.

But first, who exactly was John? He was born in 1542 in central Spain. His parents' marriage was one of love, but also one of financial struggle. John's father died when he was three. It was not an easy childhood. John had some schooling, and then worked as a nurse. But from the beginning he had a desire for solitude and a need to explore the depths of prayer. In 1563, he joined the Carmelite order.

43

Anger?
Turn the other cheek

Anxiety?
Be not anxious

Weakness?
My strength is made perfect in weakness

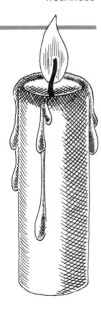

It was a time of great upheaval. Teresa of Avila was championing reform of the order, and John joined her; but there were others strongly opposed, and, like many ecclesiastical battles, powerful factions moved in to assert their strength. In 1577 John was captured by members of his order, blindfolded and put into solitary confinement in the tower of a monastery in Toledo. Flogging and fasting on bread and water were standard penalties. John was left alone in a cramped room, with little light and hardly a change of clothing, for nine months. Then, by a miracle, one hot night in August, weak and exhausted, John escaped and found refuge with Teresa's nuns in Toledo. They nursed him to health, and John returned to his life in the order. By now, the political scene had changed. John was left alone to write and to teach. Eventually he carried high office in the Reformed Carmelites, founding seven monasteries. Sadly, in 1590, the disputes rose again, and John's final months were not easy. He died in December 1591.

To understand John, we have to reflect for a moment on that imprisonment in Toledo. Imagine how we might have responded. Anger? Resentment? Heartbreak that this should be done by your own community? Fear? All of these are possibilities, but John's mind dwelt only on the pathway to God. He took the loneliness and deprivation as a gift of emptiness, divinely given. There were no consolations, no spiritual comforts, nothing in which to rest, but here was a means through which he could turn to God alone, with nothing in between: *nada* (the Spanish for 'nothing'), *nada*, *nada*, *nada*. In the darkness God is at work, teaching us the way of his love.

John is deeply rooted in the pages of the Bible. It is as if he counters every understandable, human emotion with the words of Jesus, words that we often fail to understand. Anger? *Turn the other cheek*. Anxiety? *Be not anxious*. Weakness? *My strength is made perfect in weakness*. This is John's journey—through and beyond each of these raw human emotions, with their paradoxical divine countermand, to an experience of unimaginable joy and beauty: the path to Mount Carmel. He even drew it as a map, plotting a path through all the negations.

All of this came together in the darkness of the little room. There, in his mind, John composed the first 31 verses of the 'Spiritual Canticle', one of the greatest lyrical poems of the Spanish language:

Where have you hidden,
Beloved, and left me moaning?

From this raw cry of abandonment, with its echo of the cross, John moves to a poetic affirmation that draws us to the garden of the resurrection, and the shores of Galilee:

The tranquil night,
At the time of the rising dawn,
Silent music,
Sounding solitude,
The supper that refreshes and deepens love.

This is John's path, a way to God—perhaps, for some of us, *the* way in which we can understand how God draws us to himself. What do we make of our difficult times, when anxiety, illness or depression strike, or when everything seems to collapse about us? For the most part we grin and bear it, hanging on in wavering determination, hoping for better times. John proposes something else: in the darkness God is at work. The question is, are we ready to recognize our need and to hear the answer that God

offers? We always say 'Yes' to that, of course, but John presses the question home: can you say 'Yes' to God and accept God's terms? The question is a question about space, room, emptiness for God. Could it be that through our very dereliction God is clearing a way and drawing us closer to himself?

> **In the darkness God is at work... are we ready to recognize our need?**

John tells us that God is not passive. In another poem his images are of sunlight shining, a mother feeding, water that flows—a God who initiates and invades. But also, since this is God, fire that bums into wood, making it crackle and smoke till it bursts into flame. Our encounter with the living flame of love is just that, an encounter with love, but it can never leave us unchanged. This is John's *nada*, nothing, letting go—partly our work, but mostly the work of the Spirit, making room for the gift of the Other, a gift that is utterly beyond our comprehension. 'To come to what you know not, you must go by a way where you know not.' We learn that we are not in control—a dark night of the soul. John does not minimize the loss here, but, for him, night is more than just a place of darkness. Night is Easter night—the place of resurrection, where God does work in us that we can never do.

In an unstable world and a fractious church, John brings us a word of hope, but it is a word that we are to hold in silence. When John reached the sisters after his escape, they tried to cheer him up with a song, but he asked them to stop. Clinging to a support, weeping, he stood in silence for an hour and they waited with him. We do not always understand but we can wait. God is in charge. Waiting in silence ('contemplation' is another of John's words), we can let God's love flow into us. It may be love felt as pain, but it is love. We will have the energy to go on; and more, we are on the road to discovering a quite different perspective: our essential poverty and the immense riches of God, given to those who wait.

John of the Cross is a poet and an interpreter of our deepest and most hidden experiences. He is not always easy to read at first. He needs work. But he reaches out across the centuries and he has the ability to change us whenever we read him. ■

> To come to what you know not, you must go by a way where you know not

The chase

I fled him, down the nights and down the days;
I fled him, down the arches of the years;
I fled him, down the labyrinthine ways
Of my own mind; and in the mist of tears
I hid from him, and under running laughter...
Still with unhurrying chase,
And unperturbed pace,
Deliberate speed, majestic instancy,
Came on the following feet.

FROM 'THE HOUND OF HEAVEN', FRANCIS THOMPSON (1859–1907)

Arrival

Not conscious
    that you have been seeking
      suddenly
    you come upon it

the village in the Welsh hills
      dust free
    with no road out
but the one you came in by.
    A bird chimes
    from a green tree
the hour that is no hour
    you know. The river dawdles
to hold a mirror for you
where you may see yourself
    as you are, a traveller
    with the moon's halo
    above him, who has arrived
after long journeying where he
    began, catching this
    one truth by suprise
that there is everything to look forward to.

R.S. THOMAS

My journey out of the box

Jean Watson is a writer and speaker. Her love
of fiction inspires much of her work, as
does her experience of bereavement.
Jean lives in Sevenoaks, Kent.

You got on the salvation train and the next stop was heaven. As a young child I wouldn't have put it like that, but it will do as a very brief summary of my Christian outlook at that time. I was clear about how you got on the train but unclear as to what you did or what happened between then and heaven. For reasons that I hope will become clear, I nowadays prefer, as a metaphor for the Christian life, a more winding journey—probably on foot.

Born of loving missionary parents, I spent most of my early years, from six onwards, at a Christian boarding school in China. As an adult, I have been reflecting on the strengths and weaknesses of that early upbringing and teaching, and am continuing to make adjustments in the light of 'new' truths seen and experienced.

Christ Jesus came into the world to save sinners, and I certainly knew that I was one of those! Knowing and relating to Jesus was a very natural part of my childhood—and this was great, because Jesus was good and kind and had time for little children. God, on the other hand, was somewhat scary. He was all-seeing, for one thing. I remember going through a phase of worrying about this. Could God see me when I was on the loo, for instance? Nothing wrong, perhaps, with God being awe-inspiring—'not safe', as Mr Beaver says of Aslan in C.S. Lewis' *The Lion, the Witch and the Wardrobe*—but I certainly travelled more eagerly when other aspects of his nature began to sift through to me as I grew older.

It dawned on me, for one thing, that the whole big story began not with 'miserable sinners' but with love and creativity. God—not just for a short time when Jesus was on earth, but all the time—had the

The God I travel with and towards is, I believe, behind the way that good can come out of evil...

Art may become as much a vehicle of general revelation as science and philosophy, for all truth is God's truth wherever it is found.

ARTHUR F. HOLMES

heart of a lover; and the heart of an artist too. What good news that was!

A God who is at work and evidenced in and through and throughout his creation is still awesome; but he is also creative and vulnerable and accessible. He acts in ways that are good and loving, that respect human variety and individuality and freedom. I didn't need to feel guilty about not doing specifically 'religious' things. All knowledge could be an aspect of learning more about God and his ways—through fiction, drama, history, gardening, resting, laughing, talking, visiting art galleries, as well as through the Bible, prayer, and church meetings.

> **I go through life like a transient on his way to eternity, made in the image of God but with that image debased, needing to be taught how to meditate, to worship, to think.**
>
> DONALD COGGAN

These insights, I believe, helped me begin to lose the 'split' feeling that I often had as a teenager, to integrate as a whole person without having to compartmentalize and hide different areas of my life and myself so as to fit in with or please others. However, I've still a long way to go in the business of growing more authentic as a human being, as a Christian, and as me!

Perhaps my slow progress in this area is due in part to one less-than-helpful aspect of my early background. Normal childish behaviour was, I suspect, too readily dubbed and treated as sinful. Consequently, some of us who failed to attain the required high standards were saddled with inappropriate feelings of guilt and inadequacy. Later insights on God as loving creator who made human beings in his image helped me to put a higher value on, and to be more hopeful about, myself and others. How often I had heard, 'We bring nothing to God but our sins.' But later I wondered: do we really? Surely we bring ourselves to him—his creation, albeit marred and in need of redeeming and restoring.

My experience of people, including non-believers, drew me to this 'flawed image bearers' rather than 'totally depraved' view, too. Non-believers were not, I discovered, any more obviously sinister and evil than the rest of us. Some of them were even nicer and more likable than some of the believers I knew, including myself. I could not, any longer, simply see people as in one box or another; there was more to be said about them than that, biblically, let alone psychologically. Besides, who was I to judge their relationship with God? Outward behaviour and words could be deceptive according to Jesus: not everyone calling him 'Lord, Lord' was actually on his side! (Matthew 7:21).

Back in those early boarding-school years, however, I quite often felt inadequate and vulnerable, afraid and anxious—emotions which came to the fore again strongly when, after 32 years of marriage, I was unexpectedly bereaved. On and off over the nine years since my husband Mike's death, I have been facing up to a lot of painful emotions and questions. At times, God hasn't felt close or accessible; on the contrary, he has appeared to be silent and hidden when I have most wished and needed him not to be. I have to admit that since Mike's death, I have found it much harder to feel God's love. I can believe it in my head, but to feel it in my heart and being is a different matter.

It was Mike's exclusive and cherishing love that made God's love particularly real to me. The love of parents, children, grandchildren, other family members and friends is enormously affirming and healing, but—for me—there is no substitute for that one-to-one intimacy with someone who knows the worst about you and still thinks you are wonderful, and is always there for you. However, lots of other people, many of whom I have met in recent years, have to travel with all kinds of enduring losses and handicaps. Fortunately, the one who warned us that the going would be tough understands and is close, and his agents and other resources are all around us as we journey, and grieve, with hope.

I could not, any longer, simply see people as in one box or another; there was more to be said about them than that, biblically, let alone psychologically

This has been the context in which I am learning more about God's subtler ways of working, recognizing his touch, compassion and guidance in the people I meet and the experiences I have day by day, finding 'angels' and 'means of grace' in sometimes very unexpected places. Perhaps others hear heavenly voices, see skywriting and 'feel' loved by God all the time. In all honesty I don't, but I believe that he touches, speaks to, comforts and resources me through life, through 'all good gifts around us' and through people and all the ways we interact and communicate with one another. Of course, the Bible, prayer and worship are very important, but they too, surely, are made available and accessible in those same ways.

The God I travel with and towards is, I believe, behind the way that good can come out of evil and suffering, and love can open us up to joy and pain; behind the way that certain things elude us when we pursue them but come as byproducts of our doing other worthwhile things. But he's not just the God of such paradoxes and of the gaps in our knowledge; he's also the God behind all that we do know and understand about the way the world, people, life, the environment, knowledge, science, art—everything—normally works and interconnects. To return to the journey image, the maps, the terrain, the bends, the milestones, the bypaths, the signposts and other travellers matter to us because he is interested and with us in it all. In truth, mysteriously, he is our destination and the road itself. ■

> **The pilgrim can never have everything neatly 'sewn up'—there is always the exploration, the search, the movement, the questions and the challenge.**
>
> PETER MILLAR

Lead us on our journey
to places of
resurrection,
to dwellings
of peace,
to healings
of wounds,
to joys of discovery.
RAY SIMPSON

PRAYER

Prayer journey:
the body matters

This meditation is an edited extract from 'Long Wandering Prayer',
by David Hansen (BRF, 2001). David is a Baptist pastor in Cincinnati,
Ohio, USA, having formerly worked in Montana.

Long wandering prayer… is mental wandering in the presence of God, corresponding to physical wandering in the presence of God. Long wandering prayer involves leaving our normal environment for the express purpose of spending many hours alone with God. It involves walking, or at least moving, and stopping whenever we want, to consider a lily for as long as we desire. Long wandering prayer uses the fact that our minds wander as an advantage to prayer rather than as a disadvantage. In long wandering prayer we recognize that what we want to pray about may not be what God wants us pray about. Our obsessive drive to control our minds in the presence of God, that is, to pray about one thing or stick to one list, may be a form of hiding from God. In this kind of prayer we recognize the wandering mind as a precious resource for complex and startling dialogue with God…

The body matters in prayer, as does the physical world around us. We know this and yet many of us understand prayer as an exercise in which we should ideally subdue, quiet or otherwise discipline the body so that it remains dormant while we engage in the spiritual exercise of prayer. There is no question about the fact that prayer is a spiritual exercise. Prayer is in its very essence our soul in communion with the Spirit of God. The fallacy lies in the idea that the body must be subdued in order for the soul to commune with the Spirit of God. The very term 'quiet time' (the fullest term being 'quiet time with

To pray for a community, walk through the neighbourhoods during prayer

> **In this kind of prayer we recognize the wandering mind as a precious resource for complex and startling dialogue with God**

> **Not all those who wander are lost**
> J.R.R. TOLKIEN

God') implies this very thing—that we go to a quiet place and quiet the body so that we can be with God in quiet. Why can't we call it 'noisy time'? Why can't we call it 'moving time'? Why can't we say, 'I had a great *noisy time* with God this morning'? I know of no biblical mandate for quiet time. For me, quiet time always turns into sleepy time. I think that what we have been calling quiet time should really, biblically, be termed 'alone time'.

Doesn't Jesus tell us to pray behind closed doors? Indeed. He tells us, 'But whenever you pray, go into your room and shut the door and pray to your Father who is in secret; and your Father who sees in secret will reward you' (Matthew 6:6). Jesus tells us to pray in secret, not in quiet. How quiet would that room be? He was probably referring to the pantry or storage room of a small house. The house filled with children, animals, neighbours and street noise would have provided precious little quiet time. However, alone in the pantry, hearing the glorious cry of a child at play, the parent might well have prayed more fervently for that child than if they had been praying in an insulated room.

Did not Jesus go to the mountain to pray? Absolutely. When did you last pray on a mountain? I prayed on a mountain yesterday, alone. Birds whistled, the river roared, the wind howled, and my heart thumped as I climbed the mountain. Alone with God, I felt quite free to speak out loud. It was not quiet—and my body was not subdued—and my prayers reflected invigoration.

Doesn't it say, 'Be still, and know that I am God' (Psalm 46:10)? Yes, it does. But in the context of Psalm 46 the injunction means 'be still' in the presence of war's violent destruction and mountains that are shaking and falling into the heart of the sea. It means to be still in the midst of chaos.

Many Christians report difficulty praying for more than ten minutes. Can we do anything for more than ten minutes? Of course. Most of us, whether we will admit it or not, can shop for eight hours. Yes, the same person who cannot pray for more than ten minutes can shop for eight hours…

We consume for eight hours, and we pray for ten minutes. Or is it that we have construed prayer as something so preposterously body-depriving, so mind-numbingly inactive that it is impossible to imagine praying for eight hours and still have a heartbeat? I think that's it. It's easy to say we need to spend more time praying and less time shopping. But this guilt won't help unless we find a physical way to pray more hours. We cannot pray a minute longer than our body allows us. It isn't mind over matter. The brain is matter. The body is matter. The soul isn't matter. But what the body and brain do in prayer does matter to the soul because in this life the soul needs the body and the brain to give it all things human—even in prayer. The soul cannot exult in Handel's *Messiah* without hearing, which is purely a material matter. And the soul cannot enter into the divine communion of prayer without the words and groans and work of the body and the brain. Without the body and the brain in prayer, we cannot think of God in the soul, and the soul will starve in the process...

Prayer issues from the place where we are and is affected by the places the body moves into and out of. To pray for a community, walk through the neighbourhoods during prayer. The prayer will be longer because walking keeps the body alert. The prayer will be broader because moving past dwellings, churches, schools and businesses reminds us to pray for persons and community concerns that never would have entered the mind otherwise. The prayer will be deeper because the sum total of the sights and sounds weighs heavy on the soul.

On the other hand, when the prayer is prompted by a central and demanding irritant—a child is in trouble, a dear one is sick, we are depressed, the church faces demanding times, we are at a crossroads—then getting out to pray surrounded by many sensory stimulants can keep us focused on the one issue at hand... Walking and praying in a forest alive with birds, insects, intermittent wind noises blowing through branches and reeds, and gurgling creeks, may be intensely focused. Out of the din of forest sounds, the ear is distracted by the sound of a woodpecker cracking away at an old beetle-ridden pine. The trail and the prayer diverge—the woodpecker is considered; the woodpecker pounds his head against a tree to feed; we pound our mind against a problem to solve it; we return to the irritant for prayer more intensely than before. ■

The body matters in prayer, as does the physical world around us

Dear

Dear *Quiet Spaces*,

A recent Bible study on 1 Peter reminded me of those wonderful words of verses 6–11. I realized today how much they speak into the very everyday, normal events of life.

Today started off with the usual stress of getting my four boys off to school. (Skateboard techniques practised in the living-room do not go down well at 8 in the morning!) By the time I had dropped the youngest two at the school gates, I was feeling pretty frazzled.

I was already late for 'Loose-ends', a volunteer project providing breakfasts for the homeless, and was determined not to let my stress get in the way of my joy in serving the breakfast 'customers'.

But today, twitching my way down the hill, I found a traffic jam to rest in and 'cast all my anxiety on him'. I prayed that I could arrive at the Baptist hall fully recovered from the morning's rush and stress.

So in the quiet space of my car in a traffic jam, I was very grateful to cast all the churned-up hormones, nerves, 'grrrr', on to him. I gave thanks and praised God and asked to be filled with his love so that I might share his love with the homeless. I felt a bit calmer, but still no smile. So I prayed that God would give me something to smile about. 'I really want to go in smiling today, Lord,' I prayed. 'A real, genuine smile, please, God.'

I turned in to the Baptist hall car park and there was a rather large lady in a huge brown fur coat. She looked so much like a great cuddly teddy bear that my face broke into a huge grin. Thank you, God!

I walked into the hall smiling and spotted a guy who hadn't been for ages. 'Hi, how are you?' I enquired. He looked at me with a big grin. 'What is it with you?' What could he mean? Perhaps I was still twitching... I tried to look normal. 'It's just that... well... you're always smiling.'

Hallelujah!

SUE SMITH, THATCHAM, BERKSHIRE

How this picture came to be

(or, Life can be pants!)

Quiet Spaces reader Susanna Spanring responds to last issue's theme, 'Creation and creativity'.

I am a busy teacher, the mother of three teenagers and wife of a not quite full-fledged Baptist minister, who is completing his training on the job. Sometimes I have to grab my quiet spaces in the midst of chaos. This can mean a pause for prayer outside the door of a seething classroom, before entering and facing the caged lions within. Or it can mean dragging myself out of bed extremely early in the morning and taking the trouble to for a short time and capture this wonderful moment with my paints. I left cups, crumbs, crusts and crud, locked the front door and settled down at the window to a time of marvelling at God's creation and trying to capture a little of its glory on paper.

... everything was laced with a delicate frosting of white...

pamper myself with freshly ground real coffee and a time of prayer, reflection and—let's be honest—an extra snooze in a candle-lit bath before getting down to last-minute marking and the finishing touches for the day's preparation.

In the old days, when I was only working part-time, it was easier. One morning, already exhausted after the daily onslaught of last-minute school forms to sign and the successful reclamation of several long-lost snack boxes, each complete with its ancient, moulding apple core and delicately furred piece of ham, I turned with a sigh to the unpleasant task of clearing away the breakfast things. However, a glance out of the window—initially to wave at three huffy departing backs—completely distracted my attention. It was a crispy autumn morning, everything was laced with a delicate frosting of white, and the light was stunning as it shone through the few remaining leaves on the trees, making them translucent and radiant. I was still in my pyjamas, but I made a conscious decision to forget normal everyday life

I became completely involved in my work until, coming back down to earth with a nasty jolt, I realized that it was 9.45 and that at 10.00 I was supposed to be teaching Music to Years 3 and 4 at our local village school. I left my paints scattered on the floor and rushed to get dressed.

Ten minutes later, I arrived at school. As I started to ascend the rather imposing front staircase, I felt something unfamiliar in my trouser leg. Instinctively I bent down to investigate, simultaneously greeting the headmaster as he approached from further up the stairs. It was a horrifying and embarrassing moment as I realized—too late—that the lump was actually a stray pair of knickers. Hastily I bent and pretended to polish my shoes with the offending garment and made some stupid remark like, 'Muddy today, isn't it?'

Sometimes we pay dearly for our quiet spaces, yet it was worth it. This one enabled me to hold fast to a beautiful moment and I can still relive its joy and wonder—that fascinating combination of nature sparkling outside and the inner sparkle of the creative process. It has also provided me with a funny story into the bargain. ■

Veronica Zundel is a journalist, author and contributor to BRF's 'New Daylight' Bible reading notes. She lives in north London.

Musings of a middle-aged mystic

A fellow writer recently told me she'd been reading a book called *Travels with a Tangerine*. Fortunately I worked out that this meant the author was accompanied by a person from Tangiers, not a withering piece of citrus fruit. It reminded me, however, of the period when it was a running joke in my family that whatever you might forget, you should never travel without at least a couple of satsumas!

The image of the spiritual life as a journey goes back at least to the time when Abram left Ur, if not before. Journeys in ancient times were a lot more hazardous than they are today. True, there were no crashes, but you were lucky if your camel didn't turn uncooperative, if you didn't die of

Or remember that man in Jesus' story, on a journey from Jerusalem to Jericho, waylaid by violent muggers and left for dead. (I've been on that road, and it really is very barren and frightening.)

It was as well, then, to make sure, if possible, that you had good travelling companions as well as the right supplies. What do we need for our journey with God? And what kind of journey is it?

One of the hymns I chose for our wedding was 'Father, hear the prayer we offer', with those scary lines:

Not for ever in green pastures
Do we ask our way to be,
But the steep and rugged pathway
May we tread rejoicingly.

Not for ever by still waters
Would we idly rest and stay,
But would smite the living fountains
From the rocks along our way.

Getting married on my 36th birthday, already well set in my habits, I knew that this journey to which God had clearly called me would not be a bed of roses—or, at least, that the roses might have quite a few thorns.

The journey of life is rarely smooth, and the journey of faith, swimming against the tide of society, is likely to be even less so. We need, then, a few good travelling companions, and enough spiritual food to make it to the next inn. John Bunyan's Christian, in *Pilgrim's Progress*, had Faithful by his side to lighten his load and share his setbacks. It's not always necessary to

---

> The journey of life is rarely smooth, and the journey of faith, swimming against the tide of society, is likely to be even less so

---

dehydration, if your sandals didn't wear out, and if you didn't get attacked by bandits.

Just think of the hungry Israelites remembering the garlic, leeks, cucumber and melons they used to eat in Egypt, before they set off on that crazy journey with Moses; or Balaam, faced with a donkey that simply refused to go one step further (admittedly, the donkey was wiser than Balaam about whether God wanted this particular journey).

travel in a crowd, unless you happen to be a person who likes crowds. One or two sympathetic spiritual companions—a prayer partner or a spiritual director, perhaps—may be all we need to keep us walking.

Christian, however, also had to reject some unhelpful companions, such as Talkative, who was all pious talk and no action. Occasionally (perhaps less often than we think) we may need to distance ourselves from someone who undermines our discipleship. Notice, however, that it's not a non-Christian friend whom the pilgrim has to lose, but a destructive Christian companion.

Supplies for the journey are also vital, and not everyone will thrive on the same thing. Some love satsumas, some prefer bananas; one Christian will find that his or her greatest spiritual sustenance comes from daily Bible reading, another will be refreshed by frequently taking communion. Whatever we need, we should make a habit of replenishing our supplies often as we travel on Jesus' narrow road.

There will always, of course, be times when we are weary, footsore, hungry and lonely. There will even be times when we feel that God has deserted us, and that no more food or friendship will be forthcoming. Yet God provided manna in the desert for the Israelites; and then, when they were bored with manna, down came the quails. Sometimes, when we feel that the journey will never end, when we have only the dimmest view of the

It's not always necessary to travel in a crowd

destination—somehow, amazingly, we are given new strength.

I was moved, last Advent, by a sermon from a visiting preacher at my church. This is part of what he said:

There's a passage in Genesis about Melchizedek, King of Salem, priest of God Most High. After a tremendous battle (Genesis describes it as four kings against five), Melchizedek goes out to meet Abram, gives him bread and wine, blesses him, and is never again seen in the Bible. Melchizedek is a shadowy figure, someone who stands for God, turns up at just the right time, provides food and drink for Abram, and disappears. Perhaps that is the way that some of us experience God: mysteriously, fleetingly and somehow just at the moment of most impact.

That rang lots of bells with me; looking back, I can see so many times when God provided unexpected help, sometimes from the most surprising people, and perhaps only for a moment—but just enough. Why can't

Uphill

Does the road wind uphill all the way?
  Yes, to the very end.
Will the day's journey take the whole long day?
  From morn to night, my friend.

But is there for the night a resting-place?
  A roof for when the slow, dark hours begin.
May not the darkness hide it from my face?
  You cannot miss that inn.

Shall I meet other wayfarers at night?
  Those who have gone before.
Then must I knock, or call when just in sight?
  They will keep you waiting at that door.

Shall I find comfort, travel-sore and weak?
  Of labour you will find the sum.
Will there be beds for me and all who seek?
  Yea, beds for all who come.

CHRISTINA ROSSETTI (1830–94)

Whatever we need, we should make a habit of replenishing our supplies often as we travel on Jesus' narrow road.

I remember these times when I'm feeling at my worst and don't believe that God will ever visit me again?

While compiling a women's poetry anthology many years ago, I came across a poem by Christina Rossetti, called 'Uphill'. It begins with the question, 'Does the road wind uphill all the way?', to which the response is, 'Yes, to the very end.' It's not an answer any of us would be thrilled to hear. But here's the last verse:

Shall I find comfort,
travel-sore and weak?
Of labour you shall find the sum.
Will there be beds for me and all
who seek?
Yea, beds for all who come.

There *is* a destination; there *is* an end to wandering in the desert. And meanwhile, I think I saw a plump quail or two settling over there... ■

We want to hear from you...

Have you enjoyed reading this issue of *Quiet Spaces*? We would love to have your feedback—of what would you like to see more (or less) in future issues? Which writers do you find particularly helpful and why? Write to us or e-mail with your thoughts.

We hope that in reading *Quiet Spaces*, you will want to respond to it. You may find that the prayers, reflections and features inspire you to creativity in some way. If that is the case, do visit the *Quiet Spaces* website where you will find opportunity to share your thoughts with others.

Contact us at:

Quiet Spaces,
BRF, First Floor,
Elsfield Hall,
15–17 Elsfield Way,
Oxford OX2 8FG

enquiries@brf.org.uk

In the next issue, our theme will be *The Feast*, exploring our spiritual hunger and the ways in which God offers us satisfaction.

QUIET SPACES SUBSCRIPTIONS

Quiet Spaces is published three times a year, in March, July and November. To take out a subscription, please complete this form, indicating the month in which you would like your subscription to begin.

☐ I would like to give a gift subscription (please complete both name and address sections below)

☐ I would like to take out a subscription myself (complete name and address details only once)

This completed coupon should be sent with appropriate payment to BRF. Alternatively, please write to us quoting your name, address, the subscription you would like for either yourself or a friend (with their name and address), the start date and credit card number, expiry date and signature if paying by credit card.

Gift subscription name _____

Gift subscription address _____

_____

_____ Postcode _____

Please send beginning with the next November / March / July issue: *(delete as applicable)*

(please tick box)   UK   SURFACE   AIR MAIL

Quiet Spaces   ☐ £16.95   ☐ £18.45   ☐ £20.85

Please complete the payment details below and send your coupon, with appropriate payment to: BRF, First Floor, Elsfield Hall, 15–17 Elsfield Way, Oxford OX2 8FG.

Name _____

Address _____

_____

Postcode _____ Telephone Number _____

Email _____

☐ Please do not email me any information about BRF publications

Method of payment: ☐ Cheque ☐ Mastercard ☐ Visa ☐ Postal Order ☐ Switch

Card no. ☐☐☐☐ ☐☐☐☐ ☐☐☐☐ ☐☐☐☐ ☐☐☐☐ ☐☐☐☐

Expires ☐☐ ☐☐   Issue no. of Switch card ☐☐☐

Signature _____ Date ___/___/_____

All orders must be accompanied by the appropriate payment.
Please make cheques payable to BRF

PROMO REF: QSJOURNEY

☐ Please do not send me further information about BRF publications

BRF is a Registered Charity

64

15 to 1

15 to 1

2002 for 2002

First published in 2001 by Channel 4 Books, an imprint of Pan Macmillan Ltd,
Pan Macmillan, 20 New Wharf Road, London N1 9RR, Basingstoke and Oxford.

Associated companies throughout the world.

www.panmacmillan.com

ISBN 0 7522 6148 7

Text © Channel 4 Books, 2001

9 8 7 6 5 4 3 2 1

A CIP catalogue record for this book is available from the British Library.

Design and typesetting by Ben Cracknell Studios.

Printed by Mackays of Chatham plc.

This book accompanies the television series *15 to 1* made by Regent Productions
for Channel 4.
Executive producer: William G. Stewart

15 to 1 is a Trademark of Regent Productions Limited. Licensed by Fremantle Brand
Licensing.
www.fremantlemedia.com

CONTENTS

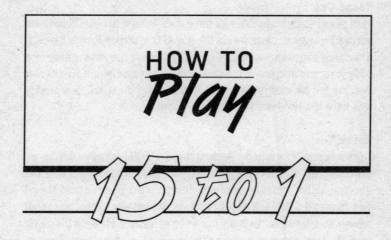

HOW TO Play

15 to 1

15 to 1: 2002 for 2002 is the ultimate challenge for you either to test your own general knowledge, or to pit your wits against friends and family. The book contains 2002 questions, all of which have featured on the television show. They are divided into three rounds, to enable you to recreate the show at home.

If you are playing in a group of three or more you need to nominate one of the players to take the role of William G. Stewart and act as questionmaster and scorekeeper. There are scoresheets at the back of the book (pages 247–268) which you can either photocopy or fill in with pencil.

For eight players upward

Although we always start with fifteen players on the programme, it is quite possible to play the same game with only eight (providing not too many players lose both their lives in Round One!).

Round One

Each player starts the game with three lives. In turn, the questionmaster asks each player a question from the Round One section (pages 11–50). If the player answers incorrectly, or does not know the answer, they lose a life. A second question is then asked of each player in turn, and again, lives are lost for incorrect answers. At the end of the round, any players who have lost two lives are out of the game.

Round Two

The remaining players begin the next round with either two or three lives, depending on whether they got both questions right in Round One. The questionmaster begins by asking the first person a question from Round Two (pages 51–135). If the player gets the answer wrong, or cannot answer, they lose a life and play moves on to the next player. If the player gives the correct answer, they can then nominate another player to answer a question. If this player gets the question right, then he or she can nominate another player and so play continues. However, if any player gets a question wrong, then he or she loses a life and play returns to the previous player to nominate another player again. Play continues until all but three of the players have lost all of their lives.

Round Three

The remaining three players proceed to the quick-fire Round Three, with three new lives. In this round, not only do the players have to avoid losing lives, they also need to gain points. The questionmaster will need a pencil and paper to keep score. For every incorrect answer the player loses a life; for every correct answer he or she gains 10 points.

The questionmaster begins play by asking questions from Round Three (pages 137–193) to the floor – the quickest correct answer gains 10 points. An incorrect answer results in a life lost. This continues until one of the players has earned 30 points.

From then on, a correct answer allows the player to either answer another question, or to nominate another player. If the player gets the question wrong, then the next question is to the floor again. If a player chooses to nominate and the second player gets the question right, then the second player has the option to take a question or nominate, and so on. If a nominated player gets the question wrong, then play returns to the previous player who can choose either to take a question or to nominate again. If the player who answered the question from the floor chooses to take a question rather than nominate, and gets this wrong, play returns to the floor.

Play continues until two of the players have lost all three lives. The questionmaster continues to ask the final player questions until either they have lost all three lives, or a total of 40 questions have been asked during Round Three. The winner is the player who has the highest score.

For five to eight players

If you have between five and eight players, including the questionmaster, then you can play a two-round game, following the instructions above for Round Two and Round Three. Each player begins Round Two (now the first round) with three lives.

For three to four players

For just three or four players, including the questionmaster, play Round Three only. If you want the game to be slightly easier, use the questions from Round One.

For two players

If there are just two players, each player should take a turn at being the questionmaster. At the beginning of the game, the players should agree which round they are going to take the questions from. The question-master asks the other player questions, awarding 10 points for a correct answer, and deducting a life for an incorrect answer. When the first player has lost all their lives or a total of 40 questions have been asked, they take a turn as the questionmaster and ask the second player questions, until all three of this player's lives are lost or 40 questions have been asked. The winner is the player with the most points.

15 to 1

ROUND ONE
Questions

1 Law ✓

Taken from the Latin for 'elsewhere', what word is used in law for a provable assertion that the accused person was somewhere else when the crime was committed?

2 History

The chief naval battle of the First World War. In Germany it is known as the Skagerrak. How is it known in Britain?

3 Art

Beata Beatrix is an idealized portrait of the artist's late wife, the former model Elizabeth Siddal. Which member of the Pre-Raphaelites painted it?

4 Africa

The name of which town in Mali has come to stand for any distant or outlandish place?

5 The Peerage ✓

Eaton Hall in Cheshire has been the seat of which ducal family since the 1440s?

6 Horse Racing

Who was the first jockey in the world to ride 4000 winners?

7 Dance ✓

In which country did the samba originate?

8 Flags

What are the colours of the national flag of the Republic of Ireland?

9 Anatomy ✓

What part of your body interests a rhinologist?

10 The UK ✓

Which picturesque village on Dartmoor, in Devon, is renowned for its annual fair?

11 France ✓

In which town in Normandy is the major tourist attraction a 23-foot-long embroidery that dates from the eleventh century?

12 Science

Taking its name from the Latin for apple, which crystalline acid is found in unripe apples and other fruits?

13 Medicine ✓

A haematologist is a doctor who specializes in diseases of?

14 *Units of Measurements*

Of what is a Hoppus foot a unit of measurement?

15 *Wine* ✓

Rioja is a wine produced in which European country?

16 *Mythology*

How many heads had the mythical dog Cerberus?

17 *Opera* ✓

Whose engravings inspired Stravinsky's opera *The Rake's Progress*?

18 *Animals*

If a dog is canine, what is a pig?

19 *The Second World War*

Who in 1940 were referred to by Churchill as 'the Few'?

20 *Football*

Which English Premiership club plays its home fixtures at Anfield?

21 *Sport* ✓

Which famous shooting range is near Woking in Surrey?

22 *Cinema* ✓

The early epic films *Intolerance* and *The Birth of a Nation* were directed by which American film-maker?

23 *Scottish History*

What is the name of the village, east of Edinburgh, where in 1745 a 3000-strong Hanoverian army was routed by a 2000-strong Jacobite force?

24 *Law* ✓

What term is used in law to refer to a wall which separates two adjoining properties (house or land) and which belongs to the owners equally?

25 *Expeditions* ✓

The *Terra Nova* ship carried whose Antarctic expedition in 1910?

26 *Science* ✓

Which acid with the formula HCOOH occurs naturally in ants?

27 Broadcasting ✓

From where did the first regular British television broadcasts start transmission in London in 1936?

28 Currency

Which country's Markka bank-notes feature portraits of the composer Sibelius, the architect Alvar Aalto and the athlete Paavo Nurmi?

29 Government

The holder of which Cabinet post is responsible for advising the Crown on the appointment of senior judges?

30 Charities

By what name is the Royal Society for Mentally Handicapped Children and Adults better known?

31 The Ancient World

Formed by the Ptolemaic rulers of the third Century BC, it was the largest library in the ancient world and said to contain between 100,000 and 700,000 manuscripts. Which library?

32 Population

Which of the five inhabited continents has the largest population?

33 Architecture

Which English palace (on the bank of the River Thames in the south-west of London) was built by Cardinal Wolsey and later enlarged by Henry VIII and altered by Sir Christopher Wren?

34 The Media ✓

What are: the Bay, based in Lancaster; the Breeze, based in Southend; and the Wave, based in Blackpool?

35 Cinema

Which character is the most famous creation of the French film actor/director Jacques Tati?

36 Animals ✓

What name is given to an otter's den or nest?

37 Geography ✓

Which stretch of water connects the Mediterranean Sea and the Atlantic Ocean?

38 Art and Design ✓

What do the letters 'ap' on an etching or print stand for?

39 People

Norman Foster, Richard Seifret and Richard Rogers are famous names in which profession?

40 Art

What was the pseudonym of the Italian painter Guido di Pietro, the Dominican friar best known for the frescoes he painted at the Monastery of San Marco in Florence, under the patronage of Cosimo de' Medici?

41 Geography

To which island group do the islands of Rhodes and Kos belong?

42 The USA ✓

What is the chief investigating branch of the US Department of Justice called?

43 Medicine

Braidism, after James Braid who introduced it into medicine, is another name for what?

44 Awards

The Golden Bear in Berlin, the Golden Shell in San Sebastian and the Golden Lion in Venice are major awards given in which area of the arts?

45 Words

What does the term 'guerilla warfare' mean literally?

46 Writers ✓

In which European capital city is Oscar Wilde buried?

47 The Commonwealth ✓

Two Commonwealth countries are islands in the Mediterranean Sea. Name either of the two.

48 US Presidents

When George W. Bush was sworn in as President, he and his father became the second father and son to be US Presidents: What is the surname of the first father and son to achieve that distinction?

49 Opera

What is the occupation of Escamillo in the opera Carmen?

50 *Acronyms*

What does CAMRA stand for?

51 *Numbers*

If you are a quinguagenarian, you are in your...?

52 *Geography* ✓

What is the capital of Saudi Arabia?

53 *Shakespeare*

In which play does the eponymous character smother his wife?

54 *Business*

With which household appliance is the businessman and inventor James Dyson chiefly associated?

55 *Quotations*

On meeting which of his wives did Henry VIII, finding her so different from her picture, swear that they had brought him a Flanders mare?

56 *Trade Unions*

ANSA is an independent trade union for the staff of which high street bank?

57 *Shipping Forecasts*

The shipping forecast areas Cromarty, Forth and Tyne are named after river estuaries. What are the shipping forecast areas Rockall, Utsire and Lundy named after?

58 *Sport*

Flushing Meadow, Roland Garros and Melbourne Park are all Grand Slam venues in which sport?

59 *The Royal Family*

Apart from Charles, the Prince of Wales has three other Christian names. What are two of the three?

60 *The United Nations* ✓

The International Court of Justice is the principal judicial organ of the UN. In which European city is it based?

61 *Food* ✓

In Scottish cuisine what is a bannock?

62 *Saints*

Which of the four British patron saints is the only one who was an apostle?

63 *Mathematics*

In a right-angled triangle, the square on the hypotenuse is equal to the sum of the square of the lengths of the other two sides. Whose theorem is this?

64 *Grammar*

Which part of speech modifies or describes a verb?

65 *Precious Stones* ✓

What name is commonly given to the red transparent variety of the mineral corundum?

66 *People*

What is the name of the Dublin-born philanthropist who, in the second half of the nineteenth century, gave up the idea of missionary work in China in order to raise money to provide homeless children with a place to sleep in London's East End?

67 *Geography* ✓

Lusaka is the capital city of which African country?

68 *Buildings* ✓

In 1988 the 600-year-old Great West Window of which minster was buried to preserve it?

69 *Relatives* ✓

Which writer is the eldest daughter of Lord Longford?

70 *Cinema*

Who won an Oscar for his telephone song 'I Just Called to Say I Love You'?

71 *Science*

What letter links an SI unit of temperature and the chemical symbol for potassium?

72 *The USA* ✓

What is the name of the range of hills in South Dakota, near the town of Deadwood, in which the Mount Rushmore National Memorial is situated?

73 *History* ✓

The Crimean War was fought by Great Britain, France, Sardinia and Turkey against which country?

74 *Architecture*

What type of architectural settlements were pioneered by Sir Ebenezer Howard at the turn of the nineteenth and twentieth centuries?

75 *History*

Which seventh-century monk was known as the 'Apostle of Northumbria'?

76 *The Media*

The BSC was established in 1997 to consider complaints about violence, sex and matters of taste and decency from viewers or listeners. What does BSC stand for?

77 *Numbers*

If you were celebrating a sesqui-centennial anniversary, how many years would you be celebrating?

78 *Mathematics*

What word describes the result of multiplying two or more numbers together?

79 *Astronomy*

In 1781 astronomer William Herschel discovered the seventh major planet from the Sun. What was it?

80 *The UK* ✓

In which British city are Cavern Walks, Strawberry Field and Penny Lane?

81 *Animals* ✓

Barnacle, Greylag, Brent and Canada are types of which bird?

82 *Religious Groups*

Which religious order was founded by Ignatius Loyola in 1534 and given a papal charter in 1540?

83 *Geography* ✓

The Isle of Man was, until 1266, a dependency of which European country?

84 *Feast Days*

What is the name of the ninth-century Bishop of Winchester whose feast day is held in England on 15th July?

85 *Literature*

The Beautiful and the Damned, Tender is the Night and *The Great Gatsby* were all written by which American author?

86 *Phobias* ✓

Sinophobia is the fear of which race or nation?

87 *Business*

Britannia, JMC and Monarch are all major companies in which area of business?

88 *Names*

What does the girl's name Verity mean?

89 *Literature*

'Or there and back again' was the subtitle of the book in which Bilbo Baggins, Gollum and Gandalf first appear. What is the book?

90 *The Peerage*

For which duke are the addresses given in *Who's Who* Arundel Castle, Sussex; Carlton Towers, Goole, North Humberside; and Bacres House, Henley-on-Thames?

91 *Films* ✓

In which classic 1960 thriller does Marion Crane steal $40,000 from her boss and unwisely make her escape via the Bates Motel?

92 *Dates*

United Nations Day falls in which month of the year?

93 *Wine*

On wine labels what is the meaning of the word recolte?

94 *Musical Instruments*

On which musical instrument would a paradiddle be played?

95 *The Commonwealth* ✓

In which Commonwealth country is there a city called Stratford, on a river called Avon, where the festival theatre regularly stages plays by William Shakespeare?

96 *British Prime Ministers*

Only one British Prime Minister of the twentieth century was in office for a complete uninterrupted decade. Which Prime Minister?

97 *Medicine*

Epistaxis is the medical name for which common condition or complaint?

98 *Phrases*

Which term, originally coined during the march on Madrid in the Spanish Civil War, refers to collaborators and the enemy within?

99 *Law*

In relation to the law and crime, what is the CICB concerned with?

100 *Geography*

If you sailed due east from Newcastle, which would be the first country you would reach?

101 *Animals*

The quokka is a member of which family of animals?

102 *Chess*

At the beginning of a chess game which two pieces flank the queen?

103 *Costume*

Worn on the head, what is a chaplet?

104 *Medicine*

If a person is suffering from aphonia, what are they unable to do?

105 *Cinema*

In the 1961 film, which guns did Gregory Peck, Anthony Quinn, David Niven and Anthony Quayle set out to demolish?

106 *Phrases*

The phrase 'the quick and the dead' appears in the Anglican Book of Common Prayer version of the Apostles' Creed. Who or what are the 'quick'?

107 *Geography*

Into which bay, part of the Indian Ocean, do the Irrawaddy, Ganges and Brahmaputra rivers flow?

108 *Words*

What would be kept in a bonbonniere?

109 *Acronyms*

A professional qualification in the world of insurance, what is denoted by the letters FIA after someone's name?

110 *Mythology*

What was the name of the wild creatures, often represented as part man and part goat, that had voracious appetites for sex, wine and revelry?

111 *Dance*

The czardas is the national dance of which country?

112 *Chemistry*

The name of which chemical element, symbol P, is derived from the Greek for 'light-bringing'?

113 *Physics*

The ampere is the SI unit of electric current; of what is the coulomb the SI unit?

114 *Food and Drink*

Pumpernickel is a type of what?

115 *Computers*

Fortran, a computer language, is an abbreviation for what?

116 *Geography*

Formerly part of Yugoslavia, but now an independent state, of which European country is Ljubljana the capital city?

117 *Medicine*

What is the popular name for the anaesthetic nitrous oxide?

118 *The Second World War*

The lives of two major protagonists of the Second World War ended within two days of each other – on 28 and 30 April 1945. Who were they?

119 *Golf*

In golf what is meant by 'the Nineteenth Hole'?

120 *Television*

Two BBC series featured the characters Bernard Woolley, James Hacker and Sir Humphrey Appleby. Name either series?

121 *Surgery*

What sort of operation is a rhytidectomy?

122 *The Monarchy*

The oldest person to have ascended the British throne did so in 1830 at the age of 64. Who was he?

123 *Sport*

Athletics: the eastern cut-off, western roll and straddle have largely been replaced by the Fosbury flop. In which field event?

124 *Mythology*

In German mythology which of the knights who sought the Holy Grail was the father of Lohengrin?

125 *Place Names*

Which English word, commonly used on its own but also as a suffix in place names, comes from the Old English for fort?

126 *The Bible*

Genesis, Exodus, Leviticus are three of The Pentateuch, or the Five Books of Moses. Name one of the other two.

127 *Business*

Which major petroleum company celebrated its centenary on 27 April 1988?

128 *Finance*

Which body has responsibility for setting interest rates in the UK?

129 *Art*

What are the first names by which the controversial artists, whose surnames are Proesch and Passmore, are more commonly known?

130 *Horticulture*

Where, near Guildford in Surrey, is the Royal Horticultural Society's principal garden, established in 1904 and now covering 240 acres?

131 *Education*

Which university, founded in 1636, is the oldest institution of higher learning in the United States?

132 *Latin Phrases*

What is the English translation of the Latin phrase 'primus inter pares' which Jeffrey Archer used as the title of one of his novels?

133 *The Decorative Arts*

Which English potter developed a black stoneware called basaltware, and a white stoneware stained blue or other colours called jasperware?

134 *Animals*

What name is given to a group of gun dogs who can be trained to indicate where game lies, by standing motionless and aligning their muzzle, body and tail with the game?

135 *The USA*

Which state is the largest producer and exporter of wine?

136 *International Organizations*

In the grounds of the headquarters of which international organization is the famous statue called *Let us Beat Swords into Plowshares*?

137 *Musical Instruments*

In which section of the orchestra do the clarinet, the bassoon and the oboe belong?

138 *Religion*

Which archangel was the 'the angel who spoke to Moses on Mount Sinai'?

139 *History*

Which French king did Henry VIII meet at the Field of Cloth of Gold in 1520?

140 *Weaponry*

What was the name of the British battleship, launched in 1906, that had ten 12-inch guns and gave its name to an entirely new class of warship?

141 *History* ✓

The London agreement of 1954 restored the city of Trieste to which country?

142 *Boats and Ships* ✓

What are the draining holes or spouts which allow water on the deck of a vessel to flow overboard?

143 *Literature* ✓

Who began writing his diary on New Year's Day 1660?

144 *The Royal Family*

Which member of the Royal Family has been Lord High Admiral of the United Kingdom since 1964?

145 *Geography*

The River Aras forms part of the border between Turkey and which other country?

146 *Religion*

The Chairman of the House of Bishops is the Archbishop of Canterbury. Who is the Vice-Chairman?

147 *Literature*

The Go-Between and the trilogy *The Shrimp and the Anemone, The Sixth Heaven* and *Eustace and Hilda* were all written by which English novelist?

148 *International Politics* ✓

Name one of the founding members of the CIS, or Commonwealth of Independent States, other than Russia.

149 *Literature*

Which of the E.M. Forster novels, which he referred to as 'the Lucy novel', features a trip to Italy by Lucy Honeychurch and her chaperone, Charlotte Bartlett?

150 *Russian History*

The murder of which ruler and his family took place in Yekaterinburg in 1918?

151 *Museums*

Where is the Black Museum?

152 *Universities*

Who is the writer, radio broadcaster and TV presenter who is the Chancellor of Leeds University?

153 *Counties*

In which county are Gravesend, Sandwich and Ramsgate?

154 *Popular Culture*

Which group of comedians had hits with 'I'm Walking Backwards for Christmas' and the 'Ying Tong Song' in the 1950s?

155 *The Monarchy*

George I (1714–27) and Queen Victoria (1837–1901) were the first and last monarchs of which royal house?

156 *History*

Who in the seventeenth century asked Sir Peter Lely to paint his portrait with 'pimples, warts and everything as you see me'?

157 *Organizations*

Members of which trade are represented by the RHA?

158 *The UK* ✓

What is the name of the lighthouse off the south-west coast of Ireland which plays an important role in the Admiral's Cup?

159 *Shakespeare*

Who wins the hand of Kate – the shrew in the title of the play, *The Taming of the Shrew*?

160 *European History* ✓

Who made his eldest brother, Joseph, King of Spain in 1808?

161 *Roman History*

By tradition St Peter was crucified around AD 64, during the reign of which Roman emperor?

162 *Geography*

What is the capital of the Italian region of Piedmont?

163 *Geography*

Which is the only continent whose mainland is made up of a single country?

164 *Playwrights*

Brighton Beach Memoirs, Biloxi Blues and *Broadway Bound*, written in the 1980s, are autobiographical comedy-dramas by which American playwright?

165 *Weather Forecasts*

What term, used by weather forecasters, may be defined as a V-shaped extension of the isobars from a centre of low pressure?

166 *Acronyms*

What, in the world of television and radio, is commonly abbreviated as OB?

167 *Cinema*

Name the tough-guy actor who became Mayor of Carmel, in California, in 1986?

168 *Etymology*

What loose-weave fabric, often used for surgical dressings, is said to derive its name from the Palestinian city of Gaza?

169 *Blue Plaques*

A blue plaque on 71 Hereford Road, London W2, commemorates the first man to transmit a radio signal across the Atlantic. What was his name?

170 *The Commonwealth*

Kuala Lumpur is the capital of which Commonwealth country?

171 *Music*

In which song did Noel Coward state 'But Englishmen detest a siesta'?

172 *Aviation*

What was the popular name of the world's first vertical take-off and landing machine, made by Rolls-Royce in 1954?

173 *Crime Fiction*

What is the name of the gentleman thief and safe-cracker who appears in the short stories of E.W. Hornung?

174 *Mythology*

Who was the wife of Jason who murdered their children after Jason deserted her to marry Glauce?

175 *Words*

What is a pen name called in French?

176 *The Bible*

Cain and Abel were two of the sons of Adam and Eve. What is the name of their third son?

177 *Shakespeare* ✓

In the title of a Shakespeare play, where do two gentlemen called Valentine and Proteus come from?

178 *Geography*

On which stretch of water is Port Said at the northern end and Port Suez at the southern?

179 *Currency* ✓

What is the currency unit of New Zealand?

180 *The USA*

Which US state is abbreviated, as part of its ZIP code, as WI?

181 *Social History*

Since the 1950s, which protest marches have gone between Aldermaston and London?

182 *Medicine* ✓

What type of medical treatment do people who suffer from tryanophobia fear?

183 *The Bible*

Which biblical patriarch has a son Ishmael by his wife's maid-servant Hagar?

184 *Geography*

What is the capital city in the state of Victoria in Australia?

185 *Flags*

What symbol appears on the national flag of Israel?

186 *Cinema* ✓

Who was John Merrick in the film starring John Hurt?

187 *History*

Who, in the sixteenth century, was the last English monarch to be excommunicated by a pope?

188 *The Monarchy*

Which of Henry VIII's wives is the only one to be buried with him in St George's Chapel, Windsor?

189 *Books*

Complete the full title of the best-selling book on how to improve relationships by John Gray: *Men Are from Mars ...*?

190 *Shakespeare*

Who, in a Shakespeare play, after the death of her lover, brings about her own death with the bite of an asp?

191 *The Ancient World*

The ruins of the ancient city of Babylon are located in which modern country?

192 *Horse Racing*

Name two of the three events which make up the Triple Crown of horse racing in the USA?

193 *Science*

Hydrolysis is the decomposition of a chemical substance by?

194 *The Royal Family*

Who is the first grandchild of George VI?

195 *Television*

In which classic television series, first produced in the 1960s, were Bob Ferris and Terry Collier the main characters?

196 *Religion*

Which river is the most sacred river of the Hindus?

197 *Dates*

In Britain, how often is there a national census?

198 *Name Connections* ✓

What name connects a popular chocolate wafer biscuit and a London club of prominent Whigs and literary figures established in the early 1700s?

199 *Literature*

Who is the author of *A Farewell to Arms, Death in the Afternoon* and *The Sun Also Rises*?

200 *Motor Cars*

The Mustang, Cortina and Escort were classic models of which motor manufacturer in the 1960s and 1970s?

201 *France*

What is the name of the large park to the west of Paris, once a royal hunting ground, and which includes the racecourses of Longchamp and Auteuil?

202 *Engineering*

In engineering, industry and manufacturing what does 'R and D' stand for?

203 *The Decorative Arts*

Cloisonné, which may be found on vases and other ornaments, is a form of what type of decoration?

204 *Literature*

Which popular fictional character, created by Washington Irving, is a cheerful ne'er-do-well who falls asleep for 20 years?

205 *Botany*

Silvaner, Syrah and Merlot are all varieties of which fruit?

206 *Religion*

In the Church of England hierarchy which bishop, in order of seniority, comes after the archbishops of Canterbury and York?

207 *Latin Phrases*

Which Latin phrase meaning 'winner of the games' is often applied to a school's sports champion?

208 *Motor Cars* ✓

The Punto, the Bravo and the Seicento are models of cars produced by which motor manufacturer?

209 *Music*

What name is given to the ability possessed by some people to identify and reproduce a note of music without reference to a tuned musical instrument?

210 *International Registration Letters*

Which European country does a car with the registration letters RSM come from?

211 *Horse Racing*

What is the minimum distance for a race on the flat under the rules of racing formulated by the Jockey Club?

212 *Medicine*

For what would a doctor use a plexor or plessor?

213 *Architecture*

What word describes a tall tapering column of stone, an example of one being Cleopatra's Needle?

214 *Words*

The followers of the Greek philosopher Zeno gave their name to a word now applied to someone showing patient endurance – what is the word?

215 *The UK* ✓

The Cheddar Gorge in Somerset cuts through which range of limestone hills?

216 *Literature*

How is Alice Liddell, daughter of the Dean of Christ Church, Oxford, now remembered in literature?

217 *Cinema*

The 1958 film *A Night to Remember* tells the story of which tragic incident in 1912, which was also the subject of an Oscar-winning 1997 film?

218 *Poetry*

Who wrote 'In the spring, a young man's fancy lightly turns to thoughts of love'?

219 *Cinema*

The Last Emperor, Last Tango in Paris and *The Conformist* are all films by which Oscar-winning director?

220 *International Organizations* ✓

Founded in 1948 to promote unity among Christian churches, in which city are the headquarters of the World Council of Churches?

221 *The UK*

Which city on the River Trent has traditionally produced cigarettes, bicycles and lace, and is the original home of Boots the Chemists?

222 *Sport*

Which team sport originated in 1895 as minonette, a game devised as a less tiring alternative to basketball?

223 *Sport*

What is the upper CC limit for speedway motorbikes?

224 *Proverbs*

According to the proverb, what do you do if you spare the rod?

225 *Physics*

The maximum constant velocity reached by an object falling through a gas or a liquid is known as?

226 *Music*

What on a written score does the Latin word TACET indicate?

227 *Mythology* ✓

What is the name of the creature which was half man and half bull, lived in the Labyrinth and was killed by Theseus?

228 *Astronomy*

Which is the only planet in our solar system with retrograde motion?

229 *Poetry and Music*

Many of the poems in which collection by A.E. Housman have been set to music by, among others, composers including Ralph Vaughan Williams, George Butterworth and Ivor Gurney?

230 *Physics*

Which form of electromagnetic radiation, with a wavelength between 1mm and 0.3m, lies between infrared and short-wave radio waves in the electromagnetic spectrum?

231 *European Landmarks*

In which European city are the Trevi Fountain, the Spanish Steps and the Forum famous landmarks?

232 *Geography*

Male is the main island of which island group in the Indian Ocean?

233 *Mathematics*

What Latin word meaning 'pebble' is given to that branch of mathematics that is concerned with the integration and differentiation of functions?

234 *Anatomy*

Associated with the eye, cilia is the anatomical name for what?

235 *Languages*

Similar to Portuguese, which regional language is spoken by an estimated three million people in the north-western corner of Spain?

236 *Horse Racing* ✓

What does it mean if a racehorse is described as a maiden?

237 *The USA*

In which mountain range is the famous resort and sports centre Lake Placid which hosted the Winter Olympics in 1932 and 1980?

238 *Dates*

The third Monday in January is a public holiday in the United States, celebrating the birthday of which civil rights leader?

239 *Ballet*

The Bolshoi Ballet is based in which Russian city?

240 *Poetry*

Which month, according to the first line of T.S. Eliot's poem *The Waste Land*, is the cruellest month?

241 *Chemistry* ✓

What is the more common name for gypsum cement, obtained by heating gypsum to approximately 150°C, and used for setting broken limbs and making moulds?

242 *Classical Drama*

Who was the ancient Greek dramatist of the tragedies *Andromache*, *The Trojan Women* and *Iphigenia in Auris?*

243 *Gilbert and Sullivan*

In which Gilbert and Sullivan operetta is the apprentice, Frederic, in love with Mabel, the Major-General's daughter?

244 *History* ✓

Two of the sons of Henry II and Eleanor of Aquitaine became kings of England. What were their names?

245 *Animals*

What is the common name of the *Musca domestica?*

246 *The Peerage*

The stylized leaves of which fruiting plant are depicted on the coronets worn by dukes, marquesses and earls?

247 *Acronyms*

Which type of weapon can be abbreviated as 'SSM'?

248 *Ships*

What was the name of the world's first nuclear-powered submarine, launched in 1954?

249 Mythology

Symbolized by the falcon, who was the son of Osiris and Isis?

250 Classical Music

Which contemporary English composer wrote the operas *Punch and Judy* and *Yan Tan Tethera*?

251 Religion

What would a censer or thurible be used for in church?

252 Education

Part of London University, Wye College near Ashford in Kent specializes in which field?

253 International Organizations

In which city is the headquarters of the European Space Agency?

254 London

Now rung mainly on ceremonial occasions, where in London does the Lutine Bell hang?

255 Royalty

King Mswati III is the king of which country in Southern Africa?

256 Art

Which English sculptor, who died in 1993, became famous for her large angular bronzes, often of horses and riders?

257 Wars ✓

Which conflict in the 1950s, was the first war in which countries fought alongside each other, as members of the United Nations?

258 France ✓

Which Channel port is the most northerly town in France?

259 Religion

Which word is used to describe the transfer of a bishop from one diocese to another?

260 Cinema

Who played Douglas Bader in the film *Reach for the Skies*?

261 Chemistry

Photochemistry is the branch of chemistry concerned with the chemical changes caused by or involving what?

262 *Classical Music*

The Fiery Angel, The Love for Three Oranges and *War and Peace* are operas by which twentieth-century Russian composer?

263 *Quotations*

According to President Calvin Coolidge, 'the chief business of the American people is…' what?

264 *Horse Racing*

Two of the five English classics are run at Epsom. Which two?

265 *Television*

How were the actors Wilfred Brambell and Harry H. Corbett known in the title of a popular BBC situation comedy (of the 1960s and 70s)?

266 *Chess*

A title awarded in the world of chess, what is indicated by the letters IGM?

267 *Latin America*

Which is the country in South America that has had no armed forces since its army was abolished in 1948 and whose President, Oscar Arias Sanchez, received the Nobel Peace Prize in 1987?

268 *The Royal Navy*

In which Devon town is the Britannia Royal Naval College based?

269 *Cinema*

Which film, based on a novel by Alex Garland, stars Leonardo DiCaprio as a backpacker who discovers a paradise community on the coast of Thailand?

270 *Taxation*

What name is given to the tax levied in the UK on the trading profits of companies and other businesses?

271 *Medicine*

What medical condition is said to be present when the body temperature falls to less than 35° Celsius?

272 *Art* ✓

Which Dutch-born artist painted the ceiling of the Banqueting House in Whitehall?

273 *History*

Which English king gave the Royal Navy its royal status?

274 *Sport*

In baseball, what name is given to the five-sided slab of white rubber, sunk into the ground in front of the catcher?

275 *Counties*

Marlow, Bletchley, Chesham and Newport Pagnell are towns in which English county?

276 *Politics*

The Bow Group, which published its *Ideas Book 2000* recently, is a think tank for which British political party?

277 *The USA*

In New York, which river separates the boroughs of Queens and Brooklyn from the Bronx and Manhattan?

278 *Parliament*

What is meant when a member of the House of Lords talks about 'the other place'?

279 *Etymology*

The German title 'Kaiser' is derived from which Roman title?

280 *Geography* ✓

Which (inland) sea borders Russia, Azerbaijan and Iran?

281 *Physics*

What is the name for the unit of pressure equal to 760 millimetres of mercury?

282 *Geography*

Bretons are native to which country?

283 *The USA*

The largest city in the state of Nevada is a world-famous gambling and entertainment centre. Which city?

284 *Shakespeare*

In *The Merchant of Venice*, the three suitors of Portia are given the choice of three caskets to win her hand: gold; silver… or what?

285 *Dates*

The Sunday that falls nearest 30 November is known as which in the Church Calendar?

286 *Costume*

What is the popular name of the piece of headwear called a catercap?

287 *Literature*

Saturday Night and Sunday Morning and *The Loneliness of the Long Distance Runner* were both written by which author?

288 *Geography*

Which famous volcano, at over 10,000 feet high, is situated on the island of Sicily north of the town of Catania?

289 *Protest Groups*

CIWF is the abbreviation for which animal rights group, concerned mainly with the welfare of commercially reared animals?

290 *Geography*

Which South American country takes its name from a line of latitude that runs through it?

291 *Measurements*

Which unit for measuring the mass of precious stones is now equivalent to 200 milligrams?

292 *The UK*

Geographically, which county lies between Cornwall and Somerset?

293 *Medicine*

Which disease was commonly known as consumption?

294 *Acronyms*

What does the acronym ZPG stand for in demographic studies?

295 *The UK*

The River Thames rises in which range of hills?

296 *Geography*

Which is the longest man-made structure ever built, extending over 4000 miles?

297 *Animals*

What is a plant-eating animal called?

298 Law

In England and Wales, people are eligible for jury service between the ages of 18 and... what?

299 Japan ✓

In Japan, what item of clothing is a zori?

300 Popular Culture

Whose pet chimp, Bubbles, is set to receive several million dollars in his owner's will?

301 Auctions

Which human object was withdrawn from auction at Bonham's in May 1988, because of a public outcry from New Zealand?

302 Aviation ✓

What were the first names of the Wright Brothers?

303 British Prime Ministers

Which Prime Minister effectively launched the modern Conservative Party with the Tamworth Manifesto of 1834?

304 Historical Terms

What term was used to describe the territory around Dublin where English law and administration were effective?

305 Ballet

Delibes' *Coppelia* and Tchaikovsky's *Nutcracker* are based on stories by which German writer?

306 Aviation

Which Italian city is served by Cristoforo Colombo airport?

307 Art

Which British sculptor created *Single Form* at the United Nations in New York, a memorial to Dag Hammarskjold?

308 Literature

The Barber of Seville and its sequel, *The Marriage of Figaro*, on which major operas are based, are works by which French playwright?

309 The Armed Forces

The Duke of Edinburgh, the Duke of Kent, Lord Carver and Lord Bramall are four of only ten men to currently hold which rank in the British armed forces?

310 Art

What is the name of the sculptor, engraver and typographer whose works include *Stations of the Cross* in Westminster Cathedral and a statue of *Prospero and Ariel* on Broadcasting House?

311 Geography

What Spanish city is the capital of the region of Catalonia?

312 Roman Britain

How many gates were there in third-century Roman London?

313 Musical Instruments

Xylophone, dulcimer and tambourine all belong in which section of an orchestra?

314 Animals

Which order makes up around half of all mammal species?

315 History

In which centuries did the Hundred Years War begin and end?

316 Science

To which metal does the adjective cupreous relate?

317 History

Who met at a famous meeting at Ujiju in Africa in 1871?

318 Words

Which French word can be used to describe: a slender spire; any of the 24 points on a backgammon board; or a running attack in fencing?

319 Mythology

What is the name of the Queen of the Amazons, whose girdle Hercules had to obtain as one of his labours?

320 Hymns

In the Christmas carol which begins 'O Little Town of Bethlehem/...' what is the next line?

321　*Poetry*

Which poet wrote 'The Dance of Death', 'Look Stranger' and 'Academic Graffiti'?

322　*The USA*　✓

Which of the 50 states is named in honour of the man who later became James II of England?

323　*Anatomy*

What is the name of the sac which surrounds the heart?

324　*Scotland*

What date is Burns Night?

325　*Measurements*

What is the SI unit of mass?

326　*Measurements*

In international paper sizes, the A series of numbers (A3, A4 for example) is for writing paper, books and magazines and the B series is for posters: what is the C series for?

327　*Newspapers*

What is the name of the French daily newspaper, published in Paris, which means 'the world'?

328　*Sport*

Luffing, tacking and gybing are all terms used in which sport?

329　*The Bible*

In the New Testament there are 21 epistles of varying lengths. They are the epistles of Paul, James, Peter and John and who?

330　*The Second World War*

What 'nickname' was given to the period between the German invasion of Poland in 1939 and the invasion of Denmark and Norway in 1940, during which there were few signs of hostilities?

331　*Literature*

By what pseudonym is the nineteenth-century English novelist Mary Ann Evans better known?

332　*Charles Dickens*

In *David Copperfield,* what is the name of the simple-minded gentleman, a 'sort of distant connexion', who lives with David's aunt, Miss Trotwood?

333 *Award Schemes*

Inaugurated in 1956, which award scheme is open to young people between the ages of 14 and 24?

334 *Nature*

The comma, false comma and southern comma are all species of what?

335 *Boxing*

The Manassa Mauler was the nickname of which world heavyweight boxing champion of 1919–26?

336 *Power and Energy* ✓

What unit of power, still used when referring to the output of a motor-car engine, is equivalent to 746 watts?

337 *The Early Church*

According to early Church tradition, at which city in Asia Minor did St John the Evangelist spend his last years?

338 *Costume* ⌐

What is the shirt worn by a jockey, displaying an owner's colours, known as?

339 *Science*

What word can be used for either, in biology, the liquid part of blood or, in physics, an ionized gas produced at very high temperatures?

340 *The Bible*

In the New Testament, in the parable in the Gospel of St Luke, what was prepared for a feast to welcome home the prodigal son?

341 *Geography*

Canada, Brazil, Morocco and Portugal all have coastlines on which ocean?

342 *Motorcar Insurance*

In terms of use, what on a motor insurance policy or certificate do the letters 'SDP' stand for?

343 *Roman Britain*

Rudchester, Housesteads, and Chesters are sites along which ancient fortification in the north of England?

344　*Etymology*

What word, derived from a name shared by popes of the seventh and sixteenth centuries, describes a form of chant and a calendar?

345　*Language*　✓

An Anglophone is an English-speaker: which language would a 'Lusophone' speak?

346　*The Bible*

In the New Testament which of the four gospels is addressed to Theophilus?

347　*Religion*

Which of Christ's apostles was beheaded by order of Herod Agrippa and his body taken, according to Spanish tradition, to Santiago de Compostela?

348　*Poetry*

In his poem 'Tam O'Shanter', what name does Robert Burns give the witch who fails to catch Tam as he rides for his life, but catches his mare's tail and pulls it off?

349　*The Monarchy*

Who was on the British throne at the time of the Battle of Trafalgar and the Battle of Waterloo?

350　*Food and Drink* ✓

From what is Laver Bread made?

351　*The UK*

Which English cathedral was built in the thirteenth century as part of a new town to replace the town of Old Sarum?

352　*Medicine*

What in surgery is a suture?

353　*National Anthems*

Sung to a tune based on a melody by Haydn, 'Unity, right and freedom' is the English translation of the first line of the national anthem of which European country?

354　*The Ancient World*

Which of the Seven Wonders of the Ancient World was the tomb of an Anatolian king, built by his widow Artemisia?

355 *Sport* ✓

In which sport would you perform manoeuvres called a Randolph or a Rudolph?

356 *Geography*

Rome is the capital of which Italian region?

357 *The Second World War*

What is the name of the Black Sea resort at which a famous conference took place in February 1945, attended by Roosevelt, Churchill and Stalin?

358 *European Landmarks*

The Charlottenborg Palace and the Little Mermaid statue are major landmarks in which European capital?

359 *Medicine*

Which organs of the body are affected by the condition pulmonary emphysema?

360 *Geography*

Darling Harbour, Mrs Macquarie's Point, and Woolloomooloo Bay are all waterfront areas of which Commonwealth city?

361 *Cinema*

Which member of a family of famous movie brothers said 'Military intelligence is a contradiction in terms'?

362 *Cinema*

The African Queen is a classic film starring Humphrey Bogart. Who wrote the novel on which the film is based?

363 *Russian History*

What was the name of the illiterate Siberian mystic who exercised extraordinary influence over Tsar Nicholas II and Tsarina Alexandra of Russia?

364 *Government*

Hillsborough Castle is the official residence of which Cabinet Minister?

365 *Shakespeare*

'Two households, both alike in dignity/In Fair Verona, where we lay our scene'. These are the opening lines of which Shakespeare play?

366 *The Royal Family*

Which monarch was the grandfather of the present Queen?

367 *Language*

Which three-letter French word is used in English to indicate the maiden name of a married woman?

368 *History*

In the twelfth century, who was the first Plantagenet king of England?

369 *Music*   ✓

What had its first recorded public performance at Drury Lane Theatre on 28 September 1745?

370 *European Politics*

Of which island country in the Mediterranean is Dr Edward Fenech Adami the Prime Minister?

371 *Food and Drink*

Which Spanish drink is made of sweetened, diluted red wine and fruit?

372 *Religion*

Used in the Roman Catholic Church, what is the meaning of the Latin invocation, 'ora pro nobis'?

373 *Gilbert and Sullivan*

Mrs Cripps, known as Little Buttercup; Ralph Rackstraw; and Dick Deadeye are characters in which Gilbert and Sullivan opera?

374 *History*

The siege of Yorktown was, in 1781, the last major engagement of which eighteenth-century conflict?

375 *Children's Literature*

Shortly before her death, Anna Sewell wrote that the special aim of her only novel was to 'induce kindness, sympathy, and understanding treatment of horses'. Which novel?

376 *Literature*

By what name was the American short-story writer William Sydney Porter better known?

377 *Physiology*

What is the more common name for the movement or reaction known correctly as 'patellar reflex'?

378 *Literature*

What is the name of the German novelist whose most famous work is *Perfume: the Story of a Murderer?*

379 *Birds*

Which common seabird has varieties called Herring, Black-headed, Bonaparte's and Sooty?

380 *Classical Music*

To which note are the instruments of an orchestra commonly tuned?

381 *Chemistry*

Which chemical element has the symbol F?

382 *Quotations*

Who wrote 'Experience is the name everyone gives to their mistakes'?

383 *Gemstones*

What name is given to the crystallized form of iron pyrites which, when faceted and polished, is used in jewellery?

384 *Acronyms*

Which government department is abbreviated as DCMS?

385 *European Royalty*

Constantine II was the last king of which European country?

386 *Charles Dickens*

Which Dickens novel is largely based on Thomas Carlyle's history of The French Revolution?

387 *The UK*

Claiming to be the oldest inn in England, the 'Trip to Jerusalem' is in which English city?

388 *Currency*

What is the basic unit of currency used in Japan?

389 *Classical Music*

Who is the composer of the operas *At The Boar's Head* and *The Perfect Fool*, and the tone poem *Egdon Heath*?

390 *The Monarchy* ✓

Who was the last British monarch to marry while on the throne?

391 *History*

Which eleventh-century king of England was nicknamed 'Ironside' because of his courage?

392 *Horse Racing*

Who was the only reigning British king to have won the Derby, as an owner?

393 *Music*

'Liberty Bell', 'The Stars and Stripes Forever' and 'The Washington Post' are all military marches written by which American composer?

394 *Literature*

Which novel by Hardy features Michael Henchard, an unemployed farmhand, who gets drunk at a fair and sells his wife and baby to a sailor named Newson?

395 *Religion*

What is the name of the doctrine of the Roman Catholic Church that encapsulates the belief that bread and wine are changed into the body and blood of Christ during the Mass?

396 *Geography*

Which major river, which flows through Germany's industrial heartland, joins the River Rhine near Duisberg?

397 *Counties*

Chelmsford, Chigwell and Chipping Ongar are towns in which county?

398 *Golf*

What's two under par in golf?

399 *Parliament*

Which government department gives its name to the front bench in the House of Commons on which government ministers sit?

400 *History*

Which side adopted the red rose as a symbol during the Wars of the Roses?

401 *Gemstones*

Nephrite is better known as what type of stone?

402 *Currency*

What is the official monetary unit of Kenya?

403 *Musicals*

Who wrote the music for *West Side Story*?

404 *Art*

Who was the sculptor of the young David which stands in the Academy in Florence?

405 *Geography*

Which port and suburb of Dublin, which is a terminal for ferries to Britain, was once known as Kingstown?

406 *Geography*

The southern tip of South Africa was once named the Cape of Storms. What is it now called?

407 *Music*

Whose three symphonies representing different times of the day are nicknamed Le Matin, Le Midi and Le Soir?

408 *Sport*

At which athletic event were Jesse Owens, Ralph Boston, Lynn Davies, Bob Beamon and Carl Lewis all Olympic champions?

409 *Science*

Discovered in 1817 by Jöns Jacob Berzelius, which element, with the atomic number 34 and the symbol Se, derives its name from the Greek for 'moon'?

410 *American History*

On which great political charter of 1776 is the signature of John Hancock the first to appear?

411 *Alphabet*

In the NATO phonetic alphabet what comes after: Echo; Foxtrot; Golf?

412 *English Law*

What Latin phrase is used in English Law and means 'by virtue of his (or her) office'?

413 *The USA*

The name of a state and a major river in the United States is derived from a Spanish word meaning 'coloured or tinted red'. What name?

414 *Counties*

Porlock Weir, Minehead, and the city of Wells are all in which county?

415 *Medicine*

What does it mean if a disease is described as idiopathic?

416 *Motor Cars*

The Inca, the Alhambra and the Toledo are models produced by which motor-car manufacturer?

417 *Geography*

Which town in Cornwall is taken by the Ordnance Survey as the basis for the mean sea level?

418 *Mythology*

Pax was the Roman goddess of what?

419 *Phrases*

What is Kentish Rag?

420 *London*

Which famous London street was named after a soldier and diplomat who was MP for Morpeth in the seventeenth century?

421 *Science*

Exobiology is the study of life which originates where?

422 *Literature*

From which east coast port did Robinson Crusoe set sail?

423 *Middle Eastern History*

What is the name of the ancient mountain-top fortress in Israel, which was the site of the Jews' last stand against the Romans after the fall of Jerusalem in AD 70?

424 *Annual Events*

At which venue on the outskirts of Birmingham is Crufts staged annually?

425 *Quotations*

'Mad, bad and dangerous to know' was a comment on Lord Byron. Who made it?

426 *Latin Phrases*

Which Latin phrase, derived from a theatrical effect in ancient Greek drama in which a god would be lowered on to the stage, is now used to describe an unexpected, improbable twist in a plot?

427 *The Royal Air Force*

Which is the most junior commissioned officer rank in the Royal Air Force?

428 *Awards*

The Prix Goncourt is France's most prestigious award in which field of the arts?

429 *Sport*

Kenny Roberts, Michael Doohan and Alex Criville are famous names in which sport?

430 *Architecture*

Ogee, stilted and lancet are all types of which architectural structure?

431 *Scottish History*

Which glen in the Highlands of Scotland was the scene of the massacre of the MacDonalds by Campbell of Glenlyon and his men in 1692?

432 *Geography*

What is the highest mountain in Africa?

433 *Charles Dickens*

The seemingly never-ending Chancery Court case of Jarndyce versus Jarndyce provides the backdrop to which Dickens novel?

434 *Botany*

The botanical name of which herb, much used in cooking, is *Salvia officinalis*?

435 *Counties*

What county are Salisbury, Stonehenge and Longleat in?

436 *Aviation*

Which Italian city is served by Galileo Galilei airport?

437 *European Landmarks*

Which is the only city gate of Berlin that still survives?

438 *Weaponry*

What sort of medieval weapon was an arbalest?

439 *Geography*

Which walled town commanding a plateau in the centre of the island was the capital of Malta until the mid-sixteenth century and was known as 'the silent city'?

440 *Roman History*

What did Julius Caesar revise in 46 BC?

441 *Acronyms*

MORI is an organization which carries out public opinion polls in the UK. What does the acronym MORI stand for?

442 *Dates*

On which date does the regnal year in the UK start?

443 *Acronyms*

A person with the letters RIBA after their name, is a member of which institute or profession?

444 *Climatology*

Vardarac, Temporales, Shamal, the Roaring Forties and the Purga are all types of what?

445 *Quotations*

In Christopher Marlowe's *Dr Faustus* whose face is said to have 'launched a thousand ships'?

446 *The USA*

What name is given to more than 2000 square miles of marshy land designated a National Park in Florida?

447 *Words*

Who would use a sharp sword called an estoque?

448 *Television*

Who in the early days of *Coronation Street* played Mr Swindley, and later Captain Mainwaring in *Dad's Army*?

449 *Science* ✓

What is the highest region of the atmosphere?

450 *Poetry*

John Keats wrote 'Thou wast not born for death, immortal bird?' Which bird?

15 to 1

ROUND TWO
Questions

451 *Pop Music* ✓

Which British group had UK number one singles in the 1990s with 'Some Might Say', 'Don't Look Back in Anger', 'D'You Know What I Mean' and 'All Around the World'?

452 *Physics* ✓

What has the symbol P, is measured in watts and is defined by the equation 'work done divided by time'?

453 *Television* ✓

Which (long-running) BBC drama series, which started in 1986, is based in Holby City hospital?

454 *Words*

What word, from the Latin for kidnapping, refers to the dishonest passing off of someone else's work as your own?

455 *British Prime Ministers*

What nickname was given to a British Prime Minister after he appeared in a newspaper cartoon by Vicky in 1958 as a caricature of Superman?

456 *Geography* ✓

Dapsang and Chogori are alternative names for which mountain in Asia?

457 *Crime Fiction* ✓

Which sleuth, created by Margery Allingham, lives in a flat next to Bottle Street Police Station, off Piccadilly?

458 *Gymnastics*

In which branch of women's gymnastics do the competitors perform on the floor with a rope, a hoop, a ball, clubs and a ribbon?

459 *People*

Jennie Jerome (1854–1921), an American-born society hostess and writer, was the mother of which famous British (statesman) politician?

460 *Martial Arts*

The name of which Chinese martial art, consisting of sequences of very slow controlled movements, translates into English as 'extreme limit' or 'great ultimate'?

461 *Inventions*

For what invention, first marketed in 1993, is James Dyson best known?

462 *Music*

Which famous orchestral suite by Handel was commissioned to accompany a pyrotechnic display in Green Park to celebrate the peace treaty of Aix-la-chapelle in 1749?

463 *Popular Fiction* ✓

Who is the creator of the Sharpe series of historical novels?

464 *French Government* ✓

In which former royal palace does the French Senate now sit?

465 *Science* ✓

Which gas is produced by the process of photosynthesis?

466 *Currency*

Algeria, Tunisia and Libya all use what as their main unit of currency?

467 *Shakespeare*

Which of Shakespeare's history plays is divided into three parts?

468 *Biology*

Which vitamin complex includes thiamine, riboflavin and niacin?

469 *Science* ✓

Discovered in the 1730s, the name of which element is derived from the German for 'goblin' and has the symbol Co?

470 *Phrases*

What general term is used by the English Tourist Board for the area of the country that includes the Cotswolds, Shakespeare Country and the Marches?

471 *Television* ✓

Which classic ITV sitcom of the 1950s was based in Hut 29 of a military camp at Nether Hopping?

472 *Opera*

Living in his gloomy castle, the duke's latest wife Judith realizes he has murdered her predecessors and that a similar fate is in store for her. Which opera?

473 *Geography*

The name of which mountain range comes from the Sanskrit for 'house of snow'?

474 *Railway Stations*

Victoria, Oxford Road and Piccadilly are railway stations serving which British city?

475 *World Politics*

PASOK and New Democracy are the two leading political parties in which European Union country?

476 *Words*

If someone is described as being stentorian, what sort of physical attribute do they possess?

477 *Entertainment Venues*

The Brangwyn Hall, the Patti Pavilion and the Dylan Thomas Theatre are all venues in which British city?

478 *Astronomy*

With a distinctive 'W' shape, which northern constellation is said to represent the mother of Andromeda in Greek mythology?

479 *Acronyms*

On migration forms, for entry to some countries, inbound travellers may select the category VFR as their primary purpose of visit. The V stands for visiting; what does the FR stand for?

480 *People*

What is the name of England's leading Shakespearean actress of the late 1700s and early 1800s, who often performed with her brother John Philip Kemble in *Macbeth*?

481 *Science*

A body which is moving at a speed greater than Mach 1 is said to be travelling at supersonic speed. What term is used for speeds greater than Mach 5?

482 *The United Nations*

Based in Montreal, which agency of the UN is abbreviated as the ICAO?

483 *Phrases*

What is a billet-doux?

484 *Cricket* ✓
Who captained the West Indies for 39 successive Tests from 1965 until his retirement in 1974?

485 *Sailing* ✓
How many masts are there on a sloop?

486 *Religion*
Ash Wednesday is the first day of Lent. What is the origin of the term Ash Wednesday?

487 *Computers* ✓
Named after the seed of a quintessentially English tree, which company produced the BBC Micro and Archimedes computers?

488 *Politics*
Charles Kennedy is the party leader of the Liberal Democrats. Who is the deputy leader?

489 *Sports* ✓
In which outdoor ball game is the final requirement to peg out?

490 *Awards*
The Victoria Cross was awarded to Lieutenant Arthur Martin-Leake in 1914, Captain Noel Chavasse in 1917 and Captain Charles Upham in 1942. What connects these winners of the Victoria Cross in these years?

491 *Opera*
Rossini's last opera is based on the story of which European folk hero?

492 *People*
What was the surname of Horace, famous for his Gothic novel *The Castle of Otranto* and his father Sir Robert, a leading minister of George I and George II?

493 *The First World War*
What is the name of the American President who, in January 1918, introduced his 14 points for postwar peace?

494 *Classic Radio* ✓
Which appropriate piece of music by Chopin is the signature tune of the radio programme 'Just a Minute'?

495 *Irish Politics*

His affair with Mrs O'Shea caused a scandal in the late nineteenth century. What was the name of this Irish nationalist leader?

496 *Ballet*

Edris Stannus was the original name of which famous ballet dancer and director?

497 *Counties*

In which county do the Beer Festival at Cleethorpes, the Spalding Flower Parade and the international airshow at RAF Waddington take place?

498 *Animals* ✓

Which breed of goat originated in the Himalayas and supplies a well-known quality wool from its fine, silky undercoat?

499 *Animals*

Which major breed of wool-producing goat is named after the old name of the Turkish province where it originated?

500 *Music*

'A good night' was a sensational type of broadside ballad between the sixteenth and nineteenth centuries. Presenting the stories of whom?

501 *Motor Vehicles*

What name is given to the combined speedometer and clock that records a vehicle's speed and the length of time the vehicle is moving or stationary?

502 *Business*

The steamship company P&O: what do the letters P & O stand for?

503 *Religion*

Which was the first Christian nation in the world to embrace Christianity officially? It adopted the new religion around 301 AD.

504 *Botany*

Which genus of redwood tree was named after a Cherokee Indian?

505 *Literature*

Which South African novelist and short story writer won the 1974 Booker prize with *The Conservationist* and the Nobel Prize for Literature in 1991?

506 *The USA*

What geographical feature was named, in 1849, by a party of gold-seeking 'forty-niners', some of whom died of thirst and exposure while trying to cross it?

507 *Religion*

Taken from the Latin meaning 'nine', what name is used in the Roman Catholic Church for a devotion consisting of special prayers or services on nine successive days?

508 *Sport*

In which sport might one of the officials signal for a ten-second violation, travelling or a double dribble?

509 *Animals*

What sort of domesticated creature is the Scottish Fold, so-called because its ears are folded forwards?

510 *London*

Which famous London landmark, based on the Arch of Constantine in Rome, was designed by John Nash?

511 *Computers*

Named after a type of tinned meat, what name is given to unwanted and unrequested e-mail sent to lots of people at the same time?

512 *Geography*

The Gambia has a short coastline on the Atlantic Ocean. It is surrounded on all the other sides by which country?

513 *Railways*

The Tan Zam railway, which opened in 1975, runs from the Copperbelt in Zambia to which seaport city in Tanzania?

514 *The Monarchy* ✓

In which London palace did Henry VIII die in 1547?

515 *British Prime Ministers* ✓

Who was the last Prime Minister to be a duke?

516 *European History* ✓

Until 1806 various German princes were entitled to call themselves Elector. Whom did they elect?

517 *Car Registration*

ROK is the international car index mark for which Asian country?

518 *Counties*

Charterhouse School, Thorpe Park and the town of Dorking are all in which county?

519 *Art*

The Italian artist Canaletto is best remembered for his paintings of which city?

520 *Theatre*

Which Arthur Miller play, based on the notorious witchcraft trials in Salem, Massachusetts, centres on the relationship of John and Elizabeth Proctor with their former servant Abigail Williams?

521 *Sports*

The Canadian Wayne Gretsky was nicknamed the Great One. In which sport is he widely regarded as the best player ever?

522 *Space Exploration*

What was the name and number designation of the huge rocket that was used to launch the Apollo missions to the Moon?

523 *Charities*

Martin Drury is the Director General of which conservation organization, a charity which has its headquarters in Queen Anne's Gate, London?

524 *The UK*

What is the name of the natural rift which runs across Scotland from south-west to north-east, in which lie Loch Linnhe, Loch Lochy and Loch Ness?

525 *Religion*

What title, derived from the Latin for 'messenger', is given to papal envoys in foreign capitals?

526 *London*

Which famous London bookshop was opened by two young brothers on failing their Civil Service examinations?

527 _Law_ ✓

What is the name of the governing body of the Scottish Bar?

528 _Animals_

Mammals are divided into three groups: placental mammals; marsupials; and monotremes such as the platypus. What does monotreme mean?

529 _Words_

Which word, derived from the Greek for 'image breakers', was originally applied to those opposed to the use of images in the Church?

530 _Astronomy_

Urbain Le Verrier and John Couch Adams are recognized as the co-discoverers of which planet in 1846?

531 _The Bible_

Bartholomew is listed as one of the 12 apostles in the gospels of Matthew, Mark and Luke. By what name is he known in John's gospel?

532 _Literature_

Which English essayist and critic became famous for his memoir _Confessions of an English Opium-Eater_, published in 1822?

533 _Roman Britain_

What is the name of the major Roman fort located near Hadrian's Wall at Chesterholm, Northumberland?

534 _Politics_

What was the name of the new political party, launched in March 1981, which merged with the Liberal Party in 1988?

535 _Education_

What is the name of the German educationalist, who founded the kindergarten movement and explained his philosophy in his work _The Education of Man_, published in 1826?

536 _European History_

What is the name of the order of distinction which was instituted by Napoleon Bonaparte in 1802?

537 *The Ancient World*

Which Athenian lawmaker, who introduced a written code of law in 621 BC, was renowned for the harshness of his punishments?

538 *Latin Phrases*

Used in law, what does the Latin phrase 'toties quoties' mean?

539 *History*

Bishops Ridley and Latimer, and Archbishop Cranmer, were burnt at the stake in the sixteenth century, on the orders of which monarch?

540 *Space Exploration*

In December 1972, which Apollo mission was the last to land men on the Moon?

541 *Radio*

Which TV personality and panel-show host also presents his own radio programme on Radio 2 from 10.00 am to 1.00 pm on Saturdays?

542 *The Armed Forces* ✓

What slang name, used by soldiers for England or home, is derived from a Hindi word for a foreign or distant land?

543 *Irish History*

Which Irish Prime Minister (1937–48, 1951–4 and 1957–9) was President of Ireland from 1959 to 1973?

544 *Physics*

What general term, expressed as a percentage, refers to the amount of energy we get out of a machine divided by the amount we put into the machine?

545 *Saints*

Which of the 12 apostles has been popularized as 'the patron saint of hopeless causes'?

546 *The Early Church*

Which Roman emperor convened the First Council of Nicaea in 325 AD, the first universal council of the Church?

547 *Geography*

Doha is the capital of which small Arab state?

548 *Literature*

If you described Charles Dickens as a Victorian writer, how would you describe Jane Austen?

549 *The UK*

The villages of Ardlui and Balloch stand at the northern and southern ends respectively of which famous Scottish loch?

550 *London* ✓

Where in London are the tombs of both the Duke of Wellington and Lord Nelson?

551 *London Transport*

What is the DLR?

552 *The Monarchy*

Who was the last British Monarch not to have been married throughout their reign?

553 *Inventions*

For the invention of what is the British inventor Trevor Baylis best known?

554 *World Politics*

What name was given to President Eisenhower's assertion that once one South-east Asian country fell to Communism, the others would follow?

555 *Radio*

Which of the Goons played Neddie Seagoon?

556 *Latin Phrases*

What does the Latin phrase 'de die in diem' mean?

557 *People*

During the American War of Independence, Admiral Lord Richard commanded the British sea forces; his brother, Sir William, commanded the land forces. What is their family name?

558 *Musicals*

A story by Damon Runyon, 'The Idyll of Miss Sarah Brown', formed the basis of which stage musical by Frank Loesser?

559 *Literature*

What is the name of the country of the giants which Gulliver visits on his second voyage in *Gulliver's Travels*?

560 *Computers*

What term is used to mean adding a website address to a directory of web links, so that the site may be easily visited again?

561 *Theatre*

The Shadow of a Gunman, The Plough and the Stars and *Within the Gates* were writen by which Irish dramatist?

562 *Science*

What is listed in a publication called the Messier catalogue?

563 *History*

In which century was the first recorded Viking raid on Britain?

564 *Quotations*

Of which famous British soldier did Margot Asquith reputedly quip 'If he was not a great man, he was, at least, a great poster'?

565 *Geography*

Which small province of Canada is separated from the mainland by a stretch of water called the Northumberland Strait?

566 *Science*

Of what is carpology the study?

567 *European History*

In which European country is the Althing, which was founded in approximately 930 AD, and is the oldest parliament in the world?

568 *Mathematics*

Which branch of mathematics, sometimes called 'rubber-sheet geometry', is concerned with the properties of geometric figures that remain unchanged when the figures are deformed by bending, stretching or twisting?

569 *Public Houses*

At which pub in Oxford, which shares its name with that of the crest of the Stanley family and earls of Derby, did C.S. Lewis, Tolkien and other members of the literary group, the Inklings, meet?

570 *Sport*

TOWA is the controlling body in England of which outdoor team sport, which was an Olympic event from 1900 until 1920?

571 *Phobias*

Ereuthophobia is a morbid fear of doing what?

572 *The Early Church*

The Christian philosopher and theologian, author of *Confessions* and *The City of God*, was St Augustine of where?

573 *Games*

What was designed for competitive purposes in 1835 by Nathaniel Cook, and named after the British master Howard Staunton?

574 *History*

In 1655 Oliver Cromwell divided England into military districts, each commanded by a officer known by what title?

575 *Geography*

Cuba, Jamaica, Hispaniola and Puerto Rico are part of which specific island group within the West Indies in the Caribbean Sea?

576 *Television*

The Fish Slapping Dance, The Lumberjack Song and the Ministry of Silly Walks were the inspiration which famous comedy team?

577 *Literature*

The thrillers *Journey into Fear*, *The Mask of Demitrios* and *The Dark Frontier* are books by which writer, who died in 1998?

578 *Medicine*

The visual disorder achromatopsia is the inability to perceive what?

579 *The UK*

What has the entrance to the Tower of London from the River Thames been commonly called for hundreds of years?

580 *Space Exploration*

Which Russian was, on 12 April 1961, the sole passenger on the record-breaking flight of Vostok 1?

581 *Acronyms*

In the context of billboards in rural areas, local councils may declare sites as ASCAs. What is an ASCA, or what do the letters ASCA stand for?

582 *Animals*

Which creatures make up the family Ursidae?

583 *Astronomy* ✓

Which constellation, the largest in the night sky, represents the mythical many-headed monster that was killed by Hercules?

584 *Art*

Which artist, who died in 1992, designed a tapestry for Chichester Cathedral and windows for Coventry Cathedral?

585 *Religious Terms*

In the Roman Catholic Church, what Latin name, meaning 'on the border', is given to the home of souls who belong neither in heaven nor in hell?

586 *Wars*

In which year did the Six Day War between Israel and the Arab states take place?

587 *Fictional Characters*

Who was the hero of a number of adventure novels by the Scottish writer John Buchan... including *The 39 Steps*?

588 *Law*

What term is used in law to describe those related by blood from a common ancestor?

589 *Finance*

Set up in 1995 and operated by the London Stock Exchange, the AIM lists small and growing companies. What do the letters AIM stand for?

590 *Phobias*

Tachophobia is an irrational fear of what sensation?

591 *The Peerage*

What relation is the Duke of York to the last person before him to be created a duke?

592 *Ships*

What traditional phrase does the *Oxford Companion to Ships and the Sea* describe as 'the correct and seamanlike reply on board ship on receipt of an order'?

593 *Politics*

Of which political party in Northern Ireland has David Trimble been leader since 1995?

594 *The UK*

St George's Chapel, The Long Walk and Legoland are features of which English town?

595 *Cinema*

'Oh no, it wasn't the airplanes. It was Beauty killed the Beast.' Those are the final words to which classic 1933 movie?

596 *Cinema*

According to Mae West in *I'm No Angel*: 'It's not the men in my life that counts – it's…' what?

597 *Blue Plaques*

The author of *North and South* is commemorated by a blue plaque at 93 Cheyne Walk, London SW10, the house in which she was born. What's her name?

598 *Science*

Which creatures belong to the class Aves?

599 *Sport*

With which sport do you associate the Pittsburgh Penguins, the Toronto Maple Leafs and the Mighty Ducks of Anaheim?

600 *Mathematics*

What are the two possible answers to the question 'What is the square root of 25'?

601 *Geography*

By what name were the United Arab Emirates known between the early nineteenth century and 1971?

602 *The Media*

Aimed at the youth market, what are: Trouble, Nickelodeon and Fox Kids?

603 *History*

Which king married Elizabeth of York, eldest daughter of Edward IV, in order to unite the Houses of York and Lancaster?

604 *Quotations*

'It is the unpleasant and unacceptable face of capitalism.' This was the verdict on the activities of an international company by which British Prime Minister?

605 *Legend and Literature*

Which legendary wicked aristocrat's home was a castle near the town of Bistritz in the Carpathian mountains?

606 *Counties*

In which English county are the towns of Bishops Stortford, Baldock, Letchworth and Hitchin?

607 *Nature*

What is the common name for the fibrous skeleton of the (cylindrical) fruit of the dishcloth gourd, normally found in the bathroom?

608 *France*

Deauville, Trouville and Fecamp are popular coastal resorts in which historical region of north-western France?

609 *Medicine*

Named after Sir Percival Pott in 1779, Pott's Disease affects which part of the human body?

610 *Diamonds*

What name does the diamond company De Beers give to the ten sessions it holds each year, at which selected clients are allowed to buy rough diamonds from them?

611 Diamonds
What name does De Beers give to the select group of people or companies who are allowed to attend the buying sessions?

612 Chemistry
Which metallic element has the chemical symbol Na?

613 Acronyms
Well known in the world of crime prevention, what does the acronym ACPO stand for?

614 Cinema
A man is prevented from committing suicide by an elderly angel, who takes him back through his life to show him what good he has done. What is the name of this classic 1946 film by Frank Capra, starring James Stewart?

615 The Ancient World
What term does Plato use to refer to the speech made by Socrates, in answer to the charge of impiety that was brought against him?

616 Children's Literature
In which story by Roald Dahl does a deprived orphan boy find friendship and happiness after a magic giant fruit grows in his garden?

617 Shakespeare
What is the name of Prospero's savage and deformed slave whose name is almost an anagram of the word 'cannibal'?

618 Mythology
Charon was a famous resident of Hades. What was his profession?

619 Literature
Voss, Riders in the Chariot and The Twyborn Affair are three of the best-known novels by which Australian writer, winner of the 1973 Nobel Prize for Literature?

620 Medicine
What is the common name for the disease infectious mononucleosis, which is characterized at the onset by fever and swollen lymph glands?

621 *Words*

Halcyon, as in the expression 'halcyon days', is an alternative (poetic) name for which bird?

622 *Dates*

Why is 30 January 1649 a famous date in British history?

623 *Awards*

Five of the six Nobel Prizes are awarded in Stockholm. Which is the only prize to be awarded in Oslo?

624 *Geography*

Cape Finisterre, after which the shipping forecast area is named, is on the north-west coast of which country?

625 *Classical Music*

Vaughan Williams' third symphony and Beethoven's sixth are both known by the same name. What name?

626 *Law*

In English law citizens of only one European Union country other than the UK are not referred to as aliens. Which country?

627 *Art*

Whose huge sculpture of St Michael and the Devil can be seen on the wall of Coventry Cathedral?

628 *Literature*

Which Russian writer wrote the novel *Fathers and Sons* and the play *A Month in the Country*?

629 *Opera*

In which (Verdi) opera is the hero buried alive in a tomb, after inadvertently betraying his army's campaign manoeuvres?

630 *Railway Stations*

Which British city in the east of England is served by Paragon railway station?

631 *Medicine*

Mogigraphia is a form of cramp, associated with what activity?

632 *National Anthems*

'King Christian stood by the lofty mast' is one of the two national anthems of which European country?

633 Music

In musical notation, Americans call it a quarter-note. What is it called in Britain?

634 Art and Artists

Nicholas Hilliard and Isaac Oliver are most closely associated with what type of paintings?

635 Political Leaders

Jorge Sampaio is the President and António Guterres is the Prime Minister of which European country?

636 Acronyms

For what phrase coined by the phonetician Daniel Jones is RP the abbreviation ?

637 Architecture

Bedford Park, London's first garden suburb, was principally designed by which British architect?

638 Geographys

Vilnius is the capital of which state on the Baltic Sea?

639 Aviation

The international airport serving the Indian capital New Delhi is named after which former Prime Minister?

640 Astronomy

What feature of a total solar eclipse is named after the English amateur astronomer Francis Baily?

641 Geography

Which strait separates Sri Lanka from India?

642 History

Two sons of Richard Plantagenet, Duke of York and Protector of England, became kings of England. Edward IV was one; who was the other?

643 The USA

For the manufacture of what is the town of Hershey in Pennsylvania famous?

644 The UK

Which cathedral in North Yorkshire dates back to 672 when St Wilfrid built the first church to stand on the site?

645 *Words*

What Russian name, meaning grandee, was given to the noble class in Russia from the eleventh century until the rank was abolished by Peter the Great?

646 *Words*

Which Russian word, meaning gift or grant of land, is used for a country house or villa?

647 *Anatomy*

What is the shape of the deltoid muscle?

648 *Parliament*

Subject to considerable time restraint in the Commons, what name is given to public bills which are introduced by backbenchers?

649 *Television*

What is the name of the comedienne, writer and actress who created the *Dinnerladies* series?

650 *Musicals*

What is the title of the Oscar Hammerstein musical which is a reworking of Bizet's *Carmen*?

651 *Geography*

The Tropic of Capricorn, at approximately 23 degrees south, passes through four African countries. Name two of the four.

652 *Anatomy*

Where in the human body are there bones known as the hammer, the anvil and the stirrup?

653 *Mythology*

Talos, the giant who guarded the island of Crete, was made of which metal?

654 *The Highway Code*

What is the minimum age at which a driver may supervise a learner driver in a car?

655 *The Highway Code*

For how many years must the supervising driver have held, and still be holding, a full British driving licence?

656 *British Prime Ministers*

Which nineteenth-century Prime Minister was known by the nicknames 'Old Pam' and 'Lord Cupid'?

657 *British Prime Ministers*

Which twentieth-century Prime Minister who held office in the 1960s had a first-class cricket record, having played several games for Middlesex?

658 *Sport*

What is the name of the ground in Edinburgh, which is the headquarters of the Scottish Rugby Union?

659 *Food and Drink*

TVP is the acronym for a common meat substitute – what does it stand for?

660 *The UK*

On which island, part of Dorset, are scouts and guides the only people allowed to camp overnight?

661 *Medicine*

Icterus is a medical term for what quite common condition, often affecting new-born babies?

662 *Politics*

Harold Wilson resigned as Prime Minister in 1976. Who succeeded him at Number 10?

663 *Pop Music*

'(Everything I Do) I Do It for You' from the film *Robin Hood: Prince of Thieves* was a UK number one single for a record 16 weeks in 1991. Who sang it?

664 *The Bible*

In the Old Testament which city was founded by King Omri as the capital of the northern kingdom of Israel?

665 *Botany*

Which plant is named from the supposed resemblance of its flower to Christ's crucifixion and the story of the Redemption?

666 *The United Nations*

At the United Nations, the United Kingdom, France, China, the USA and the Russian Federation are the five permanent members of which body?

667 *Literature*

The Pumpkin Eater, My Friend Says It's Bullet-Proof, and the autobiographical *About Time* are works by which Welsh novelist?

668 *Sport*

What is the IOC?

669 *Sport*

What is the BOA?

670 *Television*

In a recent poll conducted by the British Film Institute (among 1600 programme-makers, television executives, writers and critics) which comedy series, made in 1975 and starring John Cleese and Prunella Scales, was voted the industry's favourite British programme?

671 *Aviation*

Which British airport has the three-letter designation code ABZ?

672 *Pop Music*

'Words', 'A Different Beat' and 'All That I Need' were the first three UK number one singles for which Irish boy band?

673 *Measurements*

What commodity has measurements called double crown, royal, demy and large post?

674 *Radio*

Ken Bruce, Jimmy Young and Janice Long are regular weekday presenters on which radio network?

675 *Politics*

Of which African country is Flight Lieutenant Jerry Rawlings President?

676 *Politics*

The letters MSP after a person's name indicate membership of which body?

677 *Cinema*

Drowning By Numbers, The Cook, the Thief, His Wife and Her Lover and *Prospero's Books* are films by which British director?

678 *Poetry*

The name of which mountainous region in the central Peloponnese peninsula (of southern Greece) has been used by poets such as Virgil in his *Eclogues* to describe a rustic paradise?

679 *Driving Licences*

How often normally are you required to renew the new-style photocard driving licence if you are aged under 70?

680 *Driving Licences*

If you hold a full UK driving licence, how often past the age of 70, barring medical condition renewals, must you renew it?

681 *Geography*

The Gulf of Bothnia lies between which two European countries?

682 *Shakespeare*

Which eponymous character in a Shakespeare play inspired a concert overture by Dvorak and operas by Verdi and Rossini?

683 *Animals*

Which mammal constitutes the genus Ovis?

684 *The Mediaeval Church*

Who was the founder of the Order of Friars Preachers or Black Friars?

685 *Geometry*

What name is given to a parallelogram which has all four sides equal in length but does not contain a right angle?

686 *Cinema*

What is the name of the American film actress, who won an Oscar for *The Farmer's Daughter* in 1947, who died in August aged 87?

687 *Geography*

October Revolution Island in the Arctic Ocean belongs to which country?

688 *Law*

Two police forces are responsible for policing London: the Metropolitan Police and... which other?

689 *Literature*

Who is the captain of the *Hispaniola* which sets sail to Treasure Island in the book of the same name?

690 *Musical Instruments*

Which wind instrument is defined in the Grove *Concise Dictionary of Music* as 'the principal soprano double-reed woodwind instrument'?

691 *The UK*

What specifically are: the Cotswold Way, the Cleveland Way and the Ridgeway?

692 *Motor Cars*

The Saxo, the Xantia and the Xsara are models produced by which motor-car manufacturer?

693 *Comics and Animations*

Which character has friends called Trevor Evans, Bella Lasagne, Elvis Criddlington and Station Officer Steel?

694 *Symbols and Signs*

Maltese, Papal, Celtic and St Andrews are all types of which symbol?

695 *Law*

Which official of the High Court is responsible for arresting persons in contempt of court?

696 *Television*

What does the character Frasier Crane, played by Kelsey Grammer, do for a living?

697 *History*

Only one king from the House of Blois ruled England. What is his name?

698 *Mathematics*

What name is given to any four-sided plane figure in which the opposite sides are equal in length?

699 *Motor Cars*

In automotive engineering what do the initials BHP stand for?

700 *Football*

Which London club plays its home games at Upton Park?

701 *Education*

How many UCAS points are awarded for a B grade pass at A Level?

702 *Medicine*

Iridology is the diagnosis of disorders by the examination of what specifically?

703 *Physics*

Light travels at 186,000 miles per second. The light from which heavenly body takes approximately eight minutes and 20 seconds to reach Earth?

704 *Zoology*

What is the common name of the *Vespo crabo*, a large European wasp which has brown and yellow markings and can inflict a severe sting?

705 *Charles Dickens*

In *Nicholas Nickleby* what is the name of the Yorkshire boarding school to which unwanted boys are sent, and which is run by the brutal Wackford Squeers?

706 *Charles Dickens*

What is served to the boys because, according to Mrs Squeers, 'it spoils their appetites and comes cheaper than breakfast and dinner'?

707 *Meteorology*

What is measured by a Campbell-Stokes recorder?

708 *Geography*

Mount Ayorangi, at nearly 12,350 feet above sea level, is the highest mountain in New Zealand. By what English name is it known?

709 *Computers*

HTML is a computer language used in placing documents on the World-Wide Web. What does HTML stand for?

710 *Books*

Which TV celebrity chef, known for programmes from different parts of the world and for his enjoyment of a glass of wine, published memoirs entitled *Out of the Frying Pan*?

711 *Television*

What place in television history is held by a woman called Jasmine Bligh?

712 *Opera*

Which Wagner opera is based on the legend of a ghost ship which is said to haunt the seas round the Cape of Good Hope?

713 *Islam*

What would a Muslim known by the title Hafiz have done?

714 *Music*

In musical notation, what generic term is applied to the signs placed just before a note to indicate a temporary change in pitch, for example a sharp or flat?

715 *Grammar*

Two types of punctuation marks or devices always come in pairs. Name either of the two.

716 *Literature*

Who wrote the novel *A Clockwork Orange*?

717 *Popular Music*

What is the name of the popular music which combines Punjabi folk music with rock and roll or disco?

718 *Geography*

Which city in Thailand is known to the Thais as Krung Thep, meaning the 'City of Angels'?

719 *Battles*

'Afflavit Deus et dissipati sunt' meaning 'God blew, and they are dispersed', is an inscription on the medal Elizabeth I awarded to those who fought in which naval battle?

720 *Transport*

Some road vehicles use LPG as their fuel. What does LPG stand for?

721 *Royal Pageantry*

Which hereditary royal office, fulfilling a special function at coronations, is held by the Dymokes of Scrivelsby in Lincolnshire?

722 *Entertainment*

Active throughout the Second World War, and affectionately referred to as 'Every Night Something Awful', what did the acronym ENSA really stand for?

723 *Literature*

Which children's novel by Frances Hodgson Burnett opens thus: 'When Mary Lennox was sent to Misselthwaite Manor to live with her uncle everybody said she was the most disagreeable-looking child ever seen.'?

724 *Literature*

Which book by George Eliot ends with the lines: 'The tomb bore the names of Tom and Maggie Tulliver, and below the names it was written – In their death they were not divided.'?

725 *Mathematics*

What is the cube root of one million?

726 *Art*

What was the family name of three sixteenth-century Flemish painters, the father Pieter the Elder, and his sons Pieter the Younger and Jan?

727 *Paris Landmarks*

Which Paris square, in which stands the obelisk of Luxor, lies at the south-east end of the Champs Elysées?

728 *British Institutions*

Which British monarch founded the Royal Society in 1660?

729 *Literature*

How was Mrs Heelis who owned Hill Top Farm, in what is now Cumbria, better known?

730 *Geography*

Which city, the most populous on the South Island, stands on the shores of Pegasus Bay?

731 *The Armed Forces*

Which rank in the Army is equivalent to a Commodore in the Royal Navy and an Air Commodore in the RAF?

732 *The Bible*

In St John's gospel in the New Testament, what miracle did Jesus perform at Siloam, a pool in Jerusalem?

733 *European Government*

What is the upper house of the German Parliament called?

734 *Space Exploration*

What does the acronym NASA stand for?

735 *People*

Which actress and model is the daughter of the Hollywood star Ingrid Bergman?

736 *The UK*

Which city, other than London, has a Tate Gallery, an Albert Dock, a Fleet Street and a Wapping?

737 *Geography*

Streymoy, Eysturoy and Sandoy belong to which North Atlantic island group?

738 *The Armed Forces*

What name is given to that part of a gun carriage, consisting of an axle, pole and two wheels forming an ammunition carrier, to which horses are attached?

739 *Turkish History*

What was the surname adopted by the Turkish leader Mustapha Kemal in 1934?

740 *Classical Music*

Who is the composer of *Elegy for JFK* and *In Memoriam Dylan Thomas*?

741 *European Royalty*

Of which European country is Crown Princess Victoria the heir apparent to the throne, despite having a younger brother, Prince Carl Philip?

742 *The Ancient World*

Which Roman general defeated the Carthaginian, Hannibal, at the battle of Zama, thereby ending the Second Punic War?

743 *Anatomy*

Named after a Danish anatomist, in which part of the body can the organ of Jacobson be found?

744 *Exploration*

In 1497 Portugal mounted an expedition to reach India around the southern tip of Africa. Which famous navigator led this fleet?

745 *World Affairs*

Which UN agency did the UK withdraw from in 1985, but rejoin in July 1997?

746 *Chemistry*

Zr is the symbol for which element?

747 *Literature*

At more than a million words, which novel by Samuel Richardson, published in the late 1740s, is the longest novel in English?

748 *Phrases*

Which phrase has been applied to both the city of Lhasa and the fortress within the inner city of Beijing?

749 *The Peerage*

Colin Tennant – the man who bought, and sold the Caribbean island of Mustique – is Lord ... what?

750 *Television*

Which actor plays Charlie Fairhead in *Casualty* on BBC 1?

751 *The Second World War*

Which famous Second World War prisoner-of-war camp was located in a castle on a steep hill, 30 miles south-west of Leipzig?

752 *Food and Drink*

In which British city is the brewer Boddingtons based?

753 *Geography*

What is the collective name for the group of islands, within the Lesser Antilles, that includes Grenada, St Vincent and the Grenadines, St Lucia and Martinique?

754 *Law*

What name is given to the six divisions into which England and Wales are divided for legal purposes?

755 *Law*

What are the names of two of the six circuits?

756 *Geography*

Which two seas are linked by the Kiel Canal?

757 *Popular Culture*

'All the lonely people, where do they all come from?' is a famous line from which Beatles song of 1966?

758 *Sport*

Four cyclists share the distinction of having won the Tour de France five times. Name one of the four.

759 *Scientists*

What is the name of the American nuclear physicist who, in 1942, was made Director of the Los Alamos laboratory in New Mexico but resigned in 1945 following the first successful nuclear explosion?

760 *Geography*

If you sailed due east from Edinburgh, which European country would be your first landfall?

761 *London*

What is the name of the elected body which governs the City of London?

762 *The UK*

The remnant of which ancient forest spreads between the Lea and Roding rivers in Essex?

763 *Science*

In the context of nuclear energy, what do the letters AGR stand for?

764 *Printing*

In printing, what is a ligature?

765 *Great Britain*

Three towns make up the holiday area known collectively as Torbay. Torquay is one. What are the other two?

766 *Opera*

Which Japanese city is the setting for Puccini's *Madam Butterfly*?

767 *Science*

What word is used to describe either a series of steps that can be used to solve a problem or, in computer science, the logical sequence of operations to be performed by a program?

768 *British Prime Ministers*

Who was British Prime Minister at the turn of the nineteenth into the twentieth century?

769 *Literature*

What is the name of the linen weaver in a novel by George Eliot, whose gold is stolen by Dunstan Cass, and who adopts the daughter of Godfrey Cass?

770 *Words*

In what activity or pastime would one use something called a Claude Glass, named after Claude Lorrain, a seventeenth-century Frenchman?

771 *Food and Drink*

What name is given to the fibrous outer covering of a nutmeg when it is used as a spice?

772 *Television*

Which long-running BBC soap began in 1985 with the discovery of the body of Reg Cox?

773 *Religion*

What was the name of the Devon farmer's daughter who, in the eighteenth century, declared herself to be the woman mentioned in Chapter 12 of the Book of Revelation, and attracted many followers?

774 *Theatres*

The Tron Theatre, the Citizens Theatre, the Robin Anderson Theatre and Blackfriars theatre are all in which British city?

775 *Business*

What two-word expression is applied to the acquisition of one company by another through the use of borrowed funds?

776 *Language*

In Berlin it is called the U-Bahn; in Stockholm it is called the T-Bana. What's it called in London?

777 *Cartoon Characters*

What is the name of the work-shy Geordie, created by Reg Smythe, who, with his wife Flo, first appeared in the *Daily Mirror* in the 1950s?

778 *Exploration*

In 1494, which two European countries signed the Treaty of Tordesillas in which they agreed to share the lands they had newly discovered in the Americas and the East?

779 *Television*

Which former schoolteacher founded the National Viewers' and Listeners' Association during the 1960s?

780 *Radio*

Born in 1908 and believed to be the oldest regular voice on the national airwaves, who is the veteran presenter of 'Your Hundred Best Tunes'?

781 *Geography*

What is the name of the African capital city known until 1980 as Salisbury?

782 *Games*

In Germany, she is Fräulein Ming; in France, she is Mademoiselle Rose. How is this Cluedo suspect known in England?

783 *Shakespeare*

Which of Shakespeare's history plays includes the characters Lord Bigot, Peter of Pomfret, Cardinal Pandulph and the Bastard of Falconbridge?

784 *Government*

Three members of the Cabinet have the word 'Chancellor' as part of their title. The Chancellor of the Exchequer is one. Name the other two.

785 *The UK*

Described (by the Victorians) as 'The Windsor of the North', which castle is the main seat of the Duke of Northumberland?

786 *World Politics*

The Parliament of which Asian (Commonwealth) country is divided into two houses known as the Rajya Sabha and the Lok Sabha?

787 *Mathematics*

What name is given to any straight line that joins any two points on the circumference of a circle?

788 *Geography*

Which is the largest in area of the 16 states of Germany?

789 *Gilbert and Sullivan*

In which fictional town is *The Mikado* set?

790 *Psychology*

Sufferers from the condition SAD experience a depressed mood during autumn and winter and become more cheerful in spring and summer. What does SAD stand for?

791 *Aviation*

THF, TXL and SXF are the codes for the three airports serving which western European capital city?

792 *Fictional Detectives*

Sherlock Holmes lives at 221B Baker Street; which fictional detective, created by Dorothy L. Sayers, lives at 110A Piccadilly?

793 *Place Names*

In the name of the country Yugoslavia, what does the 'Yugo' mean?

794 *The UK*

The Tomb of the Eagles, Dwarfie Stane and Skara Brae are ancient monuments in which group of islands?

795 *Books*

Perhaps best known for his creation Paddington Bear, what's the name of Michael Bond's other well-known creation about whom he has written a series of books for adults?

796 *Art*

Who became famous as a result of his illustrations for Oscar Wilde's *Salome*?

797 *Chemistry*

Which shallow, flat-bottomed circular dish, used in laboratories, takes its name from a nineteenth/twentieth-century German bacteriologist?

798 *Australian History*

Botany Bay in Australia was so named because of the range of plants collected along its shore by which eighteenth-century botanist?

799 *The European Union*

Which is the only European Union country that does not have a land border with any other European Union country?

800 *Sport*

Which athletics event takes place over seven laps of the track and involves 28 hurdle jumps and seven water jumps?

801 *The Bible*

In the story of Noah, Noah was commanded by God to take two each of 'unclean beasts' into the Ark. How many each of 'clean beasts' was he commanded to take?

802 *Shakespeare*

Which play has inspired an opera by Gounod, a symphony by Berlioz, an overture by Tchaikovsky, a ballet by Prokofiev and a film by Franco Zeffirelli?

803 *Geography*

In French it is Mont Cervin, in Italian – Monte Cervino. By what German name do we know this Alpine peak?

804 *Opera*

What is the name of the fisherman who is the central character in Benjamin Britten's opera set in the Borough, a fishing village on the east coast of England?

805 *Children's Literature*

By what alternative title is (a boy called) Cedric Errol better known in a book by Frances Hodgson Burnett?

806 *Food and Drink*

Taken from the diminutive form of the Spanish word for 'donkey', what name is given to a tortilla rolled up with a filling of spiced beef or other ingredients?

807 *Pop Music*

'You Can't Hurry Love', 'Easy Lover' and 'A Groovy Kind Of Love' were UK number one singles in the 1980s for which British singer and songwriter?

808 *London*

The name of which area of London is derived from an ancient hunting cry?

809 *Birds*

What is the function of a bird's syrinx, found at the base of the windpipe?

810 *Aviation*

Which British airport in Leicestershire has the three-letter designation code EMA?

811 *Grammar*

The words, 'and', 'because' and 'but' are examples of which part of speech?

812 *American History*

What is the name of the Boston silversmith who carried the news of the approach of British troops to Lexington and Concord on the night of 18 April 1775, during the American Revolution?

813 *Awards*

Which nineteenth/twentieth century writer, a cousin of the Prime Minister Stanley Baldwin, refused to accept the Order of Merit three times?

814 *Literature*

What is the name of the eponymous hero of a novel by Rudyard Kipling who was nicknamed 'Little Friend of all the World'?

815 *The Royal Family*

Which breed of cattle is raised by the Queen Mother at her farm near the Castle of Mey?

816 *Words*

What word, originally referring to a Germanic tribe, is applied to novels that deal with cruelty and passion, often in a medieval setting such as a castle or monastery?

817 *Geography*

Which central European republic is composed of Bohemia and Moravia?

818 *Education*

SOAS is an acronym for which college of London University?

819 *Television*

What is the name of the prison in the classic situation comedy *Porridge*, which starred Ronnie Barker as Norman Stanley Fletcher?

820 *Royal Residences*

Which unoccupied royal palace in south-west London is also known as the Dutch House?

821 *The Twentieth Century*

When the present Queen came to the throne (in 1952), Winston Churchill was Prime Minister. Who was President of the United States?

822 *Sport*

In a game of ice hockey, what is the maximum number of players allowed on the ice at any one time?

823 *The UK*

Aysgarth, Clapham and Malham are villages in which English national park?

824 *Religion*

What is the name of the fourteenth/fifteenth-century female English mystic who recorded her experiences in works called *A Showing of God's Love* and *Revelations of Divine Love*?

825 *Food and Drink*

The name of which type of pasta translates (from Italian into English) as 'little worms'?

826 *Communications*

What is the name of the world's first privately financed communications satellite, launched in July 1962?

827 *Astronomy*

What, occurring annually, are the Orionids in October and the Leonids in November?

828 *Art*

Which art movement of the nineteenth century was founded by Dante Gabriel Rossetti, William Holman-Hunt and John Everett Millais?

829 *Science*

Lying near the Equator, what is the Aclinic line?

830 *Radio*

In which Somerset town, long associated with cider-making, is the local radio station Orchard FM based?

831 *Science*

What is the study of the shells of molluscs called?

832 *Literature*

The teenager Stella Bradshaw, is the chief character in which novel by Beryl Bainbridge, set against the backdrop of a down-at-heel Liverpudlian repertory company's production of *Peter Pan*?

833 *Islands*

The largest islands in both the Orkneys and Shetlands share the same name: what is it?

834 *Politics*

Which political party in the Republic of Ireland has a name which means 'Gaelic Nation'?

835 *Mythology*

Who, in Greek mythology, killed the hero Achilles when he shot a poisoned arrow into his heel?

836 *Shakespeare*

Who, in a Shakespeare play, has the title, 'the Thane of Fife'?

837 *Law*

What name is given to judges and senior practitioners who form governing bodies for each of the Inns of Court?

838 *Geography*

Of which former Soviet Republic, now an independent state, is Baku the capital city?

839 *The Bible*

By what Latin title, meaning 'out of the depths', is Psalm 130 known?

840 *Animals*

The stocky, bear-like scavenger known as a wolverine has an alternative common name which is also a word for an excessively greedy person. What name?

841 *The Bible*

What is the name of the wife of Isaac, and the mother of Jacob and Esau?

842 *The Highway Code*

Unless there are road signs stating otherwise, what is the maximum speed limit for all traffic on roads in England and Wales that have street lighting?

843 *Science*

What substance is obtained by heating sand, sodium carbonate and lime?

844 *Proverbs*

According to the saying, 'Man's extremity is God's...' what?

845 *World Politics*

After leading the so-called 'People Power' revolt, Cory Aquino became, in 1986, the first woman president of which Asian country?

846 *Literature*

The Brer Rabbit stories were written by Joel Chandler Harris. Who is the narrator of the stories?

847 *History*

Which nickname, given to Oliver Cromwell, was also applied to his cavalrymen in the English Civil War?

848 *Architecture*

The Guggenheim Museum in New York City was the last great work by which famous American architect?

849 *Proverbs*

According to the proverb, who is bound to appear if you talk about him?

850 *Sport*

In rugby league, what numbered shirt does the fullback usually wear?

851 *European Royalty*

Grand Duke Jean reigns the European Grand Duchy of?

852 *Phrases*

What term is used in the USA for a president in the last part of his term of office who, between the election and inauguration of the next president, lacks political clout?

853 *Astronomy*

Which American astronomer propounded the theory of the expanding universe in 1929 and has an orbiting telescope named in his honour?

854 *Imaginary Places*

What is the name of the harbour town in which Dylan Thomas' 'play for voices', *Under Milk Wood*, is set?

855 *Politics*

The name of which Irish political party translates as 'soldiers of destiny'?

856 *Comedy*

Which stage and television comedienne's catchphrase was 'She knows, y'know'?

857 *Theatres*

The Congress Theatre, the Royal Hippodrome and the Winter Garden are venues in which resort on the south coast?

858 *Wales*

Which town was formerly a Roman fort called Maridunum or Moridunum, and has the Welsh name Caerfyrddin?

859 *Medicine*

Chronic Fatigue Syndrome is also known by what two-letter term?

860 *The Bible*

Shem and Ham were two of the three sons of Noah. Who was his third son?

861 *Mythology*

Who descended into the Underworld to retrieve his wife Eurydice?

862 *Literature*

Which nineteenth-century novel opens with the lines '1801 – I have just returned from a visit to my landlord – the solitary neighbour that I shall be troubled with.'?

863 *Cinema*

In the classic comedy *Bringing Up Baby*, starring Katharine Hepburn and Cary Grant, what was 'baby'?

864 *Geography*

Which state capital is situated on the estuary of the Swan River, some ten miles from its mouth?

865 *Wildlife*

The beach at Rantau Abang in Malaysia is famous as a nesting ground for which creatures?

866 *Chemistry*

Ac is the symbol for which element?

867 *Cinema*

The Englishman Stuart Craig has won three Oscars – for *Gandhi* (1982), *Dangerous Liaisons* (1988) and *The English Patient* (1996). In which category?

868 *The Royal Family*

Who is the mother of Lady Sarah Chatto?

869 *The USA*

What is the state capital of Florida?

870 *Japanese Theatre*

What is the main feature in 'Bunraku' – a traditional and popular type of theatre in Japan?

871 *Radio*

Which American-born rock singer and guitarist, who had UK hits in the 1970s and 1980s, presented 'Suzi's Soul Serenade' on Radio 2?

872 *Quotations*

What, according to Oscar Wilde, is the 'curse of the drinking classes'?

873 *Scottish Literature*

What is the title of the Compton Mackenzie novel, later adapted as a film, which is based on a true event when a cargo of Scotch whisky ran aground on a Hebridean island during the Second World War?

874 *Musical Instruments*

From the Urdu for 'three' and 'string', what name is given to the Indian musical instrument with a long neck and up to seven strings?

875 *Wales*

The Menai Strait is crossed by two bridges: one is Thomas Telford's Menai Suspension Bridge. What is the name of the other, which is both a road and rail bridge?

876 *The Bible*

Mentioned in St Luke's gospel, what is the name of the priest who was John the Baptist's father?

877 *Arts*

In which ballet, with music by Tchaikovsky, is Princess Aurora the principal character?

878 *Animals*

What is the common name of the (flying) mammals which make up the order called Chiroptera?

879 *Recent Books*

The book *Between Extremes*, an account of travels in South America, was written by Brian Keenan and which former fellow hostage?

880 *Measurements*

Which measurement on the Celsius temperature scale is equal to 273.15 on the Kelvin scale?

881 *Geography*

On which river does Dublin stand?

882 *Business*

On an invoice or business document, what does the phrase 'E and O E' mean?

883 *Medicine*

Singultus is a medical term for what common involuntary reaction?

884 *Literature*

Matilda Jenkyns, known as Miss Matty, her dominating sister Deborah and the pompous Mrs Jamieson are all characters in which novel by Mrs Gaskell?

885 *Rock Music*

Born in the 1940s, Louis Firbank was a founder of the Velvet Underground in 1965. By what name is he better known?

886 *The USA*

As used in American detective stories and films, what names are given to unidentified male and female characters?

887 *Paris Landmarks*

Built between 1806 and 1836, which Paris landmark was commissioned to celebrate the victories of Napoleon?

888 *Sports*

Of which sporting body is John Crowther the chief executive?

889 *Road Safety* ✓

A zebra crossing derives its name from its black and white stripes. Why is a pelican crossing so called?

890 The UK ✓

On the coast of which English county are Gibraltar Point, Chapel St Leonards and Mablethorpe?

891 History

Adela, a daughter of William the Conquerer, was the mother of which English king?

892 Music

What sort of song is a berceuse?

893 Saints

In Christian tradition, what is the name of the woman who wiped Christ's face with a cloth on which an image of his face was left?

894 Geography

In terms of area, which is the largest island of the Philippines?

895 London

The US Embassy in London stands in Grosvenor Square, in which there are statues to two former US presidents: Franklin Roosevelt and...?

896 Famous Virtuosos

Itzhak Perlman, Pinchas Zukerman and Isaac Stern are distinguished twentieth-century virtuosos on which instrument?

897 Food and Drink

What name is given to the astringent blue-black berries that are the hallmark flavouring of the spirit gin?

898 Heads of State

What title is held by the sovereign ruler of Bahrain?

899 The Second World War

The D-Day Landing was a tri-phibious military operation. What does that mean?

900 London

Because of the prominent signs on the pillars at the entrance and exit, what nickname is given to the Naval and Military Club in Piccadilly, London?

901 The Church Calendar

Collop Monday is the day before which day in the religious calendar?

902 *Sport*

What acronym is used for the governing body of World Football?

903 *Geography*

Which island group, a British Crown Colony, has one town, approximately 2200 people, 750,000 sheep and no naturally growing trees?

904 *Currency*

The dong is the main unit of currency in which Asian country?

905 *British Prime Ministers*

Which Prime Minister served in two other administrations as Foreign Secretary, uniquely the first in the House of Lords and the second in the House of Commons?

906 *Languages*

What is the national language of Pakistan?

907 *Birds*

What specifically is meant by birds that are described as sedentary or sessile?

908 *Popular Fiction*

What is the name of the author of *Hold The Dream, To Be The Best* and *A Woman of Substance*?

909 *Britain*

Rusholme, Stretford and Wythenshawe are suburbs of which British city?

910 *Asia*   ✓

Malay, Mandarin (Chinese), Tamil and English are the official languages of which small South-east Asian island country?

911 *Photography*

What does the abbreviation APS stand for?

912 *History*

Catherine of Valois, daughter of the King of France, was the wife of which King of England?

913 *The Armed Forces* ✓

The badge of which commissioned rank in the British Army is a single crown?

914 *Shakespeare*

Which eponymous Shakespearean character is drawn from a legendary Roman hero of the fifth Century BC who got his name from his triumphant siege of a city of the Volsci?

915 *The European Union*

QMV is the abbreviation for a voting system used in the Council of the European Union. What does QMV stand for?

916 *Hobbies*

What would interest a gricer?

917 *Sport*

What was the profession of W.G. Grace, who took 11 years to qualify because of his preoccupation with cricket?

918 *Russian History*

Who was the first tsar to be named emperor?

919 *Famous Theatres*

Which Dublin theatre was founded in 1904 by W.B.Yeats, J.M. Synge and Lady Gregory?

920 *Phrases*

Originally a movement for reform in the Ottoman Empire, which two-word expression is now popularly used for any junior group who challenge the status quo?

921 *Imaginary Places*

In *The Lord of the Rings*, what creatures lived in the valley known as Rivendell?

922 *Geography*

Nuuk is the capital of which self-governing province of a European country?

923 *Music*

The RLPO is an abbreviation for which major regional symphony orchestra?

924 *The Bible*

In the King James version of the Bible how many books are there in the New Testament?

925 *American Institutions*

Which women's organization in the USA is known by the initials DAR?

926 *The Commonwealth*

Which is the only Commonwealth country on the mainland of South America?

927 *Art*

What in a painting is known as pentimento?

928 *European History*

The dynasty founded by Clovis which ruled France from around AD 500 to 750, was known by what name?

929 *Geography*

Akrotiri and Dhekelia are UK military base areas in which island country?

930 *The Bible*

Which gospel is (regarded as) the oldest written account of the ministry and passion of Jesus?

931 *Music*

The abbreviation SATB describes the make-up of a standard four-part choir. What do the letters SATB stand for?

932 *Motoring*

The Corsavan, the Astravan and the Combo are models of vehicles produced by which manufacturer?

933 *International Vehicle Registrations*

A car with the index mark V would have been registered... where in Europe?

934 *Botany*

Which word describes a plant that requires up to two years to complete its life cycle?

935 *Poetry*

What is the name of the Welsh poet whose works include 'Song at the Year's Turning' and 'Poetry for Supper'?

936 *Cinema*

In *The Wizard of Oz*, what is the name of Dorothy's dog?

937 *Geography*

What is the state capital of South Australia?

938 *Literature*

Which nineteenth-century writer coined the words chortle, galumph and jabberwocky?

939 *Popular Music*

Tim Rice has been awarded Oscars for his work in three films. *The Lion King* is one, what is one of the other two?

940 *Politics*

Riverside, Walton and West Derby are parliamentary constituencies in which city?

941 *Measurements* ✓

Which imperial unit of mass is equal to 635 kilograms?

942 *Religious Groups*

Which worldwide religious group takes its name from a section of Isaiah: Chapter 43 Verse 12?

943 *Anatomy*

Where on the human body would you find a whorl, a tented arch and an ulnar loop?

944 *People*

She was born Maria Cecilia Sophia Anna Kalogeropoulos. How was this famous diva known to the world?

945 *Parliament*

To be eligible for election to the Westminister Parliament, a person must be a citizen of the UK, of any Commonwealth country, or of which other country?

946 *The Second World War*

Which event in the Second World War is commemorated in the UK on 15 September each year?

947 *Literature*

What particular food does Ben Gunn, the marooned pirate in Robert Louis Stevenson's *Treasure Island*, crave?

948 *Charles Dickens*

In *A Christmas Carol* what is Tiny Tim's surname?

949 *The Peerage*

A first cousin to the Queen, what is the surname or family name of the Earl of Harewood?

950 *Canada*

Which island province, which joined the Canadian Confederation in 1873, is named after a son of George III (the father of Queen Victoria)?

951 *Phrases*

What term originated from a petition or protest on which the signatures are arranged in a circle, in order to conceal the order in which they were signed?

952 *Quotations*

Of which twentieth-century invention did the newspaper editor and Liberal MP, C.P. Scott, famously state: 'The word is half Greek, half Latin. No good can come of it'?

953 *People*

What is the name of the beautiful and witty actress with whom George Bernard Shaw had a long and famous correspondence?

954 *France*

Avignon, Arles and Lyons stand on which major river?

955 *Language*

What does it mean if something is described as homochromous?

956 *The Monarchy*

How many grandchildren of George VI were born during his lifetime?

957 *European History*

In which year did the French Revolution begin?

958 *History*

Anglo-Saxon England was divided into seven kingdoms, known as the Heptarchy. Name two of the seven.

959 *Poetry*

'And did those feet in ancient time, Walk upon England's mountains green'. Who wrote these famous words?

960 *Monastic Orders*

Which monastic order was popularly known as the 'Black Friars', and officially known as the Order of Preachers?

961 *London*

In November 1783 John Austen was the last person to be executed at which site in London?

962 *Geography*

Which range of hills extends north-south through the county of Worcestershire?

963 *Literature*

What is the title of the worldwide best-selling book by Jung Chang describing three generations of women in one Chinese family?

964 *History*

Which future royal scullion was crowned as 'Edward VI' in Dublin in 1487?

965 *Roman History*

Which philosopher and statesman was tutor to Emperor Nero?

966 *Europe*

Which European capital city took its name from two of the communities which were amalgamated in 1873, one on the right bank and one on the left of the Danube?

967 *The USA*

What is the state capital of Vermont?

968 *Cinema*

What links Bing Crosby, Bob Hope and Dorothy Lamour with Singapore, Zanzibar, Rio, Morocco and Utopia?

969 *Saints*

Which saint is often depicted in art wearing bishop's vestments and treading on snakes?

970 *The Royal Family*

The Duke of Kent who died during the Second World War had three children. The present Duke of Kent and Prince Michael of Kent are two. Who is the third?

971 Shipping Forecasts

Which shipping forecast area lies off the east coast of England between Tyne and Thames?

972 History

The eighteenth/nineteenth-century English politician and statesman William Wilberforce is best remembered for his campaign against what?

973 Motor Cars

The Galant, the Colt and the Carisma are models of motor car produced by which Japanese manufacturer?

974 Quotations

To whom in the eighteenth century are the famous words 'Let them eat cake' attributed?

975 Asia

By what name was Bangladesh known from 1947 until 1971?

976 Food and Drink

The name of which vegetable translates from the French as 'eat all'?

977 Newspapers

In which national newspaper – Monday to Friday – is the second section of the paper called The Monday Review, The Tuesday Review, etc?

978 Counties

The cathedral city of Lichfield and Tamworth, once the capital of the Saxon kingdom of Mercia, are in which English county?

979 Pop Music

Which pair of British actors, who first came to prominence in the TV series Soldier, Soldier, have had UK number one singles with 'Unchained Melody', 'I Believe' and 'What Becomes of the Brokenhearted'?

980 American History

Which massacre in 1890 was the last major confrontation between the US Army and the American Indians?

981 Medicine

MMR is the combined vaccine against which three diseases?

982 *Jazz*

What name was adopted by the jazz and blues singer who was born Eleanora Fagan and nicknamed Lady Day?

983 *Horse Racing*

Under National Hunt rules of racing, there are two kinds of races which involve jumping over obstacles. Steeplechasing is one. What is the other?

984 *Ceremonies*

The recognition, the oath, the anointing, the investiture, the enthronement and the homage are the six stages of what?

985 *Measurements*

What is the SI unit of mass?

986 *Literature*

Which novel, by Ernest Hemingway, tells the story of Robert Jordan, an idealistic American college professor who fights with the Republican army during the Spanish Civil War?

987 *Art*

What word describes the process of creating a design on a metal plate with the use of acid?

988 *American Institutions*

AP is one of the world's largest news-gathering services. What do the initials AP stand for?

989 *Children's Literature*

What is the name of the owner of the motor car Chitty-Chitty-Bang-Bang, in a series of children's stories?

990 *European Cities*

Which city is the seat of the Dutch government?

991 *Science*

For what purpose would benzoic acid, sodium benzoate or potassium benzoate be added to food?

992 *Poetry*

The opening lines from a famous ode by Shelley are 'Hail to thee blithe spirit! Bird thou never wert.' Which bird?

993 *Poetry*

To which bird did Keats write his famous ode, a bird he describes as a 'light-wingèd Dryad of the trees' that 'Singest of summer in full-throated ease'?

994 *Coins*

What are the correct terms for the head and tail sides of a coin?

995 *Mythology*

With a name meaning 'all gifts' who, according to Greek myth, was the first woman (fashioned by Hephaestus out of clay)?

996 *Organizations*

Which international and somewhat secretive organization refers to God as the 'Great Architect of the Universe'?

997 *Pop Music*

Which knight of the pop music world had the first British exhibition of his paintings at a gallery in Bristol in September?

998 *The Armed Forces*

What nickname was adopted by members of the British Expeditionary Force in France in 1914, taken from an alleged comment by the Kaiser?

999 *London*

To be born within the sound of the bells of which city church is the traditional definition of a cockney?

1000 *Charles Dickens*

In *A Tale of Two Cities* what's the name of the young French aristocrat who is saved from the guillotine by the self-sacrifice of Sydney Carton?

1001 *Crime and Punishment*

Execution Dock at Wapping on the River Thames was the traditional place of execution for what type of criminal, who would be led to his death by an official carrying a silver oar?

1002 *Cartoon Characters*

Lucy, Linus, Peppermint Patty and Woodstock are all characters in which comic strip?

1003 *Geography*

The islands of Sulawesi, Flores, Bali and Java Are part of which country?

1004 *London Airports*

LHR and LGW are London Heathrow and London Gatwick. What are STN and LTN?

1005 *Musical Instruments*

With the development of which musical instrument are the names Rickenbacher and Fender associated?

1006 *Gilbert and Sullivan*

Rose Maybud is desired by Robin Oakapple, who is actually Sir Ruthven Murgatroyd in disguise, whilst the bad baronet Despard Murgatroyd is loved by Mad Margaret. What is the Gilbert and Sullivan operetta?

1007 *Awards*

Which Italian city hosts an annual film festival, which includes the Golden Lion and Silver Lion awards?

1008 *Numbers*

How many years are there in a quadrennium?

1009 *Literature*

Which George Bernard Shaw play is named after a legendary King of Cyprus, who fell in love with an ivory statue he had carved?

1010 *Languages*

New Zealand has two official languages – English and...?

1011 *Food and Drink*

In South Africa, what Afrikaans name is given to strips of meat that have been dried and salted?

1012 *International Car Registration*

CH is the car registration mark for which European country?

1013 *Music and Film*

The Marx brothers films *A Night at the Opera* and *A Day at the Races* were also the titles of albums released in the 1970s by which British rock group (led by Freddie Mercury)?

1014 *Popular Music*

Entering the album charts in June 1967, it stayed there for 148 weeks. Acclaimed as the climax of the group's career, what is the title of this classic Beatles LP?

1015 *Words*

Which word, taken from the Greek meaning 'praise' or 'renown', is used to indicate glory or prestige?

1016 *Costume*

The name of which item of Japanese attire translates into English simply as 'wearing thing'?

1017 *Science*

What did Albert Einstein introduce as the fourth dimension in his General Theory of Relativity?

1018 *Shakespeare*

As listed in *As You Like It*, how many ages of man are there?

1019 *Universities*

Which former Governor of Hong Kong and current European Commissioner is the Chancellor of the University of Newcastle-upon-Tyne?

1020 *Place Names*

Which sea, between south-east Europe and Asia, was known to the Romans as Pontus Euxinus which means 'friendly sea'?

1021 *Food and Drink*

Solanum tuberosum is the Latin name for which popular vegetable?

1022 *Sport*

In which racquet sport is the net five feet high at the centre?

1023 *Political Societies*

What is the name of the socialist organization, founded in 1884, whose early members included George Bernard Shaw and Beatrice and Sidney Webb?

1024 *Theatres*

The Empire, the Everyman, the Neptune and the Royal Court are all theatres in which city in northern England?

1025 *The Monarchy*

Which fifteenth-century king is historically accused of the murders of the two princes in the Tower – his nephews?

1026 *The Monarchy*

What were the first names of the princes in the tower?

1027 *Theatre*

After five years of lavish living in Paris, Madame Lyubov Ranevsky and her daughter Anya return to their heavily mortgaged Russian estate which they try to save from bankruptcy. Which Chekhov play is this?

1028 *Television*

Will Preston, Alex Redman and Tom Deneley: regular characters in which ITV medical drama series?

1029 *Galleries*

The Uffizi Gallery in Florence was built in the mid-sixteenth century as government offices for the Grand Duke of Tuscany. Of which famous family was he a member?

1030 *Popular Music*

How were LaVerne, Maxene and Patti – an American vocal harmony trio at the height of their fame in the late 1930s and the 1940s – popularly known?

1031 *The Ancient World*

Who was the last ruler of the Macedonian dynasty of the Ptolemies to reign in Egypt?

1032 *The Middle East*

What is the capital of the oil-rich sultanate of Oman?

1033 *Mythology*

What is the name of the prophetic sea god, capable of changing his shape at will?

1034 *Architecture*

What type of structure is a bartizan?

1035 *France*

Which river links the city of Bordeaux with the Atlantic Ocean by way of the estuary called the Gironde?

1036 *Art*

In which of the arts was Isadora Duncan famous?

1037 *The USA*

In America, what is Old Glory?

1038 *Television*

In which country is the medical drama *The Young Doctors* set?

1039 *Measurements*

How many square inches make a square foot?

1040 *Food and Drink*

Which spirit is the basis of the liqueur Drambruie?

1041 *Quotations*

Which famous admiral is credited with the proverb 'Salt water and absence wash away love'?

1042 *Twentieth-century History*

Which country's embassy, now at 27 Prince's Gate, moved from 16 Prince's Gate after it was the scene of a violent siege in 1980?

1043 *Proverbs*

According to the proverb, what is the 'mother of invention'?

1044 *The Second World War*

In the Second World War what were 'Little Boy' and 'Fat Boy'?

1045 *The Bible*

In the New Testament whose is the first of the epistles?

1046 *Ballet*

In which Delibes ballet is a toymaker made to think that one of his dolls has come to life?

1047 *Saints*

Which saint was carried off by raiders at the age of 16 and enslaved in Ireland?

1048 *The Ancient World*

Which famous gardens, which have now disappeared, were one of the Seven Wonders of the Ancient World?

1049 *The Peerage*

Who is the hereditary Duke of Lancaster?

1050 *Science*

The optimum composition of what manufactured material is 75% silica, 10% lime and 15% soda?

1051 *Engineering*

Who designed the Clifton Suspension Bridge across the Avon Gorge?

1052 *US Politics*

What are the two major political parties in the USA?

1053 *Names*

Carlos is the Spanish equivalent of which English name?

1054 *Cinema*

In 1940 MGM honoured this inventor and film pioneer by releasing two films about his life, one starring Mickey Rooney and one Spencer Tracey. Who is he?

1055 *Politics*

In April of 1988 what Parliamentary object did MP Ron Brown pick up and drop as a protest against the poll tax?

1056 *Popular Music*

According to the folk song, what colour is the 'Rose in Texas, that I am going to see'?

1057 *Phobias*

What is chromophobia?

1058 *Animals*

What type of creature is a moccasin?

1059 *Population*

What is the most populous city in India?

1060 *Geography*

In which European country is Picardy?

1061 *Space Exploration*

What do the initials LRV stand for in transport on the Moon?

1062 *Titles*

In which year did Mr Winston Churchill become 'Sir' Winston Churchill?

1063 Motorways

Which motorway runs from near Coventry to near Leicester?

1064 Literature

Which novel by R.D. Blackmore is set in the late seventeenth century on Exmoor?

1065 Language

On what might you find a quillion, a tang and a ricasso?

1066 Politics

In what year did Margaret Thatcher become leader of the Conservative Party?

1067 Animals

What sort of animal is a Russian Blue?

1068 Saints

What Roman saint is the patron saint of girls?

1069 Trade Unions

If a person belonged to the NAS union, what would their profession be?

1070 Aviation

Its maiden flight was in 1969, but in which year did Concorde enter commercial service?

1071 Acronyms

In connection with arms treaties what is START an acronym for?

1072 The Monarchy

Who was the last Plantagenet King of England?

1073 Theatres

Which London theatre stands in Sloane Square?

1074 Sport

In which sport in the USA is the Stanley Cup the supreme professional team event?

1075 Nature

In Britain what do we commonly call the crane fly?

1076 Sport

Which player puts the ball into a set scrum in Rugby Union?

1077 *Phrases*

What French term is used for a small flat or other lodging for occasional use?

1078 *Monastic Orders*

The White Friars is an alternative name for which order of monks?

1079 *Books*

Who has written biographies of Mary Queen of Scots and Oliver Cromwell, and crime novels featuring the female detective Jemima Shore?

1080 *Flags*

The branches of which tree appear as a symbol on the United Nations flag

1081 *Poetry*

Tennyson wrote 'The mirror crack'd from side to side; "The curse is come upon me," cried…' who?

1082 *Mythology*

What is the ancient name of the Dardanelles, named in honour of the daughter of Athamas who drowned in the straits after she fell off the miraculous winged ram?

1083 *Royal Rulers*

At the time of his death in 1999, Hassan II was the longest reigning monarch in the Arab world. Of which North African country was he king for 38 years?

1084 *Geography*

The Negev Desert occupies approximately 60% of which Middle East country?

1085 *Chemistry*

Pinchbeck, which was invented and named after a London watchmaker and is used to simulate gold, is an alloy of two metals. Which two metals?

1086 *London*

Which famous London thoroughfare runs from Marble Arch to Hyde Park Corner?

1087 *The Bible*

Because Moses was 'slow of speech', who acted as his spokesman to Pharaoh and the Israelites in the events leading up to the exodus from Egypt?

1088 *Television*

Which BBC programme, first broadcast in 1979, has been presented over the years by the late Sir Robin Day, Peter Sissons and David Dimbleby?

1089 *Conservation*

Where in Gloucestshire are the headquarters of the Wildfowl and Wetlands Trust?

1090 *Mythology*

According to tradition, which king built the Hanging Gardens of Babylon for his wife Amytis, to remind her of the hills in her homeland?

1091 *Chemistry*

What Latin name is given to the mixture of concentrated nitric and hydrochloric acids, because it can disolve gold?

1092 *Cinema*

In which decade did the films *An American in Paris, From Here to Eternity* and *On the Waterfront* win Best Picture Oscars?

1093 *Football*

Feyenoord, PSV Eindhoven and Ajax are football teams in which European country?

1094 *Parliament*

What is the minimum number of MPs required for a division in the House of Commons?

1095 *The UK*

Which cathedral in Wales bears on its organ loft a sculpture by Epstein entitled *Christ in Majesty*?

1096 *Britain*

Which palace in Oxfordshire is the seat of the dukes of Marlborough?

1097 *Art*

Flatford Mill on the River Stour, The Hay Wain and *The Cornfield* are all paintings by which artist?

1098 *Mathematics*

What term is used for any whole number that can be divided only by one and itself?

1099 *Australia*

The Henley-on-Todd race, in which competitors carry bottomless boats up the dry bed of the Todd River, is an annual event in which Australian tourist centre?

1100 *Geography*

Which peninsula has coastlines on the Gulf of Suez to the west, and the Gulf of Aqaba to the east?

1101 *London*

Which London street, on which the bankruptcy court was formerly situated, is now a euphemism for the state of bankruptcy?

1102 *Counties*

Cartmel racecourse, Wordsworth's birthplace in Cockermouth and the town of Kendal are all in which county?

1103 *Opera*

In which Puccini opera does the poet Rodolfo fall in love with the seamstress Mimi?

1104 *Science*

What word is used to describe an animal that eats both plants and meat?

1105 *Harry Potter*

Sleek and shiny with a mahogany handle, Harry Potter's first what was a 'Nimbus Two Thousand'?

1106 *The UK*

St Mary's, St Agnes, St Martin's, Bryher and Tresco are the five inhabited islands in which island group?

1107 *Geography*

In which Commonwealth country are provinces grouped as the 'Atlantic Provinces' and the 'Prairie Provinces'?

1108 *The Armed Forces*

What is the curved knife traditionally carried by the Gurkhas called?

1109 *The Home*

Where in a house are parts called newel, post, baluster, riser and string?

1110 *Quotations*

Who described an English country gentleman galloping after a fox as being the 'unspeakable in full pursuit of the uneatable'?

1111 *New York*

Which area of New York City has a name which is derived from the direction 'south of Houston Street'?

1112 *The Middle East*

By what name are the Trucial States now known?

1113 *London*

Covering an area of more than 10 acres, what is the name of London's largest meat market?

1114 *Imaginary Places*

Which book, first published in 1726, describes visits to Balnibarbi, Luggnagg and Laputa?

1115 *Railway Stations*

Charing Cross Station, Central Station, High Street Station and Queen Street Station serve which British city?

1116 *London*

Commonwealth countries don't have embassies in Britain... what do they have?

1117 *Quotations*

'This is sharp remedy but it is a sure one for all ills.' These were the words of which former royal favourite as he stood on the scaffold before his execution in 1618?

1118 *Weaponry*

The American Huey Cobra and Apache and the Russian Hind are what sort of war machines?

1119 *Geography*

Only two European countries have both Atlantic and Mediterranean coastlines. Which two?

1120 *Musicals*

'Oh What a Beautiful Mornin', 'The Surrey With the Fringe on Top' and 'Kansas City' are favourite numbers from which Rodgers and Hammerstein musical?

1121 *Education*

Eight colleges and universities make up the Ivy League in the USA. Name two of the eight.

1122 *Sport*

Which sport connects Royal Lytham and St Annes, Royal St George's and Royal Birkdale?

1123 *Animals*

Frogs and toads make up the order Anura. Which amphibians make up the order Caudata?

1124 *History*

What was the name of the ship which took the Pilgrim Fathers to America in 1620?

1125 *Popular Fiction*

The Martian Chronicles, The Illustrated Man, Something Wicked This Way Comes are all science fiction novels by which popular author?

1126 *Shakespeare*

Cicero, Claudius and Calpurnia are characters in which Shakespeare play?

1127 *Judaism*

At the Passover feast a special cup of wine is poured out and the door is opened for which prophet, the forerunner of the Messiah?

1128 *Zoology*

In a colony of social insects, what name is given to the primary reproductive female?

1129 *The Commonwealth*

North and South Islands, and Stewart Island, are the three main islands of which Commonwealth country?

1130 *Medicine*

What medical term comes from two Greek words meaning 'lack of blood'?

1131 *Language*

Graphology is a study which interprets a person's character by what means?

1132 *Food and Drink*

What is the main ingredient of bouillabaisse?

1133 *Musicals*

In which Andrew Lloyd Webber musical does Christine, a member of the chorus, take over a leading role in a production of 'Hannibal' with the assistance of her mysterious music teacher?

1134 *The USA*

What is the state capital of California?

1135 *The USA*

What date is inscribed on the tablet held by the Statue of Liberty?

1136 *Roman Numerals*

Which letter of the alphabet is the Roman numeral for 500?

1137 *Animals*

Which type of large reptile has species called Nile, Orinoco and Siamese?

1138 *Poetry*

'How do I love thee? Let me count the ways.' This is the opening line from a famous sonnet by which poet, herself married to another poet?

1139 *Museums*

A museum celebrating the lives and works of which literary family is at Haworth Parsonage in Yorkshire?

1140 *Medicine*

Short for the Latin for 'holding the place', what word describes a doctor who stands in temporarily in the absence of a regular doctor?

1141 *Cinema*

Which actor won an Oscar for Best Actor in two successive years during the 1930s for his performances in *Captains Courageous* and *Boys Town*?

1142 *Birds*

The condor is the common name for two species of which bird?

1143 *Chemistry*

What is the chemical formula for ice?

1144 *Geography*

Israel has borders with four independent countries. Egypt is one. Name two of the other three.

1145 *Centuries*

Handel composed *Messiah*, Mozart, *Don Giovanni* and Vivaldi, *The Four Seasons.* In which century?

1146 *Art*

In the well-known painting *The Anatomy Lesson of Dr Tulp*, a surgeon displays the dissected arm of a male cadaver to a group of onlookers. Who was the artist?

1147 *History*

What was the family relationship between Richard I and King John?

1148 *Geography*

What is the capital of Switzerland?

1149 *Science*

Potamology is the scientific study of which geographical features?

1150 *Popular Fiction*

What is the name of the Soviet submarine that appears in the title of a Tom Clancy novel, later a film starring Sean Connery?

1151 *Geography*

The Laptev Sea and the Kara Sea lie off the coast of which country?

1152 *Exploration*

The English explorer Mathew Flinders was one of the first to circumnavigate which continent?

1153 *Art*

What scene did Leonardo da Vinci paint on the refectory wall of the Dominican convent church of Santa Maria delle Grazie in Milan?

1154 *Chemistry*

Which element is denoted by the chemical symbol F?

1155 Business

With which field of business are the names Andre Deutsch, William Heinemann and Victor Gollancz associated?

1156 Scotland

At which village do members of the MacDonald clan gather on 13 February each year, in memory of a slaughter perpetrated on the clan by the Campbells in 1692?

1157 Medicine

What is a physician who specializes in children's diseases called?

1158 Quotations

According to Lord Acton's famous dictum, 'Power tends to corrupt and absolute power corrupts...' what?

1159 Phobias

What is kenophobia the fear of?

1160 Geography

Which city, founded in 1840, replaced Auckland as the capital of New Zealand in 1865?

1161 Shakespeare

In *As You Like It*, who is the lord, attendant on the banished duke in the forest of Arden, who speaks the famous lines 'All the world's a stage, And all the men and women merely players...'?

1162 Sport

In tennis, at what 'game score' does a tie-break come into effect?

1163 Birds

Mute, Whopper and Bewick's are types of which bird?

1164 Scotland

Which saint is reputed to have brought Christianity to Scotland when he built a church at Whithorn in around AD 400?

1165 Words

A centenary is a span of 100 years. What word is used for 300 hundred years?

1166 Name Connections

Which Victorian statesman gave his name to a type of leather portmanteau?

1167 *Musicals*

Oscar Hammerstein and Jerome Kern's song *Ol' Man River* refers to which river?

1168 *Retail Technology*

EPOS systems read bar codes on retail items. What do the letters stand for?

1169 *Business*

Which English businessman and designer founded the Habitat Company in 1971?

1170 *Anatomy*

Where in the human body are the navicular bones?

1171 *Warfare*

What is the name of the chemical and biological defence research establishment in Wiltshire?

1172 *Ceremonies*

What are tested at the annual Trial of the Pyx in Goldsmith's Hall, London

1173 *London*

What is the name of the avenue in London so called because James I once kept an aviary there?

1174 *Television*

What is the name of the Amsterdam-based detective created by Nicholas Freeling and made famous on television by Barry Foster in the 1970s?

1175 *Popular Fiction*

Now and Forever, Thurston House and *A Perfect Stranger* are romantic novels set in San Francisco. Who is their best-selling author?

1176 *Pop Music*

Who duetted with John Travolta on the 1978 UK number one singles 'You're the One That I Want' and 'Summer Nights'?

1177 *Food and Drink*

Breadsticks are sometimes known by their Italian name. What is it?

1178 *Commonwealth*

Which is the only Commonwealth country with an Arctic coastline?

1179 *Music Jazz*

'Mood Indigo', 'Black and Tan' 'Fantasy' and 'Satin Doll' are works associated with which bandleader and jazz composer, who died in 1974?

1180 *Words*

The venerable Bede was a monk and early English historian, but what was a bede?

1181 *Ceremonies*

A statue of which seventeenth-century monarch stands within the grounds of the Royal Hospital, Chelsea, and is decorated with oak leaves and branches by Chelsea pensioners to mark Oak Apple Day?

1182 *American history*

The bloodiest battle ever fought on US soil, it took place over three days in early July 1863 during the US Civil War. Where, precisely?

1183 *Opera*

Which Donizetti opera is set in Windsor in 1953 with roles for, among others, Henry VIII, Jane Seymour and Richard Percy?

1184 *Education*

The pupils at which English public school are divided into Oppidans and King's Scholars?

1185 *European Royalty*

Which European monarch uses the title 'His Serene Highness'?

1186 *The Armed Forces*

In the context of the naval service, what is the RFA?

1187 *Poetry*

The owl and the pussycat went to sea in a beautiful pea-green boat. Who were sent to sea by Edward Lear in a sieve?

1188 *Latin Words*

Often seen in books of quotations, or footnotes, what does the abbreviation, IBID or IB mean in English?

1189 *Geography*

Until 1991 it was Lagos. What is now the capital city of Nigeria?

1190 *The Royal Family*

What relation is the present Prince of Wales to the last Prince of Wales?

1191 *The Arts*

With which branch of the arts are the names Anton Dolin, Anthony Dowell and Frederick Ashton associated?

1192 *Islamic Leaders*

By what hereditary title is the head of the Nizari sect of Ismali Muslims more commonly known?

1193 *Science*

What name is given to that branch of fluid physics that studies the forces exerted by air, or other gases in motion?

1194 *Children's Literature*

Written in 1877, which famous story is told autobiographically by a horse, from foal to colt, to broken-in mount, to broken-down hack?

1195 *Saints*

Which of the apostles of Jesus, sometimes called Levi, was a toll collector at Capernaum by the Sea of Galilee when Jesus met him and called him to be one of his disciples?

1196 *Scottish History*

By which nickname is Margaret, the Queen of Scots, who died in 1290 aged only seven, commonly known?

1197 *Phrases*

Which French phrase meaning 'joy of living' is used to describe a feeling of healthy and exuberant enjoyment of life?

1198 *Popular Fiction*

In which best-selling novel by Thomas Harris does the main character lie low in Italy, while a former meal seeks revenge?

1199 *Medicine*

What name is given to the inherited disease, occurring almost exclusively in males, in which the clotting ability of blood is severely impaired due to a lack of Factor 8?

1200 *Food and Drink*

What French term is used in cooking for a bunch of mixed herbs used for flavouring, often encased in a bag?

1201 *International Organizations*

In which European city do the World Health Organization, the World Meteorological Organization and the World Trade Organization have their headquarters?

1202 *Famous Publications*

What is the name of the English physician who expurgated the works of Shakespeare and published a ten-volume edition in 1818?

1203 *Surrealism*

One of Magritte's best-known paintings, *The Treachery of Images,* depicts a larger than life tobacco pipe beneath which the artist has written five words in French. Which five words?

1204 *The Royal Family*

Which year did the Queen describe as her 'annus horribilis'?

1205 *Science*

Plumbago is an alternative name for which crystalline form of carbon, used in pencils?

1206 *Music*

What is the title of the English folk song that tells of a legendary seventeenth-century churchman who held his position by changing his religious leanings to suit whatever monarch was on the throne?

1207 *Science*

Used to measure intelligent behaviour in animals used for research, the Hebb-Williams is the standard laboratory model of what?

1208 *The USA*

Which two states in the USA are named after Charles II?

1209 *Science*

Which is the main constituent metal of the alloy pewter?

1210 *Food and Drink*

Apry is an alternative name for a type of brandy flavoured with which fruit juice?

1211 *The Monarchy*

What is the name of the favourite of Edward II, who was banished by enraged English barons, and murdered by the Earl of Warwick in 1312?

1212 *The Decorative Arts*

What term is used for any kind of craftwork made on board ship, historically often a whaler, using such substances as ivory and shells?

1213 *The Armed Forces*

A break from operations or arduous training is known as 'R & R'. What does 'R & R' stand for?

1214 *France*

In which mountain range is Mount Neige the highest peak?

1215 *Royal Residences*

On which river is Balmoral Castle, holiday home of the Royal Family in Scotland?

1216 *Gilbert and Sullivan*

In a Gilbert and Sullivan opera, the profession of the character John Wellington Wells is also the title of the opera. Which opera?

1217 *The Monarchy*

Who was the husband of Mary I of England?

1218 *Poetry*

From 'The Love Song of J Alfred Prufrock': 'In the room the women come and go, talking of ...' whom?

1219 *Mythology*

The Queen of Hades, King of the Underworld, was the daughter of the goddess Demeter. What is her name?

1220 *Geography*

Which Jordanian city is known as the 'rose-red city' because of its red stone buildings and the red cliffs surrounding it?

1221 *Botany*

Used in understanding the history of plants and the environment, palynology is the study of what substance?

1222 *Communications*

At what time in the morning do both BT and Cable and Wireless start their daytime rate for telephone calls on weekdays?

1223 *Communications*

What time in the evening do both BT and Cable and Wireless change from their daytime rate to their evening and night-time rates for telephone calls?

1224 *India*

The Indian nationalist leader and social campaigner Mohandas Karamchand Gandhi was popularly known as Mahatma. What does Mahatma mean?

1225 *Computers*

What name is given to the main printed circuit board of a computer that contains most of the components and connectors for expansion boards?

1226 *The Crown Jewels*

The First Star of Africa and the Second Star of Africa are diamonds cut from which massive stone?

1227 *Equestrianism*

In equestrianism, what name is given to a bridle without a bit?

1228 Geography

Five of the Scilly Isles are inhabited: Tresco is one; Name two of the other four

1229 *Theatre*

What is the purpose of a swozzle in a Punch and Judy show?

1230 *The Second World War*

In the Second World War what German word meaning 'armour' was given to German mechanized units created by Heinz Guderian?

1231 *Art*

Which artistic attraction in London welcomed its millionth visitor only 47 days after it opened?

1232 *Law*

'Advowson' is a term for the right to nominate a person to a vacant post in which profession?

1233 Henry VIII

Which of Henry VIII's six wives had four husbands (including Henry)?

1234 Chemistry

The abbreviation NPK is often used as a synonym for artificial fertilizers – the letters refer to the chemical symbols of the three elements used in their manufacture. Name two of the three.

1235 Public Houses

The emblem of St Peter is often used as a pub sign. What is the emblem?

1236 Exploration

Which passenger liner, designed by Brunel, laid the first successful transatlantic cable in 1866?

1237 Roman History

The adopted son of Julius Caesar, Octavian ruled Rome under what name, given to him by the Senate in 27 BC?

1238 Patron Saints

Which saint is popularly regarded as the patron saint of France?

1239 National Insurance Numbers

How many letters and figures, in total, are there in a person's national insurance number?

1240 Latin Phrases

What Latin phrase meaning 'Beware of the dog' is often seen on garden gates?

1241 Classical Drama

Which Greek tragic dramatist wrote the trilogy Oresteia ?

1242 Religion

What type of religious building takes its name from the Greek for 'gathering'?

1243 Mythology

Odysseus was the father of Telemachus. Who was his mother?

1244 Languages

Dari and Pashto are the official languages of which Asian country?

1245 Geography

The name of which South American country comes from the Latin word for silver?

1246 *Science*

If a substance is described as being stannic or stannous, which metal would it contain?

1247 *Television*

In which classic television comedy series are the four main characters called Basil, Sybil, Manuel and Polly?

1248 *British Organizations*

Founded in 1965, which Building Preservation Trust administers some 200 properties including cottages, castles, lighthouses, follies, a railway station and the entire island of Lundy?

1249 *Central American History*

Tenochtitlan, on the site of present-day Mexico City, was the capital city of which ancient empire?

1250 *Ireland*

The Curragh, Leopardstown and Fairyhouse are all associated with what activity in the Republic of Ireland?

1251 *Musical Instruments*

What name is given to the piece of wood which supports the strings on a violin?

1252 *The British Armed Forces*

In the Royal Navy, what type of vessels are *Sceptre*, *Sovereign*, *Trenchant*, and *Triumph*?

1253 *American History*

What sort of business was founded in America in the 1850s by the Scottish-born Alan Pinkerton?

1254 *Counties*

Snetterton motor-racing circuit, Carrow Road football ground and Fakenham racecourse are all in which county?

1255 *US Presidents*

Benjamin Harrison, Grover Cleveland and William McKinley were all US presidents in which decade of the nineteenth century?

1256 *Philosophy*

What name is given to the philosophy of law?

1257 *US Presidents*

The father of which US president was American ambassador to Britain from 1937 to 1940?

1258 *Airlines*

Several national airlines are known by three-letter initials, KLM for example. Which Asian country's national carrier is known as PIA?

1259 *Country Music*

Literally performing in front of a captive audience, which country singer, nicknamed 'The Man in Black', released an album in 1969 that had been recorded live at San Quentin prison?

1260 *Games*

There are two tax spaces on a monopoly board. One is income tax. What is the other?

1261 *Physics*

Which Greek word for 'little' is used as a prefix meaning a millionth part?

1262 *Athletics*

Derek Ibbotson in 1957, Steve Ovett and Seb Coe in 1981 and Steve Cram in 1985 are British athletes who set world records in those years. At which distance?

1263 *Insects*

Which is the largest order of insects, with over 250,000 species of which the Whirligig, Screech and Churchyard are members?

1264 *Geography*

Which mountain range extends along the Russian/Georgian border between the Black Sea and the Caspian Sea?

1265 *Food and Drink*

What name is given to the quintessential English dessert that consists of lightly stewed soft fruit, raspberries or redcurrants, for example, chilled in a mould lined with slices of white bread?

1266 *The Bible*

The American Negro song 'Dem Bones' was inspired by a story about which Old Testament prophet?

1267 *Dates*

In Australia and New Zealand, Anzac Day, 25 April commemorates what event of the First World War?

1268 *Anatomy*

Which tube-shaped sac at the end of the large intestine is a relic of evolution, which can be dispensed with when young and shrivels up with age?

1269 *Musicals*

Which 1975 American musical tells the story of a group of dancers auditioning for a Broadway show?

1270 *Business*

Bar codes are also known by the abbreviation 'UPC'. What does UPC stand for?

1271 *Nursery Rhymes*

Which nursery rhyme commemorates an attack on London by Vikings, when a bridge over the Thames was torn down by grappling irons?

1272 *Geography*

Named the Sandwich Islands by Captain Cook, they are now known as... what?

1273 *Museums*

A museum in Scala Street, London W1, is named after Benjamin Pollock and devoted exclusively to a history of what?

1274 *Architecture*

What name is given to the part of a church which contains the altar, sanctuary, and choir?

1275 Motor Racing

Who is the only Briton to have won the World Driver's title on three occasions?

1276 The UK

The Vines, the Charles Dickens Centre and Court of Pie Powder are features of which city on the River Medway?

1277 *European Royalty*

How is the present King of Spain, Juan Carlos, related to the previous king, Alphonso XIII, who was deposed in 1931?

1278 *South American History*

Which South American empire was conquered by Francisco Pizarro in the sixteenth century?

1279 *Sport*

In which sport are penalties awarded for hooking, spearing or slashing?

1280 *Medicine*

Very specifically, what does an ocularist make?

1281 *Counties*

Dropping to approximately 7 feet below sea level, Holme Fen is the lowest area of the UK. In which county is Holme Fen?

1282 *Words*

The name of which yellowish shade of brown is derived from an Urdu word for 'dust', or 'dust coloured'?

1283 *American History*

In 1819, Florida was ceded to the United States in a treaty signed by John Quincy Adams. Which country had ruled Florida immediately prior to this date?

1284 *Religion*

In Christian tradition, which of the four evangelists is symbolized by an eagle?

1285 *Chess*

He was born Harry Weinstein in 1963, and in 1985 became the youngest ever World Chess Champion. What is his name?

1286 *Mythology*

In which mythology were Atum, Shu, Tefnut, Geb and Nut five of the nine great gods?

1287 *London*

Which royal residence in London was named after the future William IV?

1288 *Literature*

Nathanael West's novel, *The Day of the Locust*, Evelyn Waugh's *The Loved One* and F. Scott Fitzgerald's *The Last Tycoon* are all set in which American city?

1289 *History*

The Channel Islands have been part of the kingdom of England since the reign of which monarch?

1290 *Literature*

One of the four novels which make up the Raj Quartet is *The Jewel in the Crown*. Name one of the other three.

1291 *Cricket Records*

Who, in the 1986/7 England/Australia series, was the last man to lead England to victory in an Ashes series?

1292 *Playwrights*

Shakespeare is well known for his history plays – *Henry IV*, *Henry V* etc. Which sixteenth-century playwright wrote *Edward II*?

1293 *Astronomy*

Which gas is the dominant constituent of the atmospheres of both Venus and Mars?

1294 *Music*

What is the name of the Italian composer and arranger best known for his soundtracks for Sergio Leone's spaghetti westerns?

1295 *Medicine*

Nosophobia is the morbid fear of what?

1296 *Children's Literature*

What is the name of the Fat Controller who runs Thomas the Tank Engine's railway?

1297 *Phrases*

Which French phrase means someone who incites others to commit crime – a role often found in detective novels and stories of espionage?

1298 *Geography*

On which large island in the northern hemisphere are King Christian IX Land, King Christian X Land and King Frederick VIII Land?

1299 *Food and Drink*

An Arbroath Smokie is what type of smoked fish?

1300 *Acronyms*

Used mainly in the US, what does the acronym WASP stand for?

1301 *Language*

Epigraphy is the study of ancient... what?

1302 *The Royal Family*

Which member of the Royal Family is the President of the Commonwealth Games Federation?

1303 *The Monarchy*

Which British monarch of the twentieth century was the father of only daughters?

1304 *Dates*

The United Nations was inaugurated in 1945. What day of the year is United Nations Day?

1305 *The Bible*

In Matthew 27 (verses 57 to 60) who went to Pilate, asked for the body of Jesus and buried it in his own tomb?

1306 *Language*

In the English alphabet, which letter is the ante-penultimate letter?

1307 *Children's Rhymes*

According to the rhyme, which day of the week's child is 'fair of face'?

1308 *Geography*

Palermo is the capital of which Italian region?

1309 *Costume*

Used in ceremonial costumes, what is miniver?

1310 *Animals*

What name, from the Greek meaning belly-footed, is given to the large class of molluscs that includes snails, slugs and whelks, which move using one large muscular foot?

1311 *Pop Music*

'Mulder and Scully' and 'Road Rage' were Top Five singles in 1998 for which Welsh band?

1312 *Literature*

The novel *The Vicar of Wakefield* and the play *She Stoops to Conquer* are works by which eighteenth-century writer?

1313 *Cinema*

Who won his only Oscar in 1944, playing a priest in the film *Going My Way*?

1314 *Food and Drink*

Bel Paese and Roquefort are types of what?

1315 *Literature*

Which novelist and playwright invented the term Wendy house?

1316 *Art*

What nationality was the painter Paul Gaughin?

1317 *The Media*

Which international media body, based in Geneva, is known by the abbreviation EBU?

1318 *European Politics*

What was abolished by a referendum in Italy in 1946, and by decree and referendum in Greece in 1973?

1319 *Law*

What is the name of the ecclesiastical court of appeal of the Province of the Archbishop of Canterbury?

1320 *Flags*

Which bird was the ensign of the Roman Army, and also of the French Army, during the Napoleonic Empire?

1321 *The Bible*

The Decalogue is another name for what?

1322 *History*

Before the Reform Act of 1832, what name was given to an English borough-constituency controlled by one person or family who owned the land?

1323 *Biology*

A parasite is a dependent organism that lives in or on another organism. What term describes that second organism?

1324 *Fictional Characters*

Which novel by Ian Fleming first introduced the character James Bond?

1325 *Archaeology*

If an archaeologist uncovered a design made up of tesserae, what would he have found?

1326 *British Prime Ministers*

Which British Prime Minister's Cabinet purge in 1962 was nicknamed 'the Night of the Long Knives'?

1327 *Proverbs*

'When you can tread on nine daisies at once...' what?

1328 *Motoring*

What is the name of the first British magazine entirely devoted to motor cars? It appeared on 2 November 1895 and is still going strong.

1329 *Publishing*

What organization do the initials PCC stand for?

1330 *US Presidents*

George Washington was the first President of the USA. Who was elected America's first Vice-President and second President?

1331 *Television*

Jake, Fizz, Milo and Bella, four rag-doll characters with the catchphrase 'ready to play?', arrived on BBC television in September. How are they known collectively?

1332 *Latin Phrases*

What does the Latin expression 'de facto' mean?

1333 *Philosophy*

What name is given to the attitude that beliefs are to be accepted and acted upon only if they have first been confirmed by actual experience?

1334 *The Middle East*

Its Arabic name means 'House of Meat'. Its Hebrew name means 'House of Bread'. Which Middle Eastern town is this?

1335 *Art*

The American painter and naturalist John James Audubon is best known for his paintings of what?

1336 *Proverbs*

The name of which town, also the name of a county in Ireland, is given to a pair of legendary cats who fought to destruction?

1337 *Law*

In connection with property, what is curtilage?

1338 *Anatomy*

Which is the longest bone in the human skeleton?

1339 American History

Which American abolitionist was hanged for treason in 1859, following his unsuccessful raid on the US arsenal at Harpers Ferry?

1340 Poetry

'In the Spring, a young man's fancy/Lightly turns to...' What are the next three words?

1341 The Monarchy

Queen Victoria had nine children. How many daughters?

1342 Professions

In what profession has Bruce Oldfield made his name?

1343 Geography

If you sailed due east from San Francisco, which country would be your first landfall?

1344 Theatre

The Festival Theatre in Oaklands Park is the location of which annual theatre festival?

1345 Geography

Mount Cook National Park is in which country?

1346 Liquids

Which liquids have knock ratings reduced by anti-knock additives?

1347 Music

What nationality is the composer Aaron Copeland?

1348 Numbers

How many hertz are represented by one megahertz?

1349 Science

By what term is the anaesthetic nitrous oxide more commonly known?

1350 The Armed Forces

Members of the Women's Royal Naval Service are popularly known as what?

1351 Cinema

Which film actor had the real name Emmanual Goldberg, and played the title role in the 1930 film Little Caesar?

1352 Motor Cars

What car company had a model called the Uno?

1353 Measurements

What is measured in lumens?

1354 Opera

Who composed the opera *The Girl of the Golden West*

1355 Show Business

Who was the 'last of the red hot mamas'?

1356 Medicine

If you were febrile what would you have?

1357 Proverbs

According to the proverb. 'Hard words break no...' what?

1358 Pop Music

Which pop star topped the charts in the 1980s with 'Stand and Deliver', 'Prince Charming' and 'Goody Two Shoes'?

1359 Children's Literature

In *The Wizard of Oz* the Lion wants courage and the Tin Man a heart. What does the Scarecrow want?

1360 Mythology

What is the name of the beautiful youth, accidentally killed by Apollo? A flower that sprung from his blood was later named after him.

1361 Politics

What is the minimum age at which you can stand for Parliament in the United Kingdom?

1362 The Early Church

Which saint, one of the four great Doctors of the Western Church, is traditionally represented in art with a lion at his feet?

1363 Islam

What is the ninth month of the Muslim year called – a month of fasting from sunrise to sunset?

1364 History

Anne of Bohemia, known as Good Queen Anne, was the wife of Richard II. Who was Queen to Richard III?

1365 *English History*

Who in the eleventh century was the wife of Leofric, Earl of Mercia?

1366 *British Prime Ministers*

Who was the British Prime Minister at the time of the Suez crisis in the 1950s?

1367 *Shipping Forecasts*

The two shipping forecast areas North Utsire and South Utsire lie off the coast of which European country?

1368 *Word Connections*

What name is shared by a tall plant grown in India and used for making twine and rope, and a Germanic people who invaded Britain in the fifth century?

1369 *Jazz*

The American jazz musicians John Coltrane, Charlie Parker and Ornette Coleman are most closely associated with which instrument?

1370 *Meteorology*

A triple point is a point on a weather chart where three different fronts meet: a warm front, a cold front and what other kind of front?

1371 *The UK*

Temple Meads Railway Station, the M32 motorway and the Royal Portbury Dock all serve which English city?

1372 *Athletics*

In which athletics event must the implement used by the competitor weigh a minimum of 2 kilograms for men and 1 kilogram for women?

1373 *Anatomy*

What's the name of the small channel that connects the middle ear with the back of the throat, to allow the air pressure on either side of the eardrum to remain equal?

1374 *Animals*

What name is given to the creamy-white domesticated polecat used to catch rabbits?

1375 *Scotland*

Which Scottish village was the birthplace of Robert Burns, in 1759?

1376 *Harry Potter*

Albus Dumbledore is the headmaster of which school in the Harry Potter series?

1377 *The Royal Family*

What are the other two Christian names of Elizabeth II?

1378 *Physics*

What can be AC or DC?

1379 *Religion*

What is the name of the Muslim mystic fraternity whose ecstatic trances are typified by howling, dancing and whirling?

1380 *Food and Drink*

What word describes the deposit left in old port?

1381 *Cinema*

Which sort of movies were referred to as 'oaters' or 'sagebrushers'?

1382 *Saints*

Which saint in the mid-nineteenth century saw visions of the Virgin Mary at Lourdes?

1383 *Sport*

Long Jenny and Short Jenny are two types of shot in which game?

1384 *Words*

What is seersucker?

1385 *Anatomy*

Where is your radial artery?

1386 *Geography*

Egypt, Sudan, Ethiopia, Saudi Arabia and Yemen all have borders on which sea?

1387 *Literature*

"'Excellent' I cried. 'Elementary' said he." Who are the 'I' and the 'he'?

1388 *Music*

What sort of instrument is a bodhran?

1389 *Ceremonies*

Since 1678 the Godiva Procession has been held every seven or eight years in which city?

1390 *Horses*

What happens if a horse 'spreads a plate'?

1391 *American History*

What was found at Sutter's Mill, California, in 1848 which the following year gave rise to a mass migration of over 80,000 people who became known as the 'forty-niners'?

1392 *Political History*

In which country was Leon Trotsky assassinated?

1393 *Music*

What is the literal meaning of the word tempo?

1394 *Inventions*

In which field was the eighteenth/nineteenth century Frenchman called Louis Daguerre a pioneer?

1395 *The UK*

The Church Calendar: what date is Michaelmas? (St Michael and All Angels)

1396 *Education*

The teaching profession: precisely please – what does the acronym INSET stand for?

1397 *Literature*

In a quiet village, thirty one boys and thirty girls, all with golden eyes, are born: which novel?

1398 *Geometry*

What name is given to an angle greater than 180 degrees but less than 360 degrees?

1399 *English Counties*

In which county is the village of Tolpuddle, which gave its name to the six agricultural workers known as the Tolpuddle Martyrs?

1400 *Language*

Which language is commonly used to give plants and animals their scientific names?

15 to 1

ROUND THREE
Questions

1401 *Music*

The bandleaders Art Blakey, Buddy Rich and Max Roach are most closely associated with which instrument?

1402 *Television*

in 1960, Ken Irwin wrote in the *Daily Mirror* 'There is little reality in this new serial which apparently we will have to suffer twice a week. The programme is doomed from the outset with its dreary signature tune and grim scene of terraced houses.' Which programme?

1403 *The Royal Family*

Who is the Queen's only nephew?

1404 *Literature*

Which famous mystery writer created a mystery by disappearing herself in 1926?

1405 *Sport*

Three types of sword are used for competition fencing. Name two.

1406 *Art* ✓

In which art museum can you see the Venus de Milo?

1407 *Medicine* ✓

What is the more common name for pollinosis?

1408 *Cinema*

Ingrid Bergman's last film role was that of a world leader. Who did she play?

1409 *Golf*

On 6 February 1971, where was a golf ball hit for the first time?

1410 *Aiviation* ✓

Which classic aircraft, designed by Tommy Sopwith, got its name because of the hump over its gun breeches?

1411 *Mythology*

According to Greek mythology on which mountain did the gods live?

1412 *Names* ✓

What was the name of Dick Turpin's horse?

1413 *Engineering*

What was the name of the steam locomotive built by William Hedley in 1813?

1414 *Popular Music*

Which US singer made the LP *Born in the USA*?

1415 *Animals*

Which breed of toy dog is named after the Mediterranean island where it is thought to have originated about 2800 years ago?

1416 *Politics* ✓

A twentieth-century US President shared a common surname with a British Prime Minister. Who were they?

1417 *Science*

Ni is the chemical symbol for which metallic element?

1418 *Theatre*

What is the theme of a passion play?

1419 *Sport*

Which two countries compete for the Wrightman Cup in tennis, first played in 1923?

1420 *Words*

Puckle, Gatling and Mauser are all types of what?

1421 *Science*

Cartesian geometry, also known as analytical or coordinate geometry, is named after which sixteenth/seventeenth century French mathematician and philosopher?

1422 *Exploration*

Which famous English sailor and explorer died on 28 January 1596 and was buried at sea off the coast of Panama?

1423 *Sport* ✓

Which athletic event is run over 25 laps of the 400-metre track?

1424 *The Royal Family*

Which of the Queen's children was born in 1950?

1425 *Grammar* ✓

What name is given to clauses in a sentence that are introduced by the conjunctions 'if' or 'unless'?

1426 *London*

An exhibition formed by this woman is one of the major tourist attractions in London. What is her name?

1427 *Poetry*

The fate of which ship, which sank off Cape Ann, Massachusetts, in the nineteenth century, inspired the poem by Henry Wadsworth Longfellow?

1428 *British Prime Ministers*

The last words of which British Prime Minister in 1812 were 'Oh I am murdered'?

1429 *British Landmarks*

In which British city is there a cathedral known colloquially as 'Paddy's wigwam'?

1430 *Mythology*

Boreas, Notus, Euras and Zephyrus were gods of what in classical mythology?

1431 *Literature*

What is the connection between *The History of the World* by Sir Walter Raleigh and John Bunyan's *The Pilgrim's Progress?*

1432 *The Ancient World*

The Peloponnesian Wars were fought between which two ancient city states?

1433 *Religion*

The term diaconate refers to which ecclesiastical post or office?

1434 *North America*

What is the capital city of the Canadian province of Nova Scotia, sharing its name with a town in Yorkshire?

1435 *Sport*

In which decade of the twentieth century were the Summer Olympic Games held in Rome, Tokyo and Mexico City?

1436 *Music*

On a musical score, what is meant by the dynamic mark dolente?

1437 *Theatre*

In which George Bernard Shaw play is a condemned Christian rewarded for his kindness to an animal, which he has treated in the wild for a poisoned paw?

1438 *The USA*

At 20,320 feet, which is the highest mountain in the US?

1439　*The Armed Forces*

Which branch of the armed forces has been known as 'the Andrew' since the nineteenth century?

1440　*Crime Fiction*

The Big Sleep, The Long Goodbye and *Farewell My Lovely* are all books featuring which Los Angeles private eye?

1441　*Words*

A cab, the common word for a taxi, is an abbreviation of which word for a horse-drawn carriage with a hood?

1442　*European Government*

In which European capital city is Christiansborg Palace, which houses the country's Parliament and its Supreme Court?

1443　*Literature*

What is the name of the American writer whose works include *Breakfast at Tiffany's*, published in 1958, and *In Cold Blood*, published in 1966?

1444　*Food and Drink*

What is the French name of the seafood soup or stew from Provence, made with an assortment of fish and shellfish with onions, tomatoes, garlic, saffron, herbs and olive oil?

1445　*Languages*

What do we call the minority European language known to its speakers as Euskara?

1446　*The Bible*

In the New Testament St Matthew records Jesus as saying 'Blessed are the meek'. Why?

1447　*Medicine*

Anosmia is the loss of which of the senses?

1448　*Opera*

Which opera by Franz Lehar centres on the marriage prospects of the wealthy Hanna Glawari?

1449　*The USA*

Washington DC lies on the Potomac River between Maryland and which other state?

1450 *Quotations*

Which former editor of *Private Eye* said of his philosophy while working on the magazine, 'My motto is: publish and be sued'?

1451 *Quotations*

Who is the current editor of *Private Eye* who, after a libel judgement was made against the magazine, famously said, 'If this is justice, I am a banana'?

1452 *Words*

What biblical word was applied by Matthew Arnold to the English middle classes, whom he believed were uninterested in art and culture?

1453 *European Royalty*

Queen Alexandra, wife of King Edward VII, was the daughter of the king of which European country?

1454 *The UK*

Fort Augustus stands at the southern end of which Scottish loch?

1455 *Aviation*

This year is the 100th anniversary of the maiden flight of which famous airship, when it travelled a distance of 3½ miles from Lake Constance?

1456 *Shakespeare*

Which Shakespeare play was described by Laurence Olivier in his 1948 screen adaptation as, 'The tragedy of a man who could not make up his mind'?

1457 *The Bible*

In the Old Testament, which famous story is told in Genesis chapters 6,7,8 and 9?

1458 *Finance*

In the UK a 'stale cheque' is one that has not been presented for payment within how long of being written?

1459 *Organizations*

The LDOS is a society founded in 1831 to preserve Sunday as a national day of rest. What does LDOS stand for?

1460 *Geometry*

Each interior angle of a regular one is 108° and all its interior angles add up to 540°. Which geometric figure is this?

1461 *People*

Three bridges over the River Severn, the Caledonian Canal and suspension bridges over the River Conwy and the Menai Strait are the work of which eighteenth/nineteenth century Scottish civil engineer?

1462 *Jamaica*

Jamaica is the third largest island of which island group in the West Indies?

1463 *Sport*

The French Open is played at which venue in Paris?

1464 *Food and Drink*

Which famous cocktail is made with pineapple juice, rum and coconut milk?

1465 *Australian Landmarks*

Which enormous Australian landmark has an aboriginal name meaning 'great pebble'?

1466 *Australian Landmarks*

By what aboriginal name is Ayers Rock known?

1467 *Words*

Taken from a Tamil word literally meaning 'tied wood', what name is given to a type of boat with two hulls?

1468 *Name Connections*

What name connects a county in south-east Ireland and a fictional detective created by Ruth Rendell?

1469 *Scotland*

At Traquair House, one mile south of Innerleithen in the Scottish Borders, there is a set of gates called the Bear Gates. They were closed in 1745 and will not be reopened until what happens?

1470 *Charities*

The name of the sports charity, The Primary Club, refers to its membership which is nominally restricted to those batsmen who have achieved which dubious distinction in cricket?

1471 *Phrases*

What two-word expression describes the situation when the value of a property falls below the amount originally borrowed in the mortgage?

1472 *People* ✓

Which suave English actor, a former James Bond, once described his range of acting techniques as 'left eyebrow raised, right eyebrow raised'?

1473 *Words*

As nocturnal means by night, what word means by day?

1474 *Politics*

What is the name of Karl Marx's collaborator on the *Communist Manifesto* and author of the earlier *The Condition of the Working Class in England*?

1475 *Law*

What is the title given to the judge who, among his other duties, is responsible for admitting solicitors to the Roll of Solicitors?

1476 *Mythology*

What is the name of the Titan who stole fire to give it to mankind?

1477 *Language*

A Jurisconsult is a person learned in, or consulted on... which subject?

1478 *London*

At which famous north London cemetery are the Rossetti family, George Eliot and Michael Faraday all buried?

1479 *Writers*

Revolt in the Desert was the title of an abridged version of which work by T.E. Lawrence?

1480 *Children's Rhymes*

'They're changing Guard at Buckingham Palace, Christopher Robin went down with Alice'. Who was Alice?

1481 *Wales*

Which holiday resort stands on the Great Ormes Head, a promontory on the north Wales coast?

1482 *Aviation*

Which aeronautical engineer, whilst still a cadet at the RAF College at Cranwell in 1928, advanced the idea of replacing the piston engine and propeller on aircraft with a gas turbine?

1483 *The USA*

New York comprises five boroughs. The Bronx and Manhattan are two. Name two of the other three?

1484 *History*

Catherine Parr's third husband, died in 1547. Who was he?

1485 *Poetry*

Complete this line by Shelley: 'If Winter comes…'

1486 *Pop Music*

What are the first names of the Gallagher brothers?

1487 *Art*

What name is given to an abstract sculpture which has moving parts driven either by motors or by the natural force of wind?

1488 *Science*

Which acid is a constituent of vinegar?

1489 *Geography*

In which European country is the River Po the longest river?

1490 *Words*

What Italian word, literally meaning 'a person who knows', may be applied to a discerning expert?

1491 *Roman Numerals*

How is the year 2000 indicated in Roman numerals?

1492 *Roman History*

Which emperor visited Britain in 122 AD and initiated the building of a wall in the north of the country 'to separate the Romans from the barbarians'?

1493 *Organisations*

In the area of recreation what is the NPFA?

1494 *Language*

A factory in which crude oil is turned into petrol is called a… what?

1495 *Twentieth-century History*

Which Mediterranean island was invaded by Turkish forces in 1974 and is still divided into two parts?

1496 *Twentieth-century History*

The foundation of which Middle East state in 1948 could be said to be the fulfilment of the Balfour Declaration of 1917?

1497 *Taxation* ✓

Which tax was introduced in Britain 1986 to replace capital transfer tax?

1498 *Sport*

In archery, the outer scoring area is coloured white and scores one or two points: what colour is the inner scoring area that scores nine or ten points?

1499 *Awards*

Which British lyricist, a former collaborator with Andrew Lloyd Webber, has won Oscars for the songs 'A Whole New World' from *Aladdin*; 'Can You Feel the Love Tonight' from *The Lion King*; and 'You Must Love Me' from *Evita*?

1500 *Plants*

What name is given to the sugary liquid produced by flowering plants, which honey bees collect to produce honey?

1501 *The USA*

Dry Creek Valley, Santa Clara Valley and Napa Valley are wine-growing areas in which US state?

1502 *Parliament*

What cry goes up in the House of Commons, echoed by policemen, when the House has finished a sitting and is about to close its doors?

1503 *History*

In which German city did Martin Luther nail his famous 95 theses to the door of the castle church in 1517?

1504 *Television*

The Australian composer Barrington Pheloung's best-known work is the theme tune to which long-running ITV detective series starring John Thaw and Kevin Whately?

1505 *The Arts*

In which field of the arts is the Frenchwoman Sylvie Guillem a famous name?

1506 *History*

In connection with what event did a ship's surgeon by the name of Dr William Beatty earn a place in history in 1805?

1507 *Geography*

Minsk is the capital city of which former member state of the Soviet Union?

1508 *Parliament*

What traditional name is given to the public gallery in the House of Commons from which the public may observe the proceedings of the House?

1509 *Parliament* ✓

How is the Gallery above and behind the Speaker's Chair commonly referred to?

1510 *Geography*

Which Mediterranean island country has its main international airport at Larnaca?

1511 *Science*

What name is given to an electric current that regularly reverses its direction of flow?

1512 *Counties* ✓

Which is the most northerly county in England?

1513 *Food and Drink*

Under what name are the salted eggs of the sturgeon sold commercially?

1514 *Geography*

A Cairene is a native or citizen of which African capital city?

1515 *Measurements*

Which mainly nautical unit of measurement is equivalent to 1829 metres?

1516 *Football*

Which English Premiership club plays its home matches at the Dell and is nicknamed the Saints?

1517 *Football*

Which Scottish Premier Divison club plays its home fixtures at Ibrox Stadium in Glasgow?

1518 *Animals*

Which tree-dwelling mammal shares its name with one of the seven deadly sins?

1519 *The UK*

What specifically is an SSSI, a designation that may be given to particular locations?

1520 *Theatre*

Which two-act comedy by Willy Russell was adapted as a film starring Michael Caine as Frank, a university lecturer, and Julie Walters as the eponymous hairdresser and Open University student?

1521 *Geography*

You can catch a ferry from either Plymouth or Portsmouth to Santander. In which country is Santander?

1522 *Parliament*

Which member of the House of Lords, and former actor, is President of MENCAP?

1523 *British Prime Ministers*

Which twentieth-century British Prime Minister died at sea in 1937, two years after leaving office, whilst crossing the Atlantic?

1524 *Literature*

Which two eighteenth/nineteenth-century poets collaborated on the work entitled *Lyrical Ballads*, which became a publishing sensation when the first edition appeared in 1798. Name either of the two.

1525 *Pageantry*

Which carriage, the oldest in the royal collection, has been used for every coronation since 1821?

1526 *People*

Who is the famous American newspaper proprietor on whom Orson Wells based his film *Citizen Kane*?

1527 *The Armed Forces*

Lieutenant General Sir John Deverell is the current Inspector-General of which branch of the British Army, which is required to train for a minimum of 27 days of the year?

1528 *The USA*

In North America the only one of the five Great Lakes to lie entirely in the US shares its name with which American state?

1529 *People*

Which famous Hollywood swashbuckling actor built a home at Castle Comfort in Jamaica for his third wife?

1530 *Parliament*

Which large ornamental symbol of state has such significance in the House of Commons that if it is not on the table, no business can be done?

1531 *Law*

From Jowett's *Dictionary of English Law*: 'When a coroner's jury find the death of a person without saying how he came by it, this is called...' what?

1532 *The Commonwealth*

What term is used for the Queen's representative in each member country of the Commonwealth where she is head of state, other than the United Kingdom?

1533 *Universities*

By what name is the only college of Dublin University more commonly known?

1534 *Language*

Whose *Dictionary of the English Language*, the first major dictionary to use illustrative historical quotations, was published in 1755?

1535 *Television*

In which American series did three beautiful ex-policewomen work undercover for the mysterious boss of the Townsend Investigations detective agency?

1536 *Police*

In police work, toxicological examinations concern the identification of what?

1537 *Geography*

Cathay is an ancient or poetic name for which country?

1538 *France*

Which famous cathedral stands on the Île de la Cité in the River Seine in Paris?

1539 *The USA*

Which region, now a named state was bought from Napoleon by President Thomas Jefferson in 1803 for 60 million francs, in the largest land deal in American history, doubling the size of the United States at a stroke?

1540 *The Papacy*

Alexander VI, a notorious pope of the late fifteenth century, was the father of an infamous brother and sister. Name either of the two.

1541 *Proverbs*

Where does the proverb warn you never to change horses?

1542 *Astronomy* ✓

When viewed from Earth, which is the brightest planet in our Solar System?

1543 *The Early Church*

In early Christian writings, Babylon is a pejorative name for which city?

1544 *Literature*

A valuable diamond is stolen from a Hindu holy place; presented to Rachel Verinder on her eighteenth birthday, it mysteriously disappears overnight. This is the start of which novel by Wilkie Collins?

1545 *The Ancient World*

What was the name of the largest hippodrome or sports arena in ancient Rome, used particularly for chariot racing?

1546 *Business*

What Swiss-based company – the world's largest watchmaker – which was founded by the Lebanese-born engineer Nicolas Hayek, who pioneered the creation of fashionable plastic watches?

1547 *Saints*

Immortalized in a famous Christmas carol, who is the patron saint of Bohemia?

1548 *Psychology*

Which Russian scientist's experiments with dogs in the late 1890s and early 1900s led to the discovery of conditioned reflexes?

1549 *Literature*

According to J.M. Barrie, what happens when a child says 'I don't believe in fairies'?

1550 *France*

What name is given to the marshy delta area in southern France between the Great and Little Rhone rivers where horses and fighting bulls are reared?

1551 *Mathematics*

How many degrees are there in a round angle or perigon?

1552 *Education* ✓

Which public school has produced 19 British Prime Ministers?

1553 *Television*

'Gourmet Night', 'The Hotel Inspectors', and 'The Kipper and the Corpse', were three episodes in which classic 1970s comedy series?

1554 *Medicine*

In which part of the anatomy might a Colles fracture be sustained?

1555 *Meteorology*

On which scale is three a gentle breeze, four a moderate breeze and five a fresh breeze?

1556 *Animals*

Which ape is our closest genetic relative – so close, in fact, that more than 98 per cent of our DNA is the same?

1557 *Medicine*

What type of drugs are commonly used to relieve the symptoms of hayfever, urticaria and other allergic reactions?

1558 *Shipping Forecasts*

Which sea area in the BBC shipping forecasts shares its name with a river in the Republic of Ireland?

1559 *Twentieth-century History*

Why did the Queen not attend the state openings of Parliament in 1959 and 1963?

1560 *Phrases*

Which French phrase is used to describe a pair of glasses or spectacles that have no ear pieces and which are simply balanced on the bridge of the nose?

1561 *Operas*

Whose operas or operettas are known as the Savoy Operas?

1562 *Printing*

The name of which printing symbol is derived from a Greek word meaning 'little star'?

1563 *Education*

Exactly what do the letters GCSE stand for?

1564 *Cinema*

In the original film *The Pink Panther* (1964), what was the pink panther?

1565 *Theatre*

What name is given to the area above the stage from which scenery, lighting and other equipment can be suspended?

1566 *Rome*

Where, in the Vatican, do cardinals meet to elect a new pope?

1567 *The UK*

In which town on the South Coast is there an area called 'The Lanes' – a popular centre for antique shops?

1568 *Food and Drink*

Rioja is a robust red wine from which European country?

1569 *European History*

Charlemagne was, from 800 to 814, the first ruler of which European empire?

1570 *Food and Drink*

What name is given to the traditional method of cooking a hare in a tall covered pot?

1571 *Pop Groups*

If two men and a woman had used their surnames, they would have been called Yarrow, Stookey and Travers. Instead they used their first names. Which American folk trio – popular in the 1960s is this?

1572 *Anatomy*

Also called 'sinews', what is the medical term for the strong white cords that attach muscles to bones?

1573 *The USA*

Which state of the USA has the longest coastline?

1574 *American History*

In which incident in the history of the wild west did Frank and Tom McLaury and Billy Clanton die at Tombstone, Arizona, in 1881?

1575 *Musicals*

In which Lerner and Loewe musical are there characters called Arthur, Guinevere, Lancelot, Mordred and Merlin?

1576 *Motorways*

The M27 links which two cities on the south coast?

1577 *Wales*

Which town, just in Wales on the south bank of the Wye, is known for its huge sheep market, called Smithfield, and its large selection of second-hand bookshops?

1578 *Politics*

The expression 'two nations', describing a society divided into rich and poor, came from the subtitle of the nineteenth century novel *Sybil* written by which Conservative Member of Parliament, later Prime Minister?

1579 *Philately*

Whose portrait appeared on the famous Penny Black?

1580 *US Presidents*

Prior to Bill Clinton, who was the last Democrat President of the US?

1581 *Religion*

Jainism has existed as a religion for over 2500 years in which Asian country?

1582 *Geography*

Which South American country has the greatest length of Atlantic coastline?

1583 *Sport*

Bari, Lazio and Fiorentina are teams from which country?

1584 *The Monarchy*

Which African country, at the time a British colony, was Princess Elizabeth visiting when her father died and she became Queen in 1952?

1585 *Language*

Seen mainly in the countryside, smock, post, and tower are all types of what sort of structure or building?

1586 *Cinema*

The 1988 film *Bird*, directed by Clint Eastwood, was a dramatization of the life of which legendary saxophone player?

1587 *Shakespeare*

Who, in *A Midsummer Night's Dream*, is the king of the fairies?

1588 *Terms and Phrases*

Which three-word term for the human brain was coined by crime writer Agatha Christie in *The Mysterious Affair at Styles*, and is associated with her sleuth Hercule Poirot?

1589 *Italy*

The Accademia Gallery, the Correr Museum and the Treasury of St Mark's are all in which Italian city?

1590 *US Presidents*

Who is the only US president whose terms of office were exclusively within the eighteenth century?

1591 *Food and Drink*

Which restaurant chain, founded in 1894, opened its first Corner House in Coventry Street, London, in 1907 and had waitresses popularly known as 'nippies'?

1592 *Horses*

Which British military leader's horse, named Copenhagen, was buried with full military honours?

1593 *Sport*

If a hole is a par four, how many strokes would a player making a double bogey take?

1594 *Proverbs*

According to the proverb, what makes the heart grow fonder?

1595 *Writers*

The poets John Keats, Edward Lear, Ezra Pound and Elizabeth Barrett Browning are all buried in which country?

1596 *Furniture*

A heavily padded sofa with arms and back of the same height shares its name with which Derbyshire town?

1597 *Marine Life*

What is described as a hard stony substance secreted by certain aquatic invertebrates as an external skeleton, typically forming large reefs in warm seas?

1598 *Dates*

In 1752, in Great Britain, 2 September was followed by 14 September. Why?

1599 *Musicals*

Which film musical, starring Howard Keel, was adapted from a short story entitled 'The Sobbin Women', which in turn was 'inspired' by the classical tale of the rape of the Sabine women?

1600 *Religion*

Stuart Blanch, John Habgood and David Hope have all held which office in the Church of England during the past 25 years?

1601 *The Bible*

In the second book of Samuel, Which King of Israel is described in the Bible as 'the sweet psalmist of Israel'?

1602 *Inventions*

The message 'Mr Watson. Come here. I want you' is famously associated with which invention?

1603 *Business*

Price Waterhouse Coopers, KPMG and Ernst & Young are leading companies in which field?

1604 *Sport*

In Ice hockey, what is the popular name for the penalty bench or box – a rink-side area where transgressing players serve time penalties?

1605 *Radio*

What's on from Monday to Friday, on Radio 4, at seven o'clock in the evening?

1606 *Measurements*

To one decimal place, how many pounds equal one kilogram?

1607 *Landmarks*

What, in Dorset, is the Cerne Giant?

1608 *People*

Which British actor was married to Vivien Leigh from 1940 to 1961, and Joan Plowright from 1961 until his death in 1989?

1609 *Currency*

Of which European country is the zloty the main unit of currency?

1610 *Words*

A public square or marketplace is called a piazza in Italy. What is it called in Spain?

1611 *Food and Drink*

In a French restaurant, what duties are undertaken by a sommelier?

1612 *Animals*

Which two animal species belong to the order Proboscidea?

1613 *Botany*

What is the more common name for the insectivorous plant *Dionaea muscipula*, which ensnares insects between hinged leaves?

1614 *Acronyms*

ABTA is a self-regulatory organization in the travel industry. What does the acronym ABTA stand for?

1615 *The Calendar*

All Souls' Day, All Saints' Day and St Andrew's Day all fall in which month of the year?

1616 *Music*

Which section of an orchestra is also known as the batterie?

1617 *Advertising*

The United Colours of... what?

1618 *Counties*

In which English county is the southernmost point of mainland Britain?

1619 *Quotations*

Which legendary American film director and actor, whose most famous and probably finest work was his first film at the age of 26, said 'I started at the top and worked my way down'?

1620 *Phrases*

Which meteorological phrase is used to describe a relatively quiet and peaceful period before a crisis or commotion?

1621 *The Royal Family*

In which year was Prince Charles born?

1622 *Science*

After which Scottish-born inventor is the unit of sound measurement, equal to 10 decibels, named?

1623 *Geography*

Which is the main port and second largest city in Kenya?

1624 *The Decorative Arts*

First used in ancient Mesopotamia, what name is given to the decorative technique in which small pieces of coloured material (marble or stone, for example) are set tightly together to form patterns or pictures?

1625 *Aviation* ✓

Which Commonwealth country has international airports, with the codes AKL, CHC and WLG, which serve three of its major cities?

1626 *Cinema*

What is the title of the 1980s film based on the achievements of two Britons called Eric Liddell and Harold Abrahams?

1627 *Botany*

Both chlorophyll and xanthophyll are responsible for photosynthesis in plants. Chlorophyll is green, what colour is xanthophyll?

1628 *Counties*

Sudbury Hall and Hardwick Hall are stately homes in which English county?

1629 *History*

How was the ocean liner *Carpathia* involved in an event on the night of 14/15 April 1912?

1630 *Latin Words*

Which three-letter Latin word, meaning 'so' or 'thus', is placed in brackets in a quoted passage to indicate that an apparent mistake or absurdity is being quoted correctly?

1631 *American Literature*

In which Mark Twain novel does the hero live in St Petersburg, Missouri, with his Aunt Polly and brother Sid?

1632 *Geography*

Reunion, Martinique and Guadeloupe are overseas departments of which European country?

1633 *Geography*

What is the capital city of Iceland?

1634 *The Bible*

In the Old Testament which animal is the symbol of the tribe of Judah?

1635 Art

In Salford, there is a new arts centre housing the nation's largest collection of paintings and drawings by which artist, after whom the centre is named?

1636 *Latin Phrases*

What is meant by a land or region that is 'terra incognita'?

1637 *Science*

The name of which form of pure carbon is taken from the Greek meaning 'to write'?

1638 *Art*

From the French for 'pasting', what name is given to a picture made from pasted-up scraps of paper and other odds and ends?

1639 *The Second World War*

Operation Dynamo in 1940 was the name given to which major operation?

1640 *Shakespeare*

Who, in a Shakespeare play, tests the claims of a ghost by arranging a performance of a play depicting a murder?

1641 *The Monarchy*

James I, Charles I, Charles II and James II... who came next?

1642 *The European Union*

The Queen has never made a state visit to two of the 15 member states of the European Union. Name either of the two.

1643 *Literature*

Who, in his verse autobiography *Summoned by Bells*, describes his upbringing as 'safe, in a world of trains and buttered toast'?

1644 *History*

Indonesia gained its independence in 1949 from which European country?

1645 *Proverbs*

Proverbially, what is there 'twixt cup and lip'?

1646 *Communications*

In the world of the Internet, what are Yahoo!, Lycos, Hotbot and Ask Jeeves?

1647 *London*

What is the following about? Ealing Broadway to Epping – red; Hammersmith to Barking – pink; Walthamstow Central to Brixton – light blue?

1648 *Geography*

What's the capital city of Australia?

1649 *The UK*

What name is given to the day of commemoration in Britain which falls on the second Sunday in November?

1650 *Radio*

Since 1946 there have been nearly 2700 'Letters from America'. Whose letters?

1651 *Quotations*

'They also serve who only...' is from John Milton. What are the next three words?

1652 *Newspapers*

Which section of a newspaper is nicknamed 'hatches, matches and despatches'?

1653 *Geography*

Italy has two small sovereign states within its borders, San Marino and...?

1654 *Law*

In English law, what term applies to the action of confessing to a crime and then acting as witness against the other criminals involved?

1655 *Proverbs*

Complete this nineteenth century proverb, 'Speech is silver, but …'.

1656 *The European Parliament*

Prior to the 1994 European elections, Germany returned 81 MEPs; since then, it returns 99. What was the main reason for this increase?

1657 *Trade Names*

Which famous make of Swiss watch shares its name with the last letter of the Greek alphabet?

1658 *Physics*

The Greek letter Omega is used as the symbol for which unit of electric resistance?

1659 *Astronomy*

Janus and Oceanus were two suggested names for a planet discovered in 1846. What name was finally decided upon?

1660 *Language*

What is the more common name for nacre, which is found in the shells of various molluscs and is used for ornamentation?

1661 *History*

'I was not half bloody enough for him who sent me thither'. Which notorious seventeenth-century English judge said that?

1662 *Name Connections*

What name connects a brutish humanoid race in the country of the Houyhnhnms, in *Gulliver's Travels*, and an Internet search engine?

1663 *Legend*

In the collection of tales, the *Arabian Nights*, who is the mischievous son of Mustafa, a poor tailor of China?

1664 *Galleries*

Opened in 1817, which is England's oldest public picture gallery?

1665 *Theatre*

Noh Theatre is a traditional dramatic art form from which country?

1666 *Medicine*

The abbreviation PTSD describes a nervous condition that often results after a person has experienced a particularly frightening event. What do the letters PTSD stand for?

1667 *Rail Systems*

What is the name of the type of railway system on a cliff or mountain which consists of two cars connected by a wire cable wound around a drum at the summit?

1668 *Famous Scientists*

Who published his first major papers in 1905 whilst working as a clerk in the Swiss Patent Office?

1669 *Pop Music*

'Every Breath You Take', 'Walking On The Moon' and 'Message In A Bottle' are UK number one singles for which group?

1670 *Zoology*

The larva of a moth or butterfly is called a caterpillar. What is the larva of a beetle called?

1671 *Aviation*

Which British airport has the three-letter designation code CWL?

1672 *Sport*

Which sport is played by the Gloucester Gladiators, Essex Eagles, Glamorgan Dragons and Notts Outlaws?

1673 *Literature*

In James Joyce's novel *A Portrait of the Artist as a Young Man*, what is the name of the 'artist' whose childhood, school days, and early manhood are portrayed?

1674 *Scotland*

Which is the largest of the islands in the Firth of Clyde, sometimes called 'Scotland in miniature'?

1675 *European Landmarks*

What is the name of the Italian town in the region of Umbria, an important place of pilgrimage, that was the birthplace of St Francis in 1182?

1676 *Opera*

Which Gilbert and Sullivan opera has the subtitle 'The Witch's Curse'?

1677 *Judaism*

By what name is the western section of the outer wall of the Temple Mount – the only remaining structure of Herod's addition to the second 'Temple' – known?

1678 *Scientific Terms*

What is the path of a projectile called?

1679 *Sport*

On what piece of sporting equipment would you find a cantle, a pommel and a skirt?

1680 *Famous Women*

Her maiden name is Ciccone; her married name was Penn. Who is she?

1681 *Education and Universities*

Birkbeck College, Goldsmiths' College and the Royal Veterinary College are all part of which university?

1682 *Counties*

The seaside resorts of Minehead, Burnham-on-Sea and Weston-super-Mare are in which county?

1683 *Dance*

Which Spanish dance is march-like in character and has a name literally meaning 'double step'?

1684 *Quotations*

'If God did not exist, it would be necessary to invent him'. This is a famous dictum of which eighteenth-century French writer and historian?

1685 *Quotations*

The physicist Stephen Hawking said: 'Someone told me that each equation I included in the book would halve the sales'. Which best-selling book is this?

1686 *Native Peoples*

The aboriginal inhabitants of the Arctic regions of North America and Greenland are often referred to as Eskimoes. What do they call themselves?

1687 *Historic Buildings*

Which Tudor monarch built Nonsuch Palace as a hunting lodge and guest house for foreign visitors?

1688 *History*

Which town in Norfolk was known as Bishop's Lynn until its name was changed at the time of the Dissolution of the Monasteries?

1689 *London*

The Central Criminal Court in London is built on the site of which prison?

1690 *The Arts*

Which building in London houses the Royal Academy of Arts?

1691 *Geography*

What would be measured using a hypsometer?

1692 *The Olympics*

The first summer Olympics to take place outside Europe were held in 1904 in the USA. In which city?

1693 *Mythology*

What is the the name of the Athenian hero who killed the Minotaur?

1694 *Television Writers*

Name either of the two writers of *Hancock's Half Hour* and *Steptoe and Son*?

1695 *The UK*

The Hunterian Museum and the Hunterian Art Gallery were both named after Dr William Hunter, who bequeathed his collections to the university of which city?

1696 *Children's Literature*

In the books by Kathleen Hale, what is the name of the marmalade cat?

1697 *Language*

What name is given to the study of the production and description of speech sounds?

1698 *Journals*

In whose famous diary, subsequently translated into 30 languages is the first entry dated 12 June 1942 and the final entry 4 August 1944?

1699 *Playing Cards*

In the English-speaking world the picture card immediately beneath the queen is a jack. What is it called in a French pack of cards?

1700 *Theatre*

Jack is in love with Gwendolen, Algernon falls in love with Cecily, and Jack and Gwendolen cannot get married until the mystery of his parentage is settled. Which Oscar Wilde play is this?

1701 *Children's Literature*

What was the name of the famous 'son' of Gepetto the Toymaker?

1702 *Royalty*

Prince Al-Muhtadee Billah is heir to one of the oldest and richest monarchies in the world. To whom is he the heir?

1703 *Snooker*

At the start of a frame of snooker, which colour ball is placed on the spot at the apex of the triangle formed by the 15 reds?

1704 *The Royal Family*

What is the first name of the present Duke of Gloucester?

1705 *Charles Dickens*

'I only know two sorts of boys. Mealy boys, and beef-faced boys' – so says Mr. Grimwig in which Dickens novel?

1706 *Counties*

Which southern county and its inhabitants have, as one guide states, 'for some time been the butt of jokes that imply financial acuity but a lack of taste, discernment and sophistication'?

1707 *Motor Racing*

'I can't go on; I'm too emotional'. Murray Walker said this in October 1996, after who had won the Japanese Grand Prix, and with it the World Driver's title for that season?

1708 *Literature*

'...to all That', '...to Berlin', '....Mr Chips'. What word comes first in these titles of works by Robert Graves, Christopher Isherwood and James Hilton?

1709 *The UK*

Taken from the name of a loving, elderly couple in an eighteenth-century ballad by Henry Woodfall, what name is given to a social club for elderly people, usually run by volunteers who organize parties and outings?

1710 *History*

Known as 'climbing boys', their employment in the UK was banned by an Act of Parliament in 1875. What was their occupation?

1711 *Art*

Which seventeenth-century portrait painter, at the court of Charles I, had a particular style of beard named after him?

1712 *Literature*

In which Alexandre Dumas novel does Edmond Dantes make a daring escape from prison, and seek revenge on those who wrongly imprisoned him?

1713 *Languages*

English is the official language of Kenya, but what is its national language?

1714 *Mythology*

The daughter of Minos, King of Crete, fell in love with Theseus and gave him the ball of thread that helped guide him out of the Labyrinth after slaying the Minotaur. What was her name?

1715 *Writers*

Which Hampshire novelist published a novel in 1816 dedicated to the Prince Regent, who kept a set of her novels in each of his residences?

1716 *Cinema*

Ridley's films include *Alien*, *Blade Runner* and *Gladiator*, Tony's include *Top Gun* and *True Romance*. What's the surname of these British film-making brothers?

1717 *War*

What was the name of the elaborate system of routes along the South Vietnam border with Laos and Cambodia, used to bring North Vietnamese supplies to Viet Cong forces?

1718 *US Politics*

Involved in the Watergate scandal, by what acronym was the Committee for the Re-election of the President known?

1719 *Cinema*

Carl Bernstein and Bob Woodward's account of their investigation into the Watergate affair was made into a film starring Robert Redford and Dustin Hoffman. What is its title?

1720 *The UK*

The estuaries of which two rivers lie to the east and west of the Wirral Peninsula?

1721 *Astronomy*

John Flamsteed was, in 1675, the first person to be appointed to which position?

1722 *The USA*

Which American city is nicknamed 'the windy city'?

1723 *The Bible*

In the New Testament which of the 12 apostles was the brother of Simon Peter?

1724 *Geography*

Only one of the ten Canadian provinces has a motto which is not in Latin but in French. Which one?

1725 *Law*

To be liable for jury service you have to be at least 18 years of age; you must therefore have been resident for five years in the UK since reaching the age of... what?

1726 *Proverbs*

Complete this popular saying. 'If you pay peanuts...'

1727 *Awards*

In 1942, Glen Miller became the first artist to receive which award, after his recording of *Chattanooga Choo Choo* sold more than one million copies?

1728 *The Peerage*

The name of which holiday resort did Jeffrey Archer take as part of his title when he was created Baron Archer in 1992?

1729 *Art*

Which eighteenth-century English artist is best known for his landscapes and portraits, which include *The Blue Boy* and *Mr and Mrs Andrews*?

1730 *The Ancient World*

The story of which Queen of ancient Egypt has been told in drama by William Shakespeare, John Dryden and George Bernard Shaw?

1731 *Geography*

The name Bayern, as in the football team Bayern Munich, is the German name for which region of the country?

1732 *Fictional Characters*

What is the name of Sherlock Holmes' elder, and supposedly cleverer, brother in the stories by Arthur Conan Doyle?

1733 *The USA*

What stands in the middle of an 18-acre plot at 1600 Pennsylvania Avenue, Washington?

1734 *Geography*

Which is the only sea, as opposed to ocean, to wash the shores of three continents?

1735 *Food and Drink*

Cockburn's, Graham's and Taylor's are brand names associated with which drink?

1736 *Counties*

The Bleak House Dickens Maritime and Smuggling Museum, A Day at the Wells and the White Cliffs Experience are all attractions in which county?

1737 *Mythology*

Which god in Norse mythology was drawn across the sky by goats pulling a wagon that rattled and caused thunder?

1738 *The Bible*

The last supper that Jesus took with the 12 apostles was a celebration of which feast?

1739 *European Politics*

Which country split into two in January 1993 in the so-called 'velvet divorce'?

1740 *Science*

What term or word describes the conversion of a liquid to a gas?

1741 *Television*

The BBC comedy series *Only Fools and Horses* got its title from an old adage, 'Only fools and horses...' what?

1742 *Music*

He wrote over 600 songs, and is also remembered for a work he didn't complete. What is the name of this Austrian composer, who died aged 31 in 1828?

1743 *Geography*

Which African capital city stands at the confluence of the Blue Nile and the White Nile?

1744 *Children's Literature*

In the books by John Ryan, who is the captain of (the ship) the *Black Pig*?

1745 *Motorcycling*

What name is given to off-road motorbike racing, previously known as scrambling, which is held over a set distance or time, and run across country, up hills, or through mud, sand and gravel?

1746 *Geography*

What is the present name of the city formerly known as Byzantium and then Constantinople?

1747 *Language*

What does the adjective sororal or sororial mean?

1748 *Meteorology*

A violent tropical cyclone in the China Sea and adjacent regions is known as what?

1749 *Medicine*

Palpation is the act of examination by what means?

1750 *Quotations*

Complete the saying, attributed to Benjamin Disraeli, 'Never complain and never...'.

1751 *Awards*

Formerly the blue ribbon worn by the Knights of the Holy Ghost, what term describes a cook of the highest excellence?

1752 *Motorways*

Which motorway passes through the counties of Kent, Buckinghamshire, Surrey, Hertfordshire and Essex?

1753 *Literature*

What surname links the author of *The Naked Lunch* and the author of *Tarzan of the Apes*?

1754 *Food and Drink*

The name of which German wine translates as 'milk of the Blessed Virgin'?

1755 *Rock Music*

Which hugely successful band was formed in 1977, and named for the then financial situation of its members?

1756 *People*

For what, completed in the 1860s, is the name of the French diplomat Ferdinand de Lesseps best remembered?

1757 *Scotland*

A 200-foot high monument to which author stands in Princes Street in Edinburgh?

1758 *American History*

By what name is an incident which occurred in an east coast port of America, on 16 December 1773, now famously known?

1759 *Writers*

Which English writer had success in the 1960s with his novels *The Magus* and *The French Lieutenant's Woman*?

1760 *Cricket*

Which is the only first-class county not in England?

1761 *Art*

What is the name of the art historian and former Surveyor of the Queen's Pictures who was at the centre of a scandal in 1979 when his wartime spying for the Soviet Union was exposed?

1762 *Food and Drink*

What is the gastronomic connection between Whitstable in Kent and Colchester in Essex?

1763 *Language*

Pontage is a toll payable under what circumstances?

1764 *Politics*

On the door of which address in London is there a brass plate reading 'First Lord of the Treasury'?

1765 *Poetry*

What is the title of the volume of poems written by Rudyard Kipling, and published in 1892, which includes *Gunga Din*, *Mandalay* and *Tommy* ?

1766 *Geography*

Seven countries have land borders with Turkey. Name two of the seven.

1767 *Medicine*

BCG is a vaccine against which disease?

1768 *History*

Prior to 1536, the Church owned approximately 25 per cent of the land in England; by 1541, all of it had passed to the Crown. What, at the instigation of Henry VII, took place between these years to cause this?

1769 *Food and Drink*

What is the principal flavouring traditionally used in making the Italian liqueur amaretto?

1770 *Physiology*

Which glands in the body secrete tears?

1771 *Livery Companies*

Which City livery company was incorporated in England in 1327 to assay and stamp silver and gold with a leopard's head hallmark?

1772 *Nursery Rhymes*

In the nursery rhyme 'Hot Cross Buns' what should you do if your daughters do not like them?

1773 Education

In the world of further education, what do the letters GNVQ stand for?

1774 Acronyms

FRCVS, FRCS and FRCP are professional qualifications. What does the FRC stand for in each case?

1775 The Ancient World

The name of which ancient King of Lydia has, because of his immense wealth, become synonymous with any rich man?

1776 Ships

What word is used to describe the width of a ship at its widest part?

1777 Music

The word BIS on a musical score means what?

1778 Games

In Germany, she is Frau Weiss; in France, she is Madame Leblanc. How is this Cluedo suspect known in English?

1779 Pop Music

'Think Twice' and 'My Heart Will Go On' are two UK number one singles by which French-Canadian singer, who won the 1988 Eurovision Song Contest representing Switzerland?

1780 Astrology

A person born in June could have either of two birth signs. Which two?

1781 Cinema

Which muscle-bound Hollywood star played the title role in the sword-and-sorcery films *Conan the Barbarian* and *Conan the Destroyer*?

1782 Sports

In cricket, he is known as the bowler. What is the equivalent position called in baseball?

1783 The Monarchy

The adjectives 'Caroline' or 'Carolean' relate to the reigns of which two seventeenth-century monarchs?

1784 *Animals*

By what name is the black variety of leopard, jaguar or puma known?

1785 *Phrases*

Which French phrase is used for the representation or expression of the dance of death in a musical passage or piece?

1786 *Writers*

Which eighteenth/nineteenth-century novelist wrote the final versions of her six published novels at the Hampshire village of Chawton from 1809 to 1817?

1787 *Proverbs*

What, according to the famous saying, favours fools and the brave?

1788 *Organizations*

What type of organization is Green Flag?

1789 *Geography*

Which European country may be referred to by the adjective 'Hellenic'?

1790 *Cinema*

'Dozens of chorus girls arranged in kaleidoscopic but almost always symmetrical patterns'. This a description of the dance routines of which legendary Hollywood choreographer?

1791 *Ceremonies*

In which annual ceremony held in Essex do married couples swear an oath which begins 'You doe swear by custom of confession/That you ne're made Nuptiall Transgression' in hopes of being awarded a side of bacon?

1792 *The Bible*

In the Old Testament, who was the resident of Bethlehem and grandson of Ruth who was the father of King David?

1793 *Geography*

What is the name of the arm of the Mediterranean Sea that lies between Sardinia to the west, mainland Italy to the east and Sicily to the south?

1794 *Religious Leaders*

Which seventeenth-century religious leader was the founder of The Society of Friends – The Quakers?

1795 *Poetry*

Who wrote the poem, later set to music, the first line of which is 'Oh my Luve's Like a Red Red Rose' in celebration of his love for his wife, Jean?

1796 *Charities*

Made famous by Diana, Princess of Wales, with what is the Halo Trust charity concerned?

1797 *Science*

Gerontology is the scientific study of what?

1798 *Science*

What name is given in engineering to a block of iron which supports work during forging, and in anatomy to a bone in the middle ear?

1799 *Geography*

Which European capital city stands on the River Manzanares?

1800 *Cricket*

In a five-day Test match, in order to make a team 'follow on', or start its second innings straight after its first, what is the minimum first innings lead that must be held by its opponents?

1801 *Writers*

Christine, Pet Sematary and *Four Past Midnight* are works by which American horror-story writer?

1802 *The Monarchy*

Both Elizabeth I and Elizabeth II acceded to the throne at the same age. What age?

1803 *Computers*

On what number is the duodecimal number system based?

1804 *Opera*

Which religious allegorical work by John Bunyan was adapted as an opera in four acts by Vaughan Williams?

1805 *Food and Drink*

Often used in cooking, particularly in soups and salads, by what name is the herb *Rorippa nasturtium-aquaticum* better known?

1806 *Television*

Which children's character made his screen debut on BBC television with his friends Teddy and Looby Loo in 1950?

1807 *Sport*

Battledore was an early form of which racquet sport?

1808 *Scotland*

What in Scotland is a dominie?

1809 *People*

The tenor Sir Peter Pears is most closely associated with the life and work of which twentieth-century English composer?

1810 *Latin Phrases*

Which Latin phrase meaning 'good faith' can be applied to a person who acts in good faith, or to an offer which can be trusted?

1811 *Law*

What three-word term is given to a formal instrument — usually a deed poll — by which one person empowers another to represent them, or to act in their stead for certain purposes?

1812 *Cinema*

She won an Academy Award for her performance in *Darling* and went on to star in the films *Dr Zhivago*, *Far From the Madding Crowd* and *The Go-Between*. What is the name of this British actress?

1813 *Botany*

What is the common name of the *Antirrhinum majus*, so called because the flowers, which are said to look like a legendary monster, quickly shut if squeezed open and then released?

1814 *Mythology*

Who was the Roman counterpart of Artemis, the Greek goddess of hunting?

1815 *People*

Born Isabella Mary Mayson in 1836, she is best remembered for a domestic manual written in her married name and published in 1861. What name?

1816 *Art*

Whose famous painting *Guernica* was a protest at the bombing of a Basque city during the Spanish Civil War?

1817 *Music*

The musicians Andrés Segovia and Narciso Yepes are most closely associated with which instrument?

1818 *The Bible*

In the Old Testament, which of King Saul's sons was the close and loyal friend of David?

1819 *Measurements*

What imperial unit of capacity is equivalent to 568 millilitres?

1820 *Advertising*

'Pure Genius' and 'Not Everything in Black and White Makes Sense' are slogans that have been used to promote which drink?

1821 *Twentieth-Century History*

In which decade were Georges Pompidou, Edward Heath and Richard Nixon simultaneously President of France, Prime Minister of Britain and President of the United States?

1822 *International Business*

Located in the City of London, it is the world's premier maritime market for the buying, selling and chartering of ships. From which sea does it take its name?

1823 *Religion*

According to Christian tradition, which three gifts symbolize kingship, divinity and mortality?

1824 Religion

What is the official title of the person who acts as the Chairman of the annual General Assembly of the Church of Scotland?

1825 Egyptian Legend

Which animal was particularly sacred to the ancient Egyptians, the dilation and contraction of its pupils symbolizing the waxing and waning of the moon?

1826 Name Connections

Music and the Church: What links November 1st with a successful all-girl pop group?

1827 Law

After what period of time working for a company are you legally entitled to complain of unfair dismissal?

1828 Literature

The Fox, The White Peacock and The Plumed Serpent are works by which twentieth-century English novelist?

1829 The USA

Three American states between Canada and Mexico have coastlines on the Pacific Ocean. Name two of the three.

1830 History

Prince Edward, Duke of Kent, lived from 1767 to 1820. Who was his famous daughter?

1831 Food and Drink

Swan Valley, Barossa Valley and Eden Valley are wine-growing regions in which Commonwealth country?

1832 Flags

Which constellation appears on the national flag of Australia?

1833 Ships

Watched by Henry VIII, this ship sank in the Solent in 1545; she was raised in 1982. What is her name?

1834 Television

What is the name of the BBC's teletext system?

1835 *Law*

According to the legal definition, at what age does a child become classified as a young person?

1836 *Imaginary Places*

Which allegorical work, first published in the seventeenth century, features Doubting Castle, the Slough of Despond and Vanity Fair?

1837 *Botany*

What is the name of the pigment in plants which absorbs blue, violet and red light and reflects green light, which is why leaves look green?

1838 *Legal Language*

What is a recidivist?

1839 *Counties*

Trowbridge, Marlborough and Warminster are three towns in which English county?

1840 *Flags*

One of the oldest and best-known flags flown by merchant shipping consists of four triangles of white, red, yellow and blue. Which famous shipping line flies it?

1841 *Geography*

What is the name of the stretch of water that separates Tasmania from mainland Australia?

1842 *Literature*

The publication of *Jude the Obscure* in 1895, with its story of infidelity and adultery, caused such a public uproar that the author never wrote another novel. What was his name?

1843 *Exploration*

In 1773, the *Resolution* and the *Adventure* became the first known ships to sail south of the Antarctic Circle. Which famous British explorer was in charge of the *Resolution*?

1844 *History*

By what name had the Garden Tower at the Tower of London become known by the Tudor period?

1845 *Disney*

There are two major Disney attractions outside the US. One is Disneyland Paris in France. In which country is the other?

1846 *The USA*

Honolulu is the capital of which American state?

1847 *Scotland*

From the Gaelic for family or stock, what word is used for the social grouping based on kinship, familiar in the Highlands of Scotland?

1848 *The Arts*

Arabesque and entrechat are terms used in which art form?

1849 *Literature*

What is the name of the central male character in *Wuthering Heights*?

1850 *Language*

If something is described as asteroid, what shape would it be?

1851 *Phobias*

Xenophobia is a fear or dislike of what?

1852 *Parliament*

If a Member of Parliament applied for the stewardship of the Chiltern Hundreds, what would they be doing?

1853 *Literature*

Each act of a play by Samuel Beckett ends with the same exchange – 'Well, shall we go?', 'Yes, let's go' – followed by the stage direction 'They do not move'. Which play?

1854 *Decades*

In which decade of this century were the Olympic Games last held in Britain, was Prince Charles born and was the National Health Service established?

1855 *Motor Cars*

Which model of motor vehicle made by Mitsubishi is also an ancient Japanese title?

1856 *British Prime Ministers*

The Hirsel, outside Coldstream in Scotland, is the seat of which family, one of whose members was British Prime Minister in the 1960s?

1857 *Athletics*

The decathlon comprises ten events: four track events and six field events. Name two of the six field events.

1858 *The Olympics*

At which Olympics did the Britons Allan Wells win the 100 metres, Steve Ovett win the 800 metres and Daley Thompson win the decathlon?

1859 *The Alphabet*

The name of only one sport is used to denote a letter in the NATO Phonetic Alphabet. Which sport?

1860 *Ancient Literature*

The epic poem in 24 books, the *Iliad*, is traditionally attributed to which Greek poet?

1861 *The USA*

Which two of the Great Lakes of North America are linked by Niagara Falls?

1862 *Advertising*

Which tropical bird, with a large bill and brightly coloured plumage, has been a famous advertiser of Guinness over many years?

1863 *Theatre*

What is the title of the Richard Sheridan play in which Captain Jack Absolute and Bob Acres compete for the hand of Lydia Languish?

1864 *Science*

What name is given to the deceptive appearance of a distant object, caused by the bending of light rays due to particular atmospheric conditions?

1865 *Geography*

What is the name of the sea, an arm of the Pacific Ocean, that washes the eastern shore of Queensland?

1866 *The European Union*

By what name, after the Dutch city in which it was signed, is the 1992 Treaty on European Union commonly known?

1867 *European Cities*

Which German city, renowned as a centre of culture, hosts an international film festival each year in February?

1868 *Historical Terms*

Historically the nobility, the clergy and the Commons were the three estates: what has come to be known as the Fourth Estate?

1869 *Birds*

The pygostyle in birds is the remnant of the tail from which the tail feathers emanate. By what name is this fatty end-portion better known in a cooked fowl?

1870 *Film and Food*

A film director, remembered for his *Death Wish* series starring Charles Bronson, is now also known for his restaurant reviews for the *Sunday Times*. What is his name?

1871 *Test Cricket*

England and Australia compete for the Ashes. With which Test side has England competed for the Wisden trophy since 1963?

1872 *The Bible*

Which of the seven archangels is the messenger of divine comfort?

1873 *History*

What was the nickname of the notorious seventeenth/eighteenth century British pirate, Edward Teach?

1874 *Science*

The Latin name for which chemical element is hydragyrum, hence its symbol Hg?

1875 *Cinema*

The naïve young second wife of a Cornish landowner is haunted by the image of her glamorous predecessor. Which 1940 Alfred Hitchcock film, starring Laurence Olivier and Joan Fontaine, is based on this famous novel?

1876 *Place Names*

Which central American republic has a Spanish name meaning rich coast?

1877 *Britain*

Which British city is home to the Hallé Orchestra and the Royal Northern College of Music?

1878 *Food and Drink*

If a dish is served en croute, what does that mean?

1879 *Geography*

In which state is the Canadian capital Ottawa?

1880 *Medicine*

What is the familiar name for the activity known scientifically as somnambulism?

1881 *Latin Phrases*

Meaning 'at pleasure', what Latin phrase is used for a speech which is improvized?

1882 *Animal*

As canine is to dogs, so vulpine is to...which animal?

1883 *Books*

Which work of reference is often known as the OED?

1884 *Costume*

Which town in Morocco has given its name to a type of headwear, which is flat-topped, red in colour and with a tassel?

1885 *Food and Drink*

Adhering to the tradition that you should only eat oysters when there's an 'R' in the month, between which two months should you not eat them?

1886 *Proverbs*

According to the proverb, what is nine points of the law?

1887 *Competitions*

Over the years, in which competition would you have heard such 'classics' as 'Ding Ding a Dong', 'A-Ba-Ni-Bi', 'La La La' and 'Boom Bang-a-Bang'?

1888 *Law and Order*

Which (Australian) animal gives its name to improperly constituted courts that parody or disregard normal legal procedures and criteria?

1889 *Food and Drink*

What is the name of the French red wine, named after a village near Avignon, which literally translates as 'the pope's new castle'?

1890 *Science Fiction*

Which eponymous character – a biologist – in an H.G. Wells novel conducts gruesome experiments on Noble's Island?

1891 *Cinema*

Sean Connery with Claudine Auger and Adolfo Celi starred in which 1965 James Bond film?

1892 *Phrases*

What two-word phrase is now used to mean a refusal on the part of authority (especially police forces) to put up with any level of illegal activity or crime?

1893 *Law*

What is defined in law as the offence of importing or exporting prohibited goods, or of importing or exporting goods without paying the duties imposed on them?

1894 *Geography*

Which is the highest peak in the Caucasus Mountains?

1895 *Physiology*

What does the human body produce when it encounters an antigen?

1896 *Sport*

In which sport is a 'slam dunk' a shot at goal?

1897 *Science*

What name is given to the fundamental unit in which two or more atoms are bonded together?

1898 *The Bible*

In which book in the Old Testament does the story of David and Goliath appear?

1899 *Calendars*

How long a period of time is a trimester?

1900 *Opera*

On whose romantic tale was Bizet's opera *Carmen* based?

1901 *Counties*

Whitchurch, Ludlow, Bridgnorth and Market Drayton are towns in which English county?

1902 *Canada*

The Plains of Abraham are on the northern bank of the St Lawrence River. In which city?

1903 *Literature*

This man was a banker, a naval intelligence officer and the foreign manager of the *Sunday Times.* He later became one of the best-known writers in the world. What is his name?

1904 *Poetry*

'My heart aches, and a drowsy numbness pains my sense, as though of hemlock I had drunk'. These are the opening lines from an ode by John Keats to which bird?

1905 *The Monarchy*

1760–1820, a period of 59 years and three months was the reign of which British monarch?

1906 *Science*

Named after a nineteenth-century Austrian physicist, what name is given to the change in the observed frequency of waves due to the relative motion between the source of the waves and the observer?

1907 *Pop Music*

Don't Shoot Me I'm Only the Piano Player, Goodbye Yellow Brick Road and *Reg Strikes Back* are albums recorded by which singer and instrumentalist?

1908 *Jazz*

George Shearing, Art Tatum and Oscar Peterson are best known for playing which musical instrument?

1909 *Food and Drink*

The thick paste tahini is used in Middle Eastern cooking to flavour various dishes. From which seed is it made?

1910 *Music*

What term is used as the opposite of euphony and means clashing and unpleasant sounds?

1911 *Athletics*

Of the four throwing events in athletics, which is the only one which can take place at an indoor meeting?

1912 *Classical Music*

For which event in the 1950s was Benjamin Britten's opera *Gloriana* commissioned?

1913 *Literature*

How is the architect Halvard Solness known in the title of a play by Henrik Ibsen?

1914 *Geography*

Which Mediterranean island is also known as the George Cross Island?

1915 *The Monarchy*

Which English royal house had three monarchs – Edward IV, his son Edward V and his brother Richard III?

1916 *Science*

Which expression, used in nuclear physics and chemistry, has come to mean any series of rapidly occurring events which precipitate the next?

1917 *Words*

What term, used in law, commerce and economics, can be defined as 'the exclusive privilege of selling any commodity'?

1918 *Etymology*

A plumber is so called because he originally worked with which metal?

1919 *Nursery Rhymes*

In which nursery rhyme are two dozen *Turdi merulae* cooked in a savoury dish for a monarch?

1920 *Literature*

What is the novel by William Golding in which an aeroplane carrying a party of schoolboys crashes on a desert island?

1921 *Motor Cars*

The Clio, the Megane and the Laguna are models of car produced by which motor manufacturer?

1922 *Proverbs*

There's many a good tune played on what?

1923 *Education*

HND is an abbreviation for which educational qualification?

1924 *Opera*

What is the English translation of Rossini's popular opera *La Gazza Ladra*?

1925 *The Ancient World*

By what name is the ancient city of Ilium, lying near the southern entrance to the Hellespont, more usually known?

1926 *Art*

The Potato Eaters and *Starry Night* are well-known works by which post-Impressionist painter?

1927 *Geography*

Which two seas are linked by the Kiel Canal?

1928 *Counties*

The Fitzwilliam Museum, the Scott Polar Research Institute Museum and Duxford Airfield are all tourist attractions in which county?

1929 *British Isles*

Where, specifically, on the coast of England, is the coastline feature known as 'Doctor Syntax Head'?

1930 *Animals*

Which domesticated animal has breeds called Cheviot, Columbia, Corriedale and Cotswold?

1931 *London*

Which thoroughfare leads from Trafalgar Square down to Parliament Street and Parliament Square?

1932 *American History*

The Spanish-American War of 1898 began as the struggle of which Caribbean island for independence from Spain?

1933 *Animals*

Types of which family of mammals strain their food from water using a pair of horny plates called 'baleen'?

1934 *Classical Music*

What is the country of birth of the composers Bela Bartok, Zoltan Kodaly and Franz Liszt?

1935 *Paris Landmarks*

In which Paris square did the guillotine claim its victims during the French Revolution?

1936 *Sport*

Ken Doherty, Ronnie O'Sullivan and Mark Williams are famous names in which sport or game?

1937 *Transport*

How many years after its first registration must a car have its first MOT test?

1938 *Ballet*

Klara dreams that she has to defend a gift from her godfather against the King of the Mice. The gift, a household implement, then turns into a handsome prince. This is the outline of the story of which of Tchaikovsky's ballets?

1939 *Words*

Derived from an early twentieth-century French word meaning 'a dancehall woman', what word has come into use for a professional male dancing partner or escort?

1940 *Trade Names*

Which brand of frozen food products derived its name from an abbreviated form of Fruit Industries, a business formed in the Second World War?

1941 *History*

Which conspiracy against the king and government was discovered through an anonymous letter sent to Lord Monteagle in the seventeenth century?

1942 *Historical Terms*

Which president gave his name to the doctrine he first proposed in 1823, stating that the USA had an interest in preventing outside interference in the internal affairs of the Americas?

1943 *Geography*

Which geographical feature in Africa has a local name which means 'the smoke that thunders'?

1944 *Languages*

Which Commonwealth island country has the two official languages, Sinhala and Tamil?

1945 *Sport*

What name is given to the exhilarating outdoor sport in which a crew guides an inflatable raft down a fast-flowing river?

1946 *Words*

Which word, derived from the two Greek words for 'all' and 'remedy', is used for a cure for all diseases?

1947 *Literature*

Who was the author of *The Waverley Novels* published in the nineteenth century?

1948 *Human Anatomy*

To which organ of the body is the pituitary gland attached?

1949 *Pop Music*

'Knowing Me, Knowing You', 'Dancing Queen' and 'Money, Money Money' were hits for which quartet?

1950 *Geography*

What names are given to the parallels of latitude that mark the northern and southern boundaries of the tropical zone?

1951 *Mathematics*

What term describes a triangle in which the three angles are 60 degrees each?

1952 *Meteorology*

The occasional abnormal warming on the surface of the central Pacific ocean that generates huge volumes of warm air is known to meteorologists as what?

1953 *Spain*

In Spain, what type of event is known as a corrida?

1954 *The USA*

What two-word expression, involving a book and an article of clothing, is used to describe the southern states of America where fundamentalist Christianity is particularly strong?

1955 *The Monarchy*

Which group of six women had ten husbands between them, one husband being common to each of the six women?

1956 *Name Connections*

What name links a prominent member of the shadow cabinet and the destination of Old Uncle Tom Cobleigh and all in the folk ballad?

1957 *Baseball*

Since the distance between the bases is 30 yards, how far does a batter have to run to score a 'home run'?

1958 *Proverbs*

According to the eighteenth century proverb, until when should you ne'er cast a clout?

1959 *Phrases*

Which amphibious creature gives its name to an expression which means an insincere display of grief?

1960 *Popular Music*

'Crocodile Shoes', 'Love Don't Live Here Anymore' and 'Laura' are hit records by which actor, best known for his TV appearances in *Auf Wiedersehen, Pet* and *Spender*?

1961 *The Ancient World*

Which commodity was once so important that it was often used as money, and was known in Latin by a term on which the modern word 'salary' is based?

1962 *The Royal Family*

Which member of the Royal Family's entry in a book of biography begins 'royal carpenter and Harley Davidson freak'?

1963 *Geography*

Which people, who live mainly in the northern regions of Norway, Finland and Russia, are called in their own language Sami?

1964 *The Monarchy*

The coffin of which British monarch in 1910 was followed by his little terrier, Caesar, ahead of all the kings and princes in the funeral procession?

1965 *London*

On the site of St Thomas' Hospital, 2 Lambeth Palace Road in London SE1 is a museum dedicated to which famous nurse?

1966 *The UK*

Originally a Cistercian abbey, what is the name of the 3000-acre parkland and safari park in Bedfordshire near Milton Keynes?

1967 *Crime Fiction*

What is the name of the private eye and principal character in Dashiell Hammett's *The Maltese Falcon*, played by Humphrey Bogart in the famous film adaptation?

1968 *Art*

How is the painter Domenikos Theotokopoulos better known (because he was born in Crete)?

1969 *Acronyms*

The letters LLB after a person's name indicate a qualification in which profession?

1970 *Latin Phrases*

A 'Memento vivere' is a reminder of (the pleasures of) life. Which Latin phrase is used for the opposite, a warning or reminder of death?

1971 *The Bible*

In Genesis, chapter 49, whose 12 sons were the founders of the tribes of Israel?

1972 *Counties*

Launceston, Bude, Saltash and Camborne are four towns in which English county?

1973 *Shakespeare*

Whom does Hamlet describe, when addressing his skull, as 'a fellow of infinite jest, of most excellent fancy'?

1974 *Language*

What are the two official languages in Israel?

1975 *Awards*

Which medal is abbreviated as the DFC?

1976 *Science*

What is the principal explosive ingredient of dynamite?

1977 *Buildings*

What at Oxford University is named after the sixteenth/seventeenth-century English statesman and scholar Sir Thomas Bodley?

1978 *Chemistry*

Which chemical element has the symbol Kr?

1979 *People*

What was the name of the famous Scottish outlaw, known as the Robin Hood of Scotland, who was the subject of a novel published by Sir Walter Scott in 1818?

1980 *Geography*

In which African country are the provinces of Agadir and Marrakesh?

1981 *Golf*

What nationality are the golfers Peter O'Malley, Stuart Appleby, Steve Elkington and Greg Norman?

1982 *History*

Who in 1955 (after resigning as Prime Minister) was offered the dukedom of London, but refused on the grounds that it would be a blight on the prospects of his son and grandson?

1983 *Dukedoms*

The holder of which dukedom, created in 1947, also holds the titles Earl of Merioneth and Baron Greenwich, also created in 1947?

1984 *Acronyms*

LIFO is an acronym used for a redundancy policy, whereby staff who have been most recently appointed are the first to be made redundant. What does LIFO stand for?

1985 *Cinema*

Which film by Federico Fellini has an Italian title which has come into English usage to suggest a life of luxury, pleasure and self-indulgence?

1986 *Art and Literature*

What nationality by birth were the writer Georges Simenon, (creator of Maigret), the Surrealist painter René Magritte and the composer César Franck?

1987 *Animals*

Beavers, chinchillas and golden hamsters all belong to which order of mammals?

1988 *The USA*

The cities of Tucson and Phoenix are in which American state?

1989 *The Bible*

The Authorized Version of the Bible is named after which seventeenth-century British monarch?

1990 *Parliament*

What emblem is used on official House of Commons stationery?

1991 *Famous Quotations*

Mark Twain said 'There are three kinds of lies: lies, damned lies, and...' what?

1992 *Cinema*

Two unemployed musicians accidentally witness the St Valentine's Day Massacre and flee to Miami disguised as women. What is the name of this classic film comedy starring Tony Curtis, Jack Lemmon and Marilyn Monroe?

1993 *Law*

The term 'spouse-breach' is an alternative name for what?

1994 *Botany*

What do Gentius, King of Illyria in the second century BC, Michel Begon in the seventeenth century and Anders Dahl in the eighteenth century have in common specifically?

1995 *National Anthems*

'The Reign of Our Emperor' is the English translation of the national anthem, the words of which date back to the tenth century, of which country?

1996 *History*

A site, five miles east of Inverness was the location of the last battle fought on mainland Britain, in 1746. Which battle?

1997 *Famous Virtuosos*

Dinu Lipatti, Artur Rubinstein, Vladimir Horowitz are twentieth-century virtuosos on which instrument?

1998 *Religion*

With over 170 million followers, which South-east Asian country has the largest Muslim population in the world?

1999 *Science*

What generic name is given to the refined petroleum product that is used as a fuel for aircraft jet and turboprop engines?

2000 *Grammar*

What is the reflexive form of the word him?

2001 *Law*

What was set at three years duration by the Triennial Act in 1694, at seven years maximum length by the 1716 Septennial Act, and established at the present five years duration by the Parliament Act 1911?

2002 *Canada*

SK is the official abbreviation or contraction for which Canadian province?

15 to 1

ROUND ONE
Answers

1 Alibi

2 Battle of Jutland

3 Dante Gabriel Rossetti

4 Timbuktu

5 Duke of Westminster/the Grosvenor family

6 Sir Gordon Richards

7 Brazil

8 Green, white and orange vertical stripes

9 Nose

10 Widdecombe

11 Bayeux

12 Malic acid

13 Blood

14 Wood

15 Spain

16 Three

17 Hogarth's

18 Porcine

19 The pilots/airmen in the Battle of Britain

20 Liverpool

21 Bisley (home of the National Rifle Association)

22 D(avid) W(ark) Griffith

23 Prestonpans

24 'Party wall' (not common wall)

25 Robert Falcon Scott

26 Formic acid/Methanoic acid

27 Alexandra Palace

28 Finland

29 Lord Chancellor

30 Mencap

31 Library of Alexandria

32 Asia

33 Hampton Court Palace

34 Independent local radio stations (Also a 'Wave' in Swansea)

35 Monsieur Hulot

36 Holt

37 Strait of Gibraltar

38 Artist's proof

39 Architecture

40 Fra Angelico

41 Dodecanese

42 Federal Bureau of Investigation

43 Hypnotism

44 Film

45 Little war

46 Paris

47 Cyprus, Malta

48 Adams (John and John Quincey)

49 Bullfighter

50 Campaign for Real Ale

51 Fifties (50–9)

52 Riyadh

53 *Othello*

54 Vacuum cleaners

55 Anne of Cleves

56 Abbey National Group

57 Islands

58 Tennis

59 Philip, Arthur, George

60 The Hague

61 A griddle cake of oatmeal or barley or other meal

62 Scotland's St Andrew

63 Pythagoras

64 Adverb

65 Ruby

66 Dr Thomas John Barnado

67 Zambia

68 York Minster

69 Lady Antonia Fraser

70 Stevie Wonder

71 K (Kelvin)

72 Black Hills

73 Russia

74 Garden cities

75 St Aidan

76 The Broadcasting Standards Commission

77 150

78 Product

79 Uranus

80 Liverpool

81 Goose

82 The Jesuits/Society of Jesus

83 Norway

84 St Swithin

85 F Scott Fitzgerald

86 China

87 Airlines

88 Truth

89 *The Hobbit*

90 Duke of Norfolk

91 *Psycho*

92 October

93 Vintage

94 Drum

95 Canada

96 Magaret Thatcher

97 Nosebleed

98 Fifth column

99 Criminal injuries (Criminal Injuries Compensation Authority and Board)

100 Denmark

101 Kangaroo

102 The king and a bishop

103 Ornamental wreath of flowers or beads

104 Speak

105 The guns of Navarone

106 The living

107 Bay of Bengal

108 Sweets or sweetmeats

109 Fellow of the Institute of Actuaries

110 Satyrs

111 Hungary

112 Phosphorus

113 Electric charge (equal to a charge of one amp. per second)

114 Bread

115 Formula translation

116 Slovenia

117 Laughing gas

118 Benito Mussolini and Adolf Hitler

119 Clubhouse or bar.

120 *Yes, Minister, Yes, Prime Minister*

121 Facelift/operation to remove wrinkles and smooth facial skin.

122 William IV (reigned 1830–7)

123 High jump

124 Parsifal or Parzival (the Percival of Arthurian legend)

125 Borough

126 Numbers, Deuteronomy

127 Esso

128 Bank of England

129 Gilbert and George

130 Wisley

131 Harvard

132 First among equals

133 Josiah Wedgwood

134 Pointers

135 California

136 United Nations (New York)

137 Woodwind

138 Michael

139 Francis I

140 HMS *Dreadnought*

141 Italy

142 Scuppers

143 Samuel Pepys

144 The Queen

145 Armenia

146 Archbishop of York

147 L. P. Hartley

148 Belarus, Ukraine

149 *A Room with a View*

150 Tsar Nicholas II of Russia

151 New Scotland Yard

152 Lord Melvyn Bragg

153 Kent

154 The Goons

155 Hanover

156 Oliver Cromwell

157 Hauliers (Road Haulage Association)

158 Fastnet Rock

159 Petruchio

160 Napoleon Bonaparte

161 Nero

162 Turin

163 Australia

164 Neil Simon

165 Trough

166 Outside Broadcast

167 Clint Eastwood

168 Gauze

169 (Guglielmo) Marconi

170 Malaysia

171 'Mad Dogs and Englishmen'

172 Flying bedstead

173 Raffles

174 Medea

175 Nom de plume

176 Seth

177 Verona

178 Suez Canal

179 New Zealand dollar

180 Wisconsin

181 CND

182 Innoculations or injections

183 Abraham

184 Melbourne

185 Star of David

186 The elephant man

187 Elizabeth I

188 Jane Seymour (number 3 – mother of Ed VI)

189 *Women Are from Venus*

190 Cleopatra

191 Iraq

192 Kentucky Derby, Belmont Stakes, Preakness Stakes

193 Water

194 Prince Charles

195 *The Likely Lads*

196 Ganges

197 Every ten years

198 Kit Kat

199 Ernest Hemingway

200 Ford

201 Bois de Boulogne

202 Research and Development

203 Enamel

204 Rip Van Winkle

205 Grapes

206 Bishop of London

207 Victor ludorum

208 Fiat

209 Perfect pitch/absolute pitch

210 San Marino

211 5 furlongs (5/8 of a mile)

212 To elicit reflexes

213 Obelisk

214 Stoic/stoicism (from *stoa*)

215 The Mendips

216 As Alice from *Alice's Adventures in Wonderland* and *Through the Looking Glass*

217 Sinking of the *Titanic*

218 Alfred, Lord Tennyson

219 Bernardo Bertolucci

220 Geneva

221 Nottingham

222 Volleyball

223 500 CC

224 Spoil the child

225 Terminal velocity

226 That the player/singer be silent for a movement or section or time

227 Minotaur

228 Venus

229 *A Shropshire Lad*

230 Microwave

231 Rome

232 Maldives

233 Calculus

234 Eyelashes

235 Galician

236 It has never won a race

237 Adirondacks

238 Martin Luther King

239 Moscow

240 April

241 Plaster of Paris

242 Euripides

243 *The Pirates of Penzance*

244 Richard I and John

245 Housefly

246 Strawberry

247 Surface-to-surface missile

248 USS *Nautilus*

249 Horus

250 (Sir) Harrison Birtwistle

251 Burning incense

252 Agriculture

253 Paris

254 Lloyds of London

255 Swaziland

256 Dame Elisabeth Frink

257 The Korean War

258 Dunkirk

259 Translation

260 Kenneth More

261 Light

262 Sergei Prokofiev

263 Business

264 The Derby and the Oaks

265 Steptoe and son

266 International Grand Master

267 Costa Rica

268 Dartmouth

269 *The Beach*

270 Corporation tax

271 Hypothermia

272 Sir Peter Paul Rubens

273 Charles II

274 Home plate/home base/home base plate

275 Buckinghamshire

276 Conservatives

277 East River

278 House of Commons

279 Caesar

280 Caspian Sea

281 Atmosphere

282 France

283 Las Vegas

284 Lead

285 Advent Sunday

286 Mortar board

287 Alan Sillitoe

288 Mount Etna

289 Compassion in World Farming

290 Ecuador

291 Carat

292 Devon

293 Tuberculosis

294 Zero Population Growth

295 The Cotswolds

296 The Great Wall of China

297 Herbivore

298 70

299 Sandal/shoe

300 Michael Jackson

301 The steamed head of a Maori warrior, at least 160 years old

302 Orville and Wilbur

303 Sir Robert Peel

304 The Pale

305 E.T.(A) Hoffmann

306 Genoa

307 Dame Barbara Hepworth

308 Beaumarchais

309 Field Marshal

310 Arthur Eric Gill

311 Barcelona

312 Six

313 Percussion

314 Rodent

315 14th/15th (1337–1453)

316 Copper

317 Stanley and Livingstone

318 Fleché

319 Hippolyta/Hippolyte

320 'How still we see thee lie'

321 W.H. Auden

322 New York (He was Duke of York at the time)

323 Pericardium

324 25 January

325 Kilogram

326 Envelopes

327 *Le Monde*

328 Sailing/yachting (also windsurfing)

329 Jude

330 The phoney war

331 George Eliot

332 Mr Dick... (in full Mr Richard Babley)

333 Duke of Edinburgh's Award Scheme

334 Butterflies

335 Jack Dempsey

336 One horsepower

337 Ephesus

338 Silk

339 Plasma

340 The fatted calf

341 Atlantic

342 Social, Domestic and Pleasure

343 Hadrian's Wall

344 Gregorian (Gregory I and XIII)

345 Portuguese

346 Luke

347 St James

348 Cutty Sark

349 George III

350 Seaweed

351 Salisbury

352 Insertion of a stitch

353 Germany

354 Mausoleum of Halicarnassus

355 Trampolining

356 Lazio

357 Yalta

358 Copenhagen

359 Lungs

360 Sydney

361 Groucho Marx

362 C.S. Forester

363 Grigori Rasputin

364 Secretary of State for Northern Ireland

365 *Romeo and Juliet*

366 George V

367 *Née*

368 Henry II

369 The national anthem

370 Malta

371 Sangria

372 Pray for us

373 *HMS Pinafore* (or *The Lass That Loved a Sailor*)

374 The American War of Independence

375 *Black Beauty*

376 O. Henry

377 Knee-jerk

378 Patrick Suskind

379 Gull (Laridae)

380 A

381 Fluorine

382 Oscar Wilde

383 Marcasite

384 Department of Culture, Media and Sport

385 Greece

386 *A Tale of Two Cities*

387 Nottingham

388 The yen

389 (Gustav) Holst

390 Queen Victoria

391 Edmund II

392 Edward VII

393 John Philip Sousa

394 *The Mayor of Casterbridge*

395 Transubstantiation

396 Ruhr

397 Essex

398 Eagle

399 Treasury

400 Lancastrians

401 Jade

402 Kenya shilling

403 Leonard Bernstein

404 Michelangelo

405 Dun Laoghaire

406 Cape of Good Hope

407 Haydn

408 Long jump

409 Selenium

410 American Declaration of Independence

411 Hotel

412 Ex officio

413 Colorado

414 Somerset

415 The cause is unknown/It arises itself, is not symptomatic of another disease.

416 Seat

417 Newlyn

418 Peace

419 Limestone

420 Downing Street

421 Anywhere but Earth

422 Hull

423 Masada

424 NEC (National Exhibition Centre)

425 Lady Caroline Lamb

426 Deus ex machina (god from a machine)

427 Pilot Officer

428 Literature

429 Motorcycling

430 Arch

431 Glencoe

432 Mount Kilimanjaro

433 *Bleak House*

434 Sage

435 Wiltshire

436 Pisa

437 Brandenburg Gate

438 Crossbow

439 Medina

440 The calendar

441 Market and Opinion Research International

442 6 February

443 Royal Institute of British Architects

444 Winds

445 Helen of Troy

446 Everglades

447 Matador

448 Arthur Lowe

449 Exosphere

450 The nightingale (in 'ode to a Nightingale')

15 to 1

ROUND TWO
Answers

451 Oasis

452 Power

453 *Casualty*

454 Plagiarism

455 Supermac (Harold Macmillan)

456 K2

457 Albert Campion

458 Modern rhythmic gymnastics

459 Winston Churchill

460 T'ai chi

461 The bagless vacuum cleaner

462 'Music for the Royal Fireworks'

463 Bernard Cornwell

464 Palais du Luxembourg

465 Oxygen

466 Dinar (with national variations)

467 *King Henry VI* (*Henry IV* has just two parts)

468 B Complex (B1, B2 and B3 respectively)

469 Cobalt

470 Heart of England

471 *The Army Game*

472 *Duke Bluebeard's Castle*

473 Himalayas

474 Manchester

475 Greece

476 Loud voice

477 Swansea

478 Cassiopeia

479 Friends and Relatives

480 Mrs Sarah Siddons

481 Hypersonic

482 International Civil Aviation Organization

483 Love letter

484 Sir Garfield Sobers

485 One

486 Ash was placed/sprinkled on the foreheads of Christians to mark the beginning of Lent

487 Acorn (Computers)

488 Alan Beith

489 Croquet

490 Being awarded a bar to their VC

491 William Tell

492 Walpole (4th and 1st Earls of Orford respectively)

493 Woodrow Wilson

494 'The Minute Waltz'

495 Charles Stewart Parnell

496 Dame Ninette de Valois

497 Lincolnshire

498 Cashmere

499 Angora

500 Condemned criminals

501 Tachograph (*not* tachometer, which only measures speed)

502 Peninsular and Oriental (a lot more than steamships nowadays)

503 Armenia

504 Sequoia

505 Nadine Gordimer

506 Death Valley (California)

507 Novena

508 Basketball

509 Cat

510 Marble Arch

511 SPAM

512 Senegal

513 Dar es Salaam

514 Whitehall

515 Duke of Wellington

516 Holy Roman Emperor

517 South Korea (Republic of Korea)

518 Surrey

519 Venice (also painted London)

520 *The Crucible*

521 Ice hockey

522 Saturn 5

523 The National Trust

524 Great Glen

525 Nuncio

526 Foyle's

527 The Faculty of Advocates

528 Lays eggs

529 Iconoclasts

530 Neptune

531 Nathanael

532 Thomas de Quincey

533 Vindolanda

534 Social Democratic Party

535 Friedrich (Wilhelm) Froebel

536 Legion of Honour

537 Draco (aka Drakon)

538 'As often as necessary'

539 Mary I

540 Apollo 17

541 Jonathan Ross

542 Blighty

543 Eamonn de Valera

544 Efficiency

545 St Jude

546 Constantine the Great

547 Qatar (Dawlat Qatar)

548 Georgian

549 Loch Lomond

550 St Paul's Cathedral

551 Docklands Light Railway

552 Edward VIII

553 Clockwork radio

554 Domino Theory

555 (Sir) Harry Secombe

556 From day to day

557 Howe

558 *Guys and Dolls*

559 Brobdingnag

560 Bookmarking

561 Sean O'Casey (real name John Casey)

562 Celestial objects

563 Eighth

564 Field Marshal Kitchener

565 Prince Edward Island

566 Fruits and seeds

567 Iceland

568 Topology

569 The Eagle and Child

570 Tug of war (Tug of War Association)

571 Blushing

572 Hippo

573 The Staunton Chess Set

574 Major General

575 Greater Antilles

576 Monty Python

577 Eric Ambler

578 Colour

579 Traitors' Gate (Water Gate)

580 Yuri Gagarin

581 Area of Special Control of Advertising

582 Bears

583 Hydra

584 John Piper

585 Limbo

586 1967

587 Richard Hannay

588 Consanguinity

589 Alternative Investment Market

590 Speed

591 Son

592 'Aye, Aye Sir'

593 Ulster Unionist Party

594 Windsor

595 *King Kong*

596 '... the life in my men'

597 Mrs Elizabeth Gaskell

598 Birds

599 Ice hockey

600 +5 or -5

601 Trucial States

602 Satellite TV channels or children/youth television channels

603 Henry VII

604 Edward Heath

605 Count Dracula (in Bram Stoker's *Dracula*)

606 Hertfordshire

607 Loofah (not sponge)

608 Normandy

609 Spine

610 Sights

611 Sightholders

612 Sodium (from 'natrium')

613 Association of Chief Police Officers

614 *It's a Wonderful Life*

615 The 'Apology' of Socrates

616 *James and the Giant Peach*

617 Caliban

618 Ferryman

619 Patrick White

620 Glandular fever

621 Kingfisher

622 Execution of Charles I

623 Peace

624 Spain

625 Pastoral

626 Republic of Ireland

627 Sir Jacob Epstein

628 Ivan Turgenev

629 *Aida*

630 Hull

631 Writing (writer's cramp)

632 Denmark

633 Crotchet

634 Miniatures/miniature portraits

635 Portugal

636 Received Pronunciation

637 Richard Norman Shaw

638 Lithuania

639 Indira Gandhi

640 Baily's Beads (spots of sunlight seen on the edge of the Moon before and after a total eclipse of the Sun)

641 Palk Strait

642 Richard III

643 Chocolate bars

644 Ripon

645 Boyar

646 Dacha

647 Triangular

648 Private Members' Bills

649 Victoria Wood

650 *Carmen Jones*

651 Namibia, Botswana, South Africa, Mozambique

652 Ear

653 Bronze

654 21

655 At least three years

656 Lord Palmerston

657 Sir Alec Douglas-Home

658 Murrayfield

659 Textured Vegetable Protein

660 Brownsea Island

661 Jaundice

662 James Callaghan

663 Bryan Adams

664 Samaria

665 Passionflower/passiflora

666 The Security Council

667 Penelope Mortimer

668 International Olympic Committee

669 British Olympic Association

670 *Fawlty Towers*

671 Aberdeen

672 Boyzone

673 Paper

674 Radio 2

675 Ghana

676 Scottish Parliament (Member of the Scottish Parliament)

677 Peter Greenaway

678 Arcadia

679 Every ten years

680 Every three years

681 Sweden and Finland

682 Othello

683 Sheep

684 St Dominic

685 Rhombus

686 Loretta Young

687 Russia

688 City of London Police

689 Captain Smollett (Alexander)

690 Oboe

691 National trails

692 Citroen

693 Fireman Sam

694 The cross

695 Tipstaff

696 Psychiatrist

697 Stephen (1135–54)

698 Parallelogram

699 Brake Horse Power

700 West Ham United

701 Eight

702 Iris of the eye

703 Sun

704 Hornet

705 Dotheboys Hall

706 Brimstone and treacle

707 Sunshine

708 Mount Cook

709 Hypertext Mark-up Language

710 Keith Floyd

711 First female announcer

712 *The Flying Dutchman*

713 Learnt the Koran by heart

714 Accidental

715 Brackets or parentheses; quotation marks or inverted commas

716 Anthony Burgess

717 Bhangra

718 Bangkok

719 Armada

720 Liquified Petroleum Gas

721 Queen's or King's Champion

722 Entertainments National Service Association

723 *The Secret Garden*

724 *The Mill on the Floss*

725 100

726 Brueghel

727 Place de la Concorde

728 Charles II

729 Beatrix Potter

730 Christchurch

731 Brigadier

732 Cured a blind man

733 Bundesrat/Federal Council

734 National Aeronautics and Space Administration

735 Isabella Rossellini

736 Liverpool

737 Faeroes

738 Limber

739 Ataturk ('father of the Turks')

740 Igor Stravinsky

741 Sweden

742 Scipio (Africanus the Elder)

743 The nose

744 Vasco da Gama

745 UNESCO

746 Zirconium

747 *Clarissa*

748 Forbidden city

749 Glenconner

750 Derek Thompson

751 Colditz

752 Manchester

753 Windward Islands

754 Circuits

755 Midland and Oxford; North-Eastern; Northern; South-Eastern; Wales and Chester; Western

756 North Sea and Baltic Sea

757 'Eleanor Rigby'

758 Miguel Indurain, Bernard Hinault, Eddy Merckx, Jacques Anquetil

759 J. Robert Oppenheimer

760 Denmark

761 Court of Common Council

762 Epping Forest

763 Advanced Gas-cooled Reactor

764 A character formed from two or more letters or characters. e.g. the ae in Caesar or encyclopaedia, or a monogram

765 Paignton and Brixham

766 Nagasaki

767 Algorithm

768 The Marquess of Salisbury

769 Silas Marner

770 Painting, it's a small convex mirror used to reflect the landscape in miniature

771 Mace

772 *EastEnders*

773 Joanna Southcott

774 Glasgow

775 Leveraged buyout

776 Underground/tube

777 Andy Capp

778 Spain and Portugal

779 Mary Whitehouse

780 Alan Keith

781 Harare

782 Miss Scarlett

783 *King John*

784 Lord Chancellor and Chancellor of the Duchy of Lancaster

785 Alnwick Castle

786 India

787 Chord

788 Bavaria

789 Titipu

790 Seasonal Affective Disorder

791 Berlin (Tempelhof, Tegel and Schonefeld)

792 Lord Peter Wimsey

793 Southern

794 The Orkneys

795 Monsieur Pamplemousse

796 Aubrey Beardsley

797 Petri dish

798 Sir Joseph Banks

799 Greece

800 (3000 metre) steeplechase

801 Seven

802 *Romeo and Juliet*

803 Matterhorn

804 Peter Grimes

805 Little Lord Fauntleroy

806 Burrito

807 Phil Collins

808 Soho

809 Vocal or singing organ

810 East Midlands

811 Conjunctions

812 Paul Revere

813 Rudyard Kipling

814 Kim

815 Aberdeen Angus

816 Gothic

817 Czech Republic

818 School of Oriental and African Studies

819 HMP Slade

820 Kew Palace

821 Harry S. Truman

822 12

823 Yorkshire Dales National Park

824 Julian of Norwich

825 Vermicelli

826 Telstar 1

827 Meteor showers

828 Pre-Raphaelite Brotherhood

829 The magnetic equator

830 Taunton

831 Conchology

832 *An Awfully Big Adventure*

833 Mainland

834 Fine Gael

835 Paris

836 Macduff

837 Benchers

838 Azerbaijan

839 De Profundis

840 Glutton

841 Rebecca

842 30 mph

843 Glass

844 Opportunity

845 The Philippines

846 Uncle Remus

847 Ironsides

848 Frank Lloyd Wright

849 The devil

850 No. 1

851 Luxemburg

852 Lame duck

853 Edwin Hubble

854 Llareggub or Llaregyb

855 Fianna Fail

856 Hylda Baker

857 Eastbourne

858 Carmarthen

859 ME (Myalgic Encephalomyelitis)

860 Japheth

861 Orpheus

862 *Wuthering Heights*

863 Pet leopard

864 Perth

865 Giant leatherback turtles/ sea turtles (green turtles)

866 Actinium

867 Art direction

868 Princess Margaret

869 Tallahassee

870 Puppets/puppet show/ 'doll theatre'

871 Suzi Quatro

872 Work

873 *Whisky Galore*

874 Sitar

875 Britannia Bridge

876 Zachariah

877 *Sleeping Beauty*

878 Bats

879 John McCarthy

880 0°C

881 River Liffey

882 Errors and Omissions Excepted

883 Hiccup

884 *Cranford*

885 Lou Reed

886 John and Jane Doe

887 Arc de Triomphe

888 Lawn Tennis Association (LTA)

889 Pe(destrian) li(ght)- con(trolled crossing)

890 Lincolnshire

891 Stephen

892 A lullaby or cradle song

893 Veronica

894 Luzon

895 Dwight D. Eisenhower

896 Violin

897 Juniper berry

898 Emir

899 It took place on land, sea and air

900 In and Out

901 Shrove Tuesday/Mardi Gras

902 FIFA (Federation Internationale de Football Association)

903 Falklands

904 Vietnam

905 Sir Alec Douglas-Home

906 Urdu

907 They do not migrate

908 Barbara Taylor Bradford

909 Manchester

910 Singapore

911 Advanced Photo System

912 Henry V

913 Major

914 Coriolanus (from Corioli)

915 Qualified Majority Voting

916 Trains

917 Doctor of medicine

918 Peter the Great

919 Abbey Theatre

920 Young Turks

921 Elves

922 Greenland

923 Royal Liverpool Philharmonic Orchestra

924 27

925 Daughters of the American Revolution

926 Guyana

927 The reappearance through a painting of an earlier painting beneath

928 Merovingians

929 Cyprus

930 Mark

931 Soprano, Alto, Tenor, Bass

932 Vauxhall

933 Vatican City

934 Biennial

935 Rev. R.S. Thomas

936 Toto

937 Adelaide

938 Lewis Carroll

939 *Aladdin, Evita*

940 Liverpool

941 1 stone

942 Jehovah's Witnesses

943 On fingertips as part of a fingerprint

944 Maria Callas

945 Republic of Ireland

946 Battle of Britain (Day)

947 Toasted cheese

948 Cratchit

949 Lascelles

950 Prince Edward Island

951 Round Robin

952 Television

953 Mrs Patrick Campbell

954 River Rhone

955 Only one colour

956 Two (Prince Charles and Princess Anne)

957 1789

958 East Anglia, Essex, Kent, Mercia, Northumbria, Sussex, Wessex

959 William Blake

960 The Dominicans

961 Tyburn

962 Malvern Hills

963 *Wild Swans*

964 Lambert Simnel

965 Lucius Annaeus Seneca the Younger

966 Budapest

967 Montpelier

968 They were all films in the *Road* series in which all three starred

969 St Patrick

970 Princess Alexandra

971 Humber

972 The slave trade and slavery

973 Mitsubishi

974 Marie Antoinette

975 East Pakistan

976 Mangetout

977 The *Independent*

978 Staffordshire

979 Robson and Jerome

980 Wounded Knee

981 Measles, mumps and rubella

982 Billie Holiday

983 Hurdles/hurdling

984 The coronation of a British monarch

985 Kilogram

986 *For Whom the Bell Tolls*

987 Etching

988 Associated Press

989 Commander Caractacus Potts

990 The Hague (Den Haag)

991 Preservatives

992 Skylark ('Ode to a Skylark')

993 Nightingale ('Ode to a Nightingale')

994 Obverse/reverse

995 Pandora

996 Freemasons

997 Sir Paul McCartney

998 Old Contemptibles

999 St Mary-le-Bow

1000 Charles Darnay

1001 Pirate

1002 Peanuts

1003 Indonesia

1004 Stansted and Luton

1005 Electric guitar

1006 *Ruddigore*

1007 Venice

1008 Four

1009 *Pygmalion*

1010 Maori

1011 Biltong

1012 Switzerland

1013 Queen

1014 Sgt. Pepper's Lonely Hearts Club Band

1015 Kudos

1016 Kimono

1017 Time

1018 Seven

1019 Chris Patten

1020 Black Sea

1021 Potato

1022 Badminton

1023 Fabian Society

1024 Liverpool

1025 Richard III

1026 Edward and Richard

1027 *The Cherry Orchard*

1028 *Peak Practice*

1029 Medici

1030 The Andrews Sisters

1031 Cleopatra

1032 Muscat

1033 Proteus

1034 Small turret

1035 River Garonne

1036 Dance

1037 The national flag

1038 Australia

1039 144

1040 Scotch whisky

1041 Horatio Nelson

1042 Iran

1043 Necessity

1044 The atomic bombs dropped on Hiroshima and Nagasaki

1045 St Paul's

1046 *Coppelia*

1047 St Patrick

1048 Hanging Gardens of Babylon

1049 The Queen

1050 Glass

1051 Isambard Kingdom Brunel

1052 Republican and Democratic

1053 Charles

1054 Thomas Alva Edison

1055 The Speaker's Mace

1056 Yellow

1057 Fear of colour

1058 Snake

1059 Bombay

1060 France

1061 Lunar Roving Vehicle

1062 1953

1063 M69

1064 *Lorna Doone*

1065 Sword

1066 1975

1067 Cat

1068 St Agnes

1069 Teaching

1070 1976

1071 Strategic Arms Reduction Treaty

1072 Richard III

1073 The Royal Court

1074 Ice hockey

1075 Daddy-long-legs

1076 Scrum half

1077 Pied-á-terre

1078 Carmelites

1079 Antonia Fraser

1080 Olive

1081 The lady of Shalott

1082 Hellespont

1083 Morocco

1084 Israel

1085 Copper and zinc

1086 Park Lane

1087 Aaron

1088 *Question Time*

1089 Slimbridge

1090 Nebuchadnezzar

1091 Aqua Regia

1092 The 1950s

1093 The Netherlands

1094 40

1095 Llandaff

1096 Blenheim Palace

1097 John Constable

1098 Prime number

1099 Alice Springs

1100 Sinai

1101 Carey Street

1102 Cumbria

1103 *La Bohème*

1104 Omnivore

1105 Broomstick

1106 The Scilly Isles

1107 Canada

1108 Kukri

1109 Staircase

1110 Oscar Wilde

1111 SoHo

1112 United Arab Emirates

1113 Smithfield

1114 *Gulliver's Travels*

1115 Glasgow

1116 High Commissions

1117 Sir Walter Raleigh

1118 Assault and attack helicopters

1119 France and Spain

1120 *Oklahoma!*

1121 Harvard, Yale, Princeton, Pennsylvania, Columbia, Brown, Dartmouth, Cornell

1122 Golf

1123 Salamanders and newts

1124 The *Mayflower*

1125 Ray Bradbury

1126 *Julius Caesar*

1127 Elijah

1128 Queen

1129 New Zealand

1130 Anaemia

1131 Handwriting

1132 Fish

1133 *Phantom of the Opera*

1134 Sacramento

1135 July the Fourth 1776

1136 D

1137 Crocodile

1138 Elizabeth Barrett Browning

1139 Brontë family

1140 Locum

1141 Spencer Tracy

1142 Vulture

1143 H_2O

1144 Lebanon, Syria, Jordon

1145 Eighteenth

1146 Rembrandt

1147 Brothers

1148 Bernt

1149 Rivers

1150 *Red October*

1151 Russia

1152 Australia

1153 The Last Supper

1154 Fluorine

1155 Publishing

1156 Glencoe

1157 Paediatrician

1158 Absolutely

1159 Empty spaces/voids

1160 Wellington

1161 Jacques

1162 Six games all

1163 Swan

1164 St Ninian

1165 Tricentenary

1166 William Gladstone

1167 Mississippi

1168 Electronic Point-Of-Sale

1169 Sir Terence Conran

1170 Wrist or ankle

1171 Porton Down

1172 Coins

1173 Birdcage Walk

1174 Van der Valk

1175 Danielle Steel

1176 Olivia Newton-John

1177 Grissini

1178 Canada

1179 Duke Ellington

1180 A prayer

1181 Charles II

1182 Gettysburg

1183 *Anna Bolena*

1184 Eton

1185 Prince Rainer

1186 Royal Fleet Auxiliary

1187 The Jumblies

1188 In the same place i.e. from the same source

1189 Abuja

1190 Great-nephew

1191 Ballet

1192 Aga Khan

1193 Aerodynamics

1194 *Black Beauty*

1195 St Matthew

1196 Maid of Norway

1197 Joie de vivre

1198 *Hannibal*

1199 Haemophilia

1200 Bouquet garni

1201 Geneva

1202 Thomas Bowdler

1203 Ceci n'est pas une pipe

1204 1992

1205 Graphite

1206 *The Vicar of Bray*

1207 Maze

1208 North and South Carolina

1209 Tin

1210 Apricot

1211 Piers Gaveston

1212 Scrimshaw

1213 Rest and Recuperation

1214 Jura Mountains

1215 River Dee

1216 *The Sorcerer*

1217 Philip II of Spain

1218 Michelangelo

1219 Persephone

1220 Petra

1221 Pollen

1222 8.00 am

1223 6.00 pm

1224 Great soul

1225 Motherboard

1226 Cullinan Diamond

1227 Hackamore

1228 Bryher, St Mary's, St Martin's, St Agnes

1229 To produce the voice of Mr Punch

1230 Panzer

1231 Tate Modern

1232 The Church

1233 Catherine Parr

1234 Nitrogen (N), Phosphorus (P) and Potassium (K)

1235 Crossed Keys

1236 SS *Great Eastern*

1237 Augustus

1238 St Denis

1239 Nine (six figures and three letters)

1240 Cave canem

1241 Aeschylus

1242 Synagogue

1243 Penelope

1244 Afghanistan

1245 Argentina

1246 Tin

1247 *Fawlty Towers*

1248 The Landmark Trust

1249 Aztec

1250 Horse racing

1251 Bridge

1252 Submarines

1253 Detective agency

1254 Norfolk

1255 The 1890s

1256 Jurisprudence

1257 John F. Kennedy

1258 Pakistan (Pakistan International Airlines)

1259 Johnny Cash

1260 Supertax

1261 Micro

1262 Mile

1263 Beetles

1264 Caucasus

1265 Summer pudding

1266 Ezekiel

1267 Gallipoli Landings (1915)

1268 Appendix

1269 *A Chorus Line*

1270 Universal Product Code

1271 'London Bridge is Falling Down'

1272 Hawaii

1273 Toys (Pollock's Toy Museum)

1274 Chancel

1275 Jackie Stewart

1276 Rochester

1277 Grandson

1278 Inca

1279 Ice hockey

1280 Artificial eyes

1281 Cambridgeshire

1282 Khaki

1283 Spain

1284 St John

1285 Garri Kasporov

1286 Egyptian

1287 Clarence House

1288 Los Angeles

1289 William the Conqueror

1290 *The Day of the Scorpion, The Towers of Silence, A Division of the Spoils*

1291 Mike Gatting

1292 Christopher Marlowe

1293 Carbon dioxide

1294 Ennio Morricone

1295 Being ill; contracting a disease

1296 Sir Topham Hatt

1297 Agent provocateur

1298 Greenland

1299 Haddock

1300 White Anglo-Saxon Protestant

1301 Inscriptions

1302 Prince Edward

1303 George VI

1304 24 October

1305 Joseph of Arimathea

1306 X

1307 Monday's

1308 Sicily

1309 White fur

1310 Gastropods

1311 Catatonia

1312 Oliver Goldsmith

1313 Bing Crosby

1314 Cheese

1315 J.M. Barrie

1316 French

1317 European Broadcasting Union

1318 Monarchy

1319 Court of Arches

1320 Eagle

1321 Ten Commandments

1322 Pocket borough

1323 The host

1324 *Casino Royale*

1325 Mosaic

1326 Harold Macmillan

1327 'Spring has come'

1328 *Autocar*

1329 Press Complaints Commission

1330 John Adams

1331 The Tweenies

1332 In fact

1333 Empiricism

1334 Bethlehem

1335 Birds

1336 Kilkenny

1337 The land round a house

1338 Femur

1339 John Brown

1340 Thoughts of Love

1341 Five

1342 Fashion

1343 Japan

1344 The Chichester Festival

1345 New Zealand

1346 Gasoline and diesel fuels

1347 American

1348 One million

1349 Laughing gas

1350 Wrens

1351 Edward G. Robinson

1352 Fiat

1353 Luminous flux

1354 Puccini

1355 Sophie Tucker

1356 Raised temperature

1357 Bones

1358 Adam Ant

1359 A brain

1360 Hyacinthus

1361 21

1362 Jerome

1363 Ramadan

1364 Anne Neville

1365 Lady Godiva

1366 Anthony Eden

1367 Norway

1368 Jute

1369 Saxophone

1370 Occluded front

1371 Bristol

1372 Discus

1373 Eustachian tube

1374 Ferret

1375 Alloway

1376 Hogwarts

1377 Alexandra and Mary

1378 Electric current

1379 Dervishes

1380 Crust

1381 Westerns/cowboy films

1382 St Bernadette

1383 Billiards

1384 Material

1385 Arm

1386 Red Sea

1387 Doctor Watson and Sherlock Holmes

1388 Drum

1389 Coventry

1390 It loses a shoe

1391 Gold

1392 Mexico

1393 Speed, rate or pace

1394 Photography ('daguerreotype')

1395 29 September

1396 IN-SErvice Training

1397 *The Midwich Cuckoos*

1398 Reflex Angle

1399 Dorset

1400 Latin

ROUND THREE
Answers

1401 Drums

1402 *Coronation Street*

1403 Viscount Linley

1404 Agatha Christie

1405 Épée, foil and sabre

1406 Louvre, Paris

1407 Hay fever

1408 Golda Meir

1409 On the Moon

1410 Sopwith Camel

1411 Olympus

1412 Black Bess

1413 Puffing Billy

1414 Bruce Springsteen

1415 Maltese

1416 Woodrow Wilson and Harold Wilson

1417 Nickel

1418 The passion of Christ from the Last Supper to the Crucifixion.

1419 USA and Great Britain

1420 Machine gun

1421 René Descartes

1422 Sir Francis Drake

1423 10,000 metres

1424 Princess Anne

1425 Conditional

1426 Madame Tussaud

1427 *Hesperus*

1428 Spencer Perceval

1429 Liverpool

1430 Winds

1431 Both were written in gaol

1432 Sparta and Athens

1433 Deacon

1434 Halifax

1435 1960s

1436 Mournful or sorrowful

1437 *Androcles and the Lion*

1438 Mount McKinley

1439 Royal Navy (after Andrew Miller, the press-gang leader)

1440 Philip Marlowe

1441 Cabriolet

1442 Copenhagen

1443 Truman Capote

1444 Bouillabaisse

1445 Basque

1446 'For they shall inherit the earth'

1447 Smell

1448 *The Merry Widow*

1449 Virginia

1450 Richard Ingrams

1451 Ian Hislop

1452 Philistine

1453 Denmark

1454 Loch Ness

1455 Zeppelin LZ-1 Luftfahrzug

1456 *Hamlet*

1457 Noah and the Flood

1458 Six months

1459 Lord's Day Observance Society

1460 Pentagon or five-sided plane figure

1461 Thomas Telford

1462 Greater Antilles

1463 Roland Garros

1464 Pina colada

1465 Ayers Rock

1466 Uluru

1467 Catamaran

1468 Wexford (Chief Inspector Reginald Wexford)

1469 A Stuart ascends the throne

1470 Been out first ball

1471 Negative equity

1472 Roger Moore

1473 Diurnal

1474 Friedrich Engels

1475 Master of the Rolls

1476 Prometheus

1477 The law

1478 Highgate

1479 *Seven Pillars of Wisdom*

1480 His nanny

1481 Llandudno

1482 Sir Frank Whittle

1483 Brooklyn, Queens and Staten Island

1484 Henry VIII

1485 '...can Spring be far behind?'

1486 Liam, Noel

1487 Mobile or kinetic sculpture

1488 Acetic acid

1489 Italy

1490 Cognoscenti

1491 MM

1492 Hadrian

1493 National Playing Fields Association

1494 Refinery

1495 Cyprus

1496 Israel

1497 Inheritance tax

1498 Gold

1499 Sir Tim Rice

1500 Nectar

1501 California

1502 'Who goes home?'

1503 Wittenberg

1504 *Inspector Morse*

1505 Ballet

1506 He tended the fatally wounded Nelson after the battle of Trafalgar, and reported the famous words Nelson addressed to Captain Hardy

1507 Belarus

1508 Strangers' Gallery

1509 Press Gallery

1510 Cyprus

1511 Alternating current

1512 Northumberland

1513 Caviar

1514 Cairo

1515 1 fathom

1516 Southampton

1517 Glasgow Rangers

1518 Sloth

1519 Site of Special Scientific Interest

1520 *Educating Rita*

1521 Spain

1522 Lord Brian Rix

1523 James Ramsay MacDonald

1524 Samuel Taylor Coleridge and William Wordsworth

1525 Gold state coach

1526 William Randolph Hearst

1527 Territorial Army

1528 Michigan

1529 Errol Flynn

1530 Mace

1531 Open verdict

1532 Governor General

1533 Trinity College

1534 Samuel Johnson's

1535 *Charlie's Angels*

1536 Drugs or poisons

1537 China

1538 Notre Dame

1539 Louisiana

1540 Cesare and Lucrezia Borgia

1541 Mid-stream (or crossing a stream)

1542 Venus (maximum magnitude of -4.4)

1543 Rome

1544 *The Moonstone*

1545 Circus Maximus

1546 Swatch Group

1547 St Wenceslas

1548 Ivan Pavlov

1549 A fairy dies ('falls down dead')

1550 Camargue

1551 360

1552 Eton College

1553 *Fawlty Towers*

1554 Wrist

1555 Beaufort Scale

1556 Chimpanzee

1557 Antihistamines

1558 Shannon

1559 She was pregnant: expecting Andrew and Edward, respectively

1560 Pince-nez

1561 Gilbert and Sullivan

1562 Asterisk

1563 General Certificate of Secondary Education

1564 Priceless diamond

1565 Flies

1566 Sistine Chapel

1567 Brighton

1568 Spain

1569 Holy Roman Empire

1570 Jugging

1571 Peter, Paul and Mary

1572 Tendons

1573 Alaska

1574 Gunfight at the OK Corral

1575 *Camelot*

1576 Portsmouth and Southampton

1577 Hay-on-Wye

1578 Benjamin Disraeli

1579 Queen Victoria

1580 Jimmy Carter

1581 India

1582 Brazil

1583 Italy

1584 Kenya

1585 Windmill

1586 Charlie Parker

1587 Oberon

1588 Little grey cells

1589 Venice

1590 Washington

1591 Lyons

1592 Duke of Wellington's

1593 Six

1594 Absence

1595 Italy

1596 Chesterfield

1597 Coral

1598 Calendar changed from Julian to Gregorian

1599 *Seven Brides for Seven Brothers*

1600 Archbishop of York

1601 David

1602 Telephone (first words spoken by A.G. Bell to his assistant)

1603 Accountancy

1604 Sin bin

1605 *The Archers*

1606 2.2

1607 A large chalk carving of a man in the hillside

1608 Laurence Olivier

1609 Poland

1610 Plaza

1611 Wine waiter or wine steward

1612 African and Asian/Indian elephant

1613 Venus fly-trap

1614 Association of British Travel Agents

1615 November

1616 Percussion/drums

1617 Benetton

1618 Cornwall

1619 Orson Welles (*Citizen Kane*)

1620 Calm before the storm

1621 1948

1622 Alexander Graham Bell (unit is the bel)

1623 Mombasa

1624 Mosaic

1625 New Zealand (Auckland, Christchurch, Wellington)

1626 *Chariots of Fire*

1627 Yellow

1628 Derbyshire

1629 Picked up some 700 *Titanic* survivors

1630 Sic

1631 *The Adventures of Tom Sawyer*

1632 France

1633 Reykjavik

1634 Lion

1635 L.S. Lowry (The Lowry)

1636 It is unknown or unexplored

1637 Graphite

1638 Collage

1639 Evacuation of Dunkirk

1640 Hamlet

1641 William and Mary (William III, Mary II)

1642 Republic of Ireland, Greece

1643 John Betjeman

1644 The Netherlands

1645 Many a slip

1646 Search engines

1647 The colours used for underground lines between these termini

1648 Canberra

1649 Remembrance Sunday

1650 Alistair Cooke's

1651 Stand and wait

1652 Births, marriages and deaths

1653 Vatican City

1654 Turning Queen's evidence

1655 Silence is golden

1656 The reunification of Germany

1657 Omega

1658 Ohm

1659 Neptune

1660 Mother-of-pearl

1661 Judge Jeffreys

1662 Yahoo

1663 Aladdin

1664 Dulwich Picture Gallery

1665 Japan

1666 Post Traumatic Stress Disorder

1667 Funicular

1668 Albert Einstein

1669 The Police

1670 Grub

1671 Cardiff International

1672 Cricket

1673 Stephen Dedalus

1674 Arran

1675 Assisi

1676 *Ruddigore*

1677 The wailing wall

1678 Trajectory

1679 Riding saddle

1680 Madonna

1681 London University

1682 Somerset

1683 Pasodoble

1684 Voltaire

1685 *A Brief History of Time*

1686 Inuit

1687 Henry VIII

1688 King's Lynn

1689 Newgate

1690 Burlington House

1691 Heights or altitudes above sea level; land elevations/heights of mountains

1692 St Louis

1693 Theseus

1694 Ray Galton, Alan Simpson

1695 Glasgow

1696 Orlando

1697 Phonetics

1698 *The Diary of Anne Frank*

1699 Valet

1700 *The Importance of Being Ernest*

1701 Pinocchio

1702 Sultan of Brunei

1703 Pink

1704 Richard

1705 Oliver Twist

1706 Essex

1707 Damon Hill

1708 Goodbye

1709 Darby and Joan

1710 Chimney sweeps

1711 (Sir Anthony) Van Dyck

1712 *The Count of Monte Cristo*

1713 Swahili

1714 Ariadne

1715 Jane Austen (*Emma*)

1716 Scott

1717 Ho Chi Minh Trail

1718 CREEP

1719 *All the President's Men*

1720 Dee and Mersey

1721 Astronomer Royal

1722 Chicago

1723 Andrew

1724 Quebec

1725 13

1726 You get monkeys

1727 Golden Disc

1728 Weston-super-Mare

1729 Thomas Gainsborough

1730 Cleopatra

1731 Bavaria

1732 Mycroft

1733 The White House

1734 Mediterranean

1735 Port

1736 Kent

1737 Thor

1738 Passover (the feast of the unleavened bread)

1739 Czechoslovakia

1740 Evaporation

1741 Work

1742 Franz Schubert

1743 Khartoum (Sudan)

1744 Captain Pugwash

1745 Motocross

1746 Istanbul

1747 Sisterly; of the nature of a sister

1748 Typhoon

1749 Touching with the hands

1750 Explain

1751 Cordon Bleu

1752 M25

1753 Burroughs (William and Edgar Rice)

1754 Liebfraumilch

1755 Dire Straits

1756 Designing and building the Suez Canal

1757 Sir Walter Scott

1758 Boston Tea Party

1759 John Fowles

1760 Glamorgan

1761 Anthony Blunt

1762 Oysters

1763 When crossing a bridge

1764 10 Downing Street (PM's official title)

1765 *Barrack Room Ballads*

1766 Iran, Iraq, Syria, Greece, Bulgaria, Armenia, Georgia

1767 Tuberculosis

1768 Dissolution of the Monasteries

1769 Almonds

1770 Lacrimal

1771 Goldsmiths' Company

1772 Give them to your sons

1773 General National Vocational Qualification

1774 Fellow of the Royal College (of Veterinary Surgeons, Surgeons, Physicians)

1775 Croesus

1776 Beam

1777 To be repeated

1778 Mrs White

1779 Celine Dion

1780 Gemini, Cancer

1781 Arnold Schwarzenegger

1782 Pitcher

1783 Charles I and Charles II

1784 Black panther

1785 Danse macabre

1786 Jane Austen

1787 Fortune

1788 Motoring assistance/Breakdown service

1789 Greece

1790 Busby Berkeley

1791 Dunmow Flitch

1792 Jesse

1793 Tyrrhenian Sea

1794 George Fox

1795 Robert Burns

1796 Landmine clearance

1797 Ageing and problems associated with elderly people and old age

1798 Anvil

1799 Madrid

1800 200 runs

1801 Stephen King

1802 25

1803 12

1804 *The Pilgrim's Progress*

1805 Watercress/white watercress

1806 Andy Pandy

1807 Badminton

1808 Schoolmaster

1809 Benjamin Britten

1810 Bona fide

1811 Power of attorney

1812 Julie Christie

1813 Snapdragon

1814 Diana

1815 Mrs Beeton

1816 Pablo Picasso

1817 Guitar

1818 Jonathan

1819 1 pint

1820 Guinness

1821 1970s

1822 Baltic

1823 Gold, frankincense and myrrh

1824 Moderator

1825 Cat

1826 All Saints

1827 One year

1828 D.H. Lawrence

1829 California, Oregon, Washington

1830 Queen Victoria

1831 Australia

1832 Southern Cross

1833 *Mary Rose*

1834 Ceefax

1835 14

1836 *The Pilgrim's Progress*

1837 Chlorophyll

1838 An habitual offender

1839 Wiltshire

1840 P & O Line

1841 Bass Strait

1842 Thomas Hardy

1843 James Cook

1844 Bloody Tower

1845 Japan (Tokyo Disneyland)

1846 Hawaii

1847 Clan

1848 Ballet

1849 Heathcliff

1850 Star-shaped

1851 Foreigners/strangers

1852 Resigning

1853 *Waiting for Godot*

1854 1940s

1855 Shogun

1856 Douglas-Home

1857 Long jump, High jump, Shot put, Discus, Pole Vault, Javelin

1858 1980 Moscow

1859 Golf

1860 Homer

1861 Erie and Ontario

1862 Toucan

1863 *The Rivals*

1864 Mirage

1865 Coral Sea

1866 Maastricht Treaty

1867 Berlin

1868 The Press

1869 Parson's nose or pope's nose

1870 Michael Winner

1871 West Indies

1872 Gabriel

1873 Blackbeard

1874 Mercury

1875 *Rebecca*

1876 Costa Rica

1877 Manchester

1878 Wrapped in pastry

1879 Ontario

1880 Sleepwalking

1881 Ad lib

1882 Fox

1883 *Oxford English Dictionary*

1884 Fez

1885 May to August

1886 Possession

1887 Eurovision Song Contest

1888 Kangaroo

1889 Chateauneuf-du-Pape

1890 Dr Moreau

1891 *Thunderball*

1892 Zero tolerance

1893 Smuggling

1894 Mount Elbrus

1895 Antibodies

1896 Basketball

1897 Molecule

1898 The first book of Samuel

1899 Three months

1900 Prosper Mérimée

1901 Shropshire

1902 Quebec

1903 Ian Fleming

1904 Nightingale

1905 George III

1906 Doppler effect (after Christian Doppler)

1907 Sir Elton John

1908 Piano

1909 Sesame

1910 Cacophony

1911 Shot put

1912 Coronation of Elizabeth II

1913 *The Master Builder*

1914 Malta

1915 York

1916 Chain reaction

1917 Monopoly

1918 Lead (plumbum is Latin for lead)

1919 'Sing a Song of Sixpence' [*Turdus merulae* are blackbirds]

1920 *Lord of the Flies*

1921 Renault

1922 An old fiddle

1923 Higher National Diploma

1924 *The Thieving Magpie*

1925 Troy

1926 Vincent van Gogh

1927 North Sea and Baltic Sea

1928 Cambridgeshire

1929 Land's End

1930 Sheep

1931 Whitehall

1932 Cuba

1933 Whales

1934 Hungary

1935 Place de la Concorde

1936 Snooker

1937 Three years

1938 *The Nutcracker*

1939 Gigolo

1940 Findus

1941 Gunpowder Plot

1942 President Monroe (the Monroe Doctrine)

1943 Victoria Falls

1944 Sri Lanka

1945 Whitewater rafting

1946 Panacea

1947 Sir Walter Scott

1948 Brain

1949 Abba

1950 Tropics of Cancer and Capricorn

1951 Equilateral triangle

1952 El Nino effect

1953 Bullfight

1954 Bible Belt

1955 The six wives of Henry VIII

1956 (Anne) Widdecombe/ Widdicombe (Fair)

1957 120 yards (there is a home base and first, second and 3rd base)

1958 Till May be/is out

1959 Crocodile (crocodile tears)

1960 Jimmy Nail

1961 Salt

1962 Viscount Linley

1963 Lapps/Laplanders

1964 Edward VII

1965 Florence Nightingale

1966 Woburn Abbey

1967 Sam Spade

1968 El Greco

1969 Law (Bachelor of Laws)

1970 Memento mori

1971 Jacob's

1972 Cornwall

1973 Yorick

1974 Hebrew and Arabic

1975 Distinguished Flying Cross

1976 Nitroglycerine

1977 Bodleian Library

1978 Krypton

1979 Rob Roy

1980 Morocco

1981 Australian

1982 Sir Winston Churchill

1983 Duke of Edinburgh

1984 Last In First Out

1985 *La Dolce Vita*

1986 Belgian

1987 Rodentia (rodents)

1988 Arizona

1989 James I

1990 Portcullis

1991 Statistics

1992 *Some Like It Hot*

1993 Adultery

1994 They all have species of flowers named after them (gentian, begonia and dahlia).

1995 Japan

1996 Culloden (Moor)

1997 Piano

1998 Indonesia

1999 Kerosene

2000 Himself

2001 Duration of Parliament

2002 Saskatchewan

15 to 1

Scoresheets

HOW TO USE THE
ROUNDS ONE & TWO
Scoresheets

The questionmaster should shade in the bars as the players lose their lives.

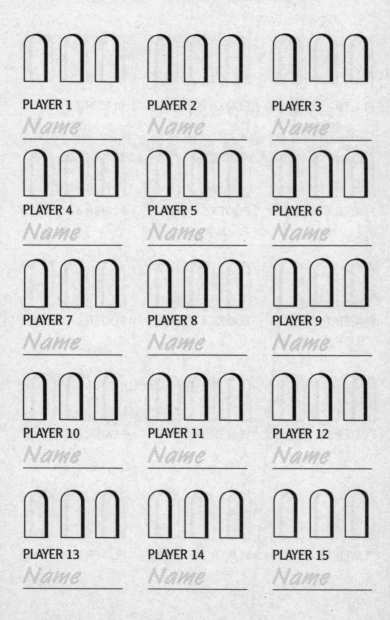

PLAYER 1

Name

PLAYER 2

Name

PLAYER 3

Name

PLAYER 4

Name

PLAYER 5

Name

PLAYER 6

Name

PLAYER 7

Name

PLAYER 8

Name

PLAYER 9

Name

PLAYER 10

Name

PLAYER 11

Name

PLAYER 12

Name

PLAYER 13

Name

PLAYER 14

Name

PLAYER 15

Name

PLAYER 1

Name

PLAYER 2

Name

PLAYER 3

Name

PLAYER 4

Name

PLAYER 5

Name

PLAYER 6

Name

PLAYER 7

Name

PLAYER 8

Name

PLAYER 9

Name

PLAYER 10

Name

PLAYER 11

Name

PLAYER 12

Name

PLAYER 13

Name

PLAYER 14

Name

PLAYER 15

Name

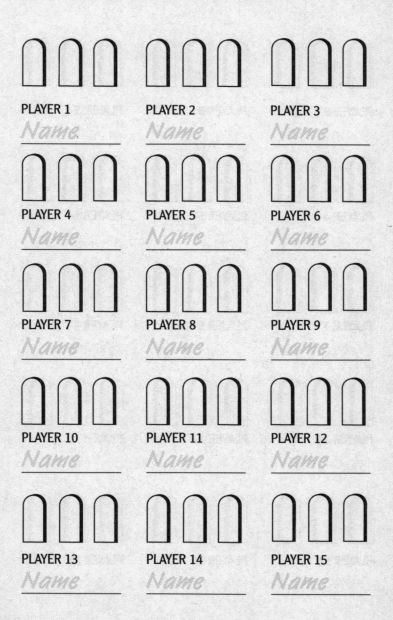

PLAYER 1
Name

PLAYER 2
Name

PLAYER 3
Name

PLAYER 4
Name

PLAYER 5
Name

PLAYER 6
Name

PLAYER 7
Name

PLAYER 8
Name

PLAYER 9
Name

PLAYER 10
Name

PLAYER 11
Name

PLAYER 12
Name

PLAYER 13
Name

PLAYER 14
Name

PLAYER 15
Name

PLAYER 1
Name

PLAYER 2
Name

PLAYER 3
Name

PLAYER 4
Name

PLAYER 5
Name

PLAYER 6
Name

PLAYER 7
Name

PLAYER 8
Name

PLAYER 9
Name

PLAYER 10
Name

PLAYER 11
Name

PLAYER 12
Name

PLAYER 13
Name

PLAYER 14
Name

PLAYER 15
Name

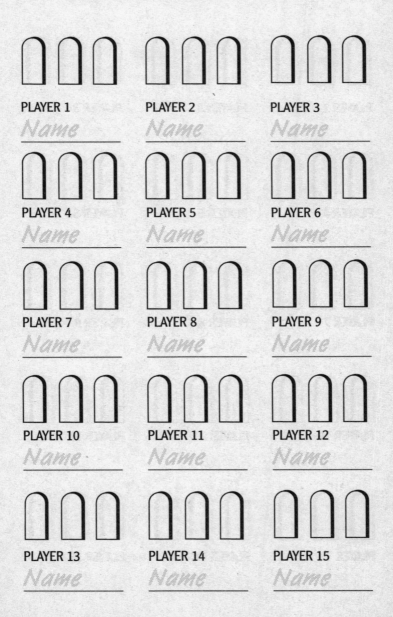

PLAYER 1

Name

PLAYER 2

Name

PLAYER 3

Name

PLAYER 4

Name

PLAYER 5

Name

PLAYER 6

Name

PLAYER 7

Name

PLAYER 8

Name

PLAYER 9

Name

PLAYER 10

Name

PLAYER 11

Name

PLAYER 12

Name

PLAYER 13

Name

PLAYER 14

Name

PLAYER 15

Name

PLAYER 1

Name

PLAYER 2

Name

PLAYER 3

Name

PLAYER 4

Name

PLAYER 5

Name

PLAYER 6

Name

PLAYER 7

Name

PLAYER 8

Name

PLAYER 9

Name

PLAYER 10

Name

PLAYER 11

Name

PLAYER 12

Name

PLAYER 13

Name

PLAYER 14

Name

PLAYER 15

Name

PLAYER 1
Name

PLAYER 2
Name

PLAYER 3
Name

PLAYER 4
Name

PLAYER 5
Name

PLAYER 6
Name

PLAYER 7
Name

PLAYER 8
Name

PLAYER 9
Name

PLAYER 10
Name

PLAYER 11
Name

PLAYER 12
Name

PLAYER 13
Name

PLAYER 14
Name

PLAYER 15
Name

PLAYER 1

Name

PLAYER 2

Name

PLAYER 3

Name

PLAYER 4

Name

PLAYER 5

Name

PLAYER 6

Name

PLAYER 7

Name

PLAYER 8

Name

PLAYER 9

Name

PLAYER 10

Name

PLAYER 11

Name

PLAYER 12

Name

PLAYER 13

Name

PLAYER 14

Name

PLAYER 15

Name

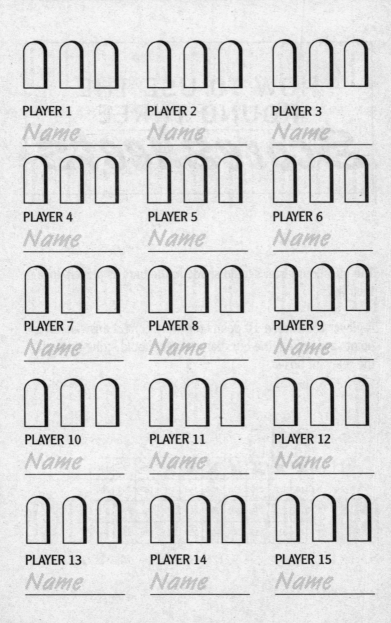

PLAYER 1
Name

PLAYER 2
Name

PLAYER 3
Name

PLAYER 4
Name

PLAYER 5
Name

PLAYER 6
Name

PLAYER 7
Name

PLAYER 8
Name

PLAYER 9
Name

PLAYER 10
Name

PLAYER 11
Name

PLAYER 12
Name

PLAYER 13
Name

PLAYER 14
Name

PLAYER 15
Name

HOW TO USE THE ROUND THREE
Scoresheets

The questionmaster should shade in the bars as players lose their lives.

A player is awarded 10 points for every correct answer. As points are scored, the question master should strike through the relevant boxes.

X	X	X	X	X	X	X	80	90	100
110	120	130	140	150	160	170	180	190	200
210	220	230	240	250	260	270	280	290	300
310	320	330	340	350	360	370	380	390	400

Name _____

10	20	30	40	50	60	70	80	90	100
110	120	130	140	150	160	170	180	190	200
210	220	230	240	250	260	270	280	290	300
310	320	330	340	350	360	370	380	390	400

Name _____

10	20	30	40	50	60	70	80	90	100
110	120	130	140	150	160	170	180	190	200
210	220	230	240	250	260	270	280	290	300
310	320	330	340	350	360	370	380	390	400

Name _____

10	20	30	40	50	60	70	80	90	100
110	120	130	140	150	160	170	180	190	200
210	220	230	240	250	260	270	280	290	300
310	320	330	340	350	360	370	380	390	400

Name _____

10	20	30	40	50	60	70	80	90	100
110	120	130	140	150	160	170	180	190	200
210	220	230	240	250	260	270	280	290	300
310	320	330	340	350	360	370	380	390	400

Name _____

10	20	30	40	50	60	70	80	90	100
110	120	130	140	150	160	170	180	190	200
210	220	230	240	250	260	270	280	290	300
310	320	330	340	350	360	370	380	390	400

Name _____

10	20	30	40	50	60	70	80	90	100
110	120	130	140	150	160	170	180	190	200
210	220	230	240	250	260	270	280	290	300
310	320	330	340	350	360	370	380	390	400

Name _____

10	20	30	40	50	60	70	80	90	100
110	120	130	140	150	160	170	180	190	200
210	220	230	240	250	260	270	280	290	300
310	320	330	340	350	360	370	380	390	400

Name _____

10	20	30	40	50	60	70	80	90	100
110	120	130	140	150	160	170	180	190	200
210	220	230	240	250	260	270	280	290	300
310	320	330	340	350	360	370	380	390	400

Name _____

10	20	30	40	50	60	70	80	90	100
110	120	130	140	150	160	170	180	190	200
210	220	230	240	250	260	270	280	290	300
310	320	330	340	350	360	370	380	390	400

Name _____

10	20	30	40	50	60	70	80	90	100
110	120	130	140	150	160	170	180	190	200
210	220	230	240	250	260	270	280	290	300
310	320	330	340	350	360	370	380	390	400

Name _____

10	20	30	40	50	60	70	80	90	100
110	120	130	140	150	160	170	180	190	200
210	220	230	240	250	260	270	280	290	300
310	320	330	340	350	360	370	380	390	400

Name _____

10	20	30	40	50	60	70	80	90	100
110	120	130	140	150	160	170	180	190	200
210	220	230	240	250	260	270	280	290	300
310	320	330	340	350	360	370	380	390	400

Name

10	20	30	40	50	60	70	80	90	100
110	120	130	140	150	160	170	180	190	200
210	220	230	240	250	260	270	280	290	300
310	320	330	340	350	360	370	380	390	400

Name

10	20	30	40	50	60	70	80	90	100
110	120	130	140	150	160	170	180	190	200
210	220	230	240	250	260	270	280	290	300
310	320	330	340	350	360	370	380	390	400

Name

10	20	30	40	50	60	70	80	90	100
110	120	130	140	150	160	170	180	190	200
210	220	230	240	250	260	270	280	290	300
310	320	330	340	350	360	370	380	390	400

Name

10	20	30	40	50	60	70	80	90	100
110	120	130	140	150	160	170	180	190	200
210	220	230	240	250	260	270	280	290	300
310	320	330	340	350	360	370	380	390	400

Name

10	20	30	40	50	60	70	80	90	100
110	120	130	140	150	160	170	180	190	200
210	220	230	240	250	260	270	280	290	300
310	320	330	340	350	360	370	380	390	400

Name

10	20	30	40	50	60	70	80	90	100
110	120	130	140	150	160	170	180	190	200
210	220	230	240	250	260	270	280	290	300
310	320	330	340	350	360	370	380	390	400

Name _____

10	20	30	40	50	60	70	80	90	100
110	120	130	140	150	160	170	180	190	200
210	220	230	240	250	260	270	280	290	300
310	320	330	340	350	360	370	380	390	400

Name _____

10	20	30	40	50	60	70	80	90	100
110	120	130	140	150	160	170	180	190	200
210	220	230	240	250	260	270	280	290	300
310	320	330	340	350	360	370	380	390	400

Name _____

10	20	30	40	50	60	70	80	90	100
110	120	130	140	150	160	170	180	190	200
210	220	230	240	250	260	270	280	290	300
310	320	330	340	350	360	370	380	390	400

Name

10	20	30	40	50	60	70	80	90	100
110	120	130	140	150	160	170	180	190	200
210	220	230	240	250	260	270	280	290	300
310	320	330	340	350	360	370	380	390	400

Name

10	20	30	40	50	60	70	80	90	100
110	120	130	140	150	160	170	180	190	200
210	220	230	240	250	260	270	280	290	300
310	320	330	340	350	360	370	380	390	400

Name

10	20	30	40	50	60	70	80	90	100
110	120	130	140	150	160	170	180	190	200
210	220	230	240	250	260	270	280	290	300
310	320	330	340	350	360	370	380	390	400

Name

10	20	30	40	50	60	70	80	90	100
110	120	130	140	150	160	170	180	190	200
210	220	230	240	250	260	270	280	290	300
310	320	330	340	350	360	370	380	390	400

Name

10	20	30	40	50	60	70	80	90	100
110	120	130	140	150	160	170	180	190	200
210	220	230	240	250	260	270	280	290	300
310	320	330	340	350	360	370	380	390	400

Name

10	20	30	40	50	60	70	80	90	100
110	120	130	140	150	160	170	180	190	200
210	220	230	240	250	260	270	280	290	300
310	320	330	340	350	360	370	380	390	400

ROUND THREE SCORESHEET

Name

10	20	30	40	50	60	70	80	90	100
110	120	130	140	150	160	170	180	190	200
210	220	230	240	250	260	270	280	290	300
310	320	330	340	350	360	370	380	390	400

Name

10	20	30	40	50	60	70	80	90	100
110	120	130	140	150	160	170	180	190	200
210	220	230	240	250	260	270	280	290	300
310	320	330	340	350	360	370	380	390	400

Name

10	20	30	40	50	60	70	80	90	100
110	120	130	140	150	160	170	180	190	200
210	220	230	240	250	260	270	280	290	300
310	320	330	340	350	360	370	380	390	400

Player	Score
Name	
Name	
Name	
Name	
Name	
Name	
Name	
Name	
Name	
Name	
Name	
Name	
Name	
Name	

Player	Score
Name	
Name	
Name	
Name	
Name	
Name	
Name	
Name	
Name	
Name	
Name	
Name	
Name	
Name	

Player	Score
Name	
Name	
Name	
Name	
Name	
Name	
Name	
Name	
Name	
Name	
Name	
Name	
Name	
Name	

Player	Score
Name	
Name	
Name	
Name	
Name	
Name	
Name	
Name	
Name	
Name	
Name	
Name	
Name	
Name	